A GUIDE TO THE BRITISH ARMY'S LINE INFANTRY REGIMENTS
1881–1914

by Ray Westlake

The Naval & Military Press

For Claire, my ever-loving Guide in all things

© Ray Westlake 2020

Published by

The Naval & Military Press Ltd
Unit 5 Riverside
Bellbrook Industrial Estate
Uckfield, East Sussex
TN22 1QQ England

Tel: +44 (0) 1825 749494
www.naval-military-press.com

CONTENTS

Acknowledgments viii

Introduction ix

Infantry Regiments 1

Bibliography 220

ACKNOWLEDGMENTS

For their generosity in allowing me to include images from their collections I must thank Alan Seymour, a special friend for almost thirty years, new friend Bruce Bassett-Powell, the creator of the superb Uniformology website, and the ever helpful Anne SK Brown Military Collection held at the Brown University Library, Providence, Rhode Island. Illustrations play an important part of this book and without their help it would have been difficult to include such a wide variety. And of course, my wonderful wife Claire without whom none of this would have been possible.

INTRODUCTION

The purpose of this book is to set out in an easily readable and well-illustrated form the structure of each line infantry regiment from 1881 up until the beginning of the First World War, a setup which can often be seen referred to as the 'Regimental Family'. The book will follow on from *A Guide to the British Army's Numbered Infantry Regiments of 1751–1881*, published by The Naval & Military Press in 2018. As we saw from that volume, the numbered infantry regiments (1st to 109th) existing in 1881 provided the Regular battalions of the now, sixty-nine in number, 'Territorial' or 'Country Regiments' that went on to fight in the Great War of 1914–1918. I have not made any attempt to record war or overseas service unless reference to it is relevant when describing the illustrations.

The several Victorian county Militia and Volunteer regiments were also affected by the 1881 reorganisation, the former losing their old tiles for battalion numbers following on from those of the Regulars, while the Volunteers were included as numbered 'Volunteer Battalions' within a separate sequence. This change of designation was gradual, however, some corps choosing to retain their Rifle Volunteer Corps styling.

Under the Territorial and Reserve Forces Act of 1907, the Volunteer Force ceased to exist on 31 March 1908. On the following day, 1 April, the Territorial Force was born and the old Volunteers invited to enlist. The change was not a popular one with the Volunteers as the new system often necessitated the reorganisation, and in some cases, disbandment of many of the existing companies. Some infantry battalions were even required to convert to artillery or some other arm of service. The new force was soon established, however, and the majority of battalions were to transfer *en bloc*. The new TF battalions were, unlike those of the Volunteers which had their own sequence, numbered on from the old Militia.

In 1863 cadet units were first sanctioned by the Government, Volunteer Regulations in that year directing that groups of boys could be formed in connection with existing volunteer companies and battalions. Many of these would be raised from within the Public Schools and it would be these that in 1908 provided the several contingents of the Junior Division of the Officers' Training Corps. Under the direct control of the War Office, the purpose of the OTC was as a supply of officers to both the Regular and Auxillary forces.

It was not until 1910, however, that the remaining cadet corps of the Volunteer Force were catered for by the formation of a new organisation to be known as the Territorial Cadet Force. Responsible for each cadet formation was its local County Territorial Force Association, these bodies having the power to grant (or not) official recognition or to cancel that already given. Over the coming years recognition of units was notified via Army Orders, along with any changes in establishment, amalgamations or disbandments.

Under the titles in use in 1914, the sixty-nine regiments have been listed according to order of precedence.

ROYAL SCOTS (LOTHIAN REGIMENT)

The original title was to be the Lothian Regiment, but this was, however, changed to that above before the end of 1881.

1st (The Royal Scots) Regiment

'It is not for nothing,' points out Lawrence Weaver in his 1915 regimental history, 'that The Royal Scots have pride of place in the Army List at the head of the roster of infantry regiments.' He tells how with 'authentic truth' the regiment can trace its origin as a military unit to the year 1421 when a large Scots force first took a permanent place in the service of France. Onward some 200 years and John Hepburn's name enters the history of the Royal Scots, for it would be he that the King directed by Royal Warrant to raise, in 1633, Hepburn's Regiment. There would be a succession of colonels' names as a regimental title—Sir John Hepburn, George Hepburn, Lord James Douglas, Archibald Douglas, Lord George Douglas, Frederick Herman Schomberg (killed at the Battle of the Boyne), Sir Robert Douglas (killed at Steinkirk), George Hamilton and James St Clair—the Royal Regiment appearing in 1688, the 1st or the Royal Regiment of Foot in 1751. Royal Scots was added in 1871, ten years before becoming the Royal Scots (Lothian Regiment) in 1881.

The Clothing Warrant of 14 September 1743 gives the King's Cypher within the circle and motto of St Andrew (*Nemo me impune lacessit,* No one provokes me with impunity) with crown above as the regiment's badge. The Star of the Order of the Thistle is also a feature of the insignia worn, as is the Thistle. For services in Egypt (1801) the Sphinx superscribed Egypt was authorized 6 July 1802. Uniform historian WY Carman noted that the first coats had white facings, the permitted blue, upon the 1st being made a royal regiment, not being taken into use until the last years of the seventeenth century.

Regular Battalions

1st and 2nd Battalions Formed from the 1st and 2nd Battalions of the 1st (The Royal Scots) Regiment. Richard Simkin's 'Military Types' series of chromoliths were issued as supplements to the *Army and Navy Gazette* between 1888 and 1902, that featuring a piper, private and officer of the Royal Scots appearing on 7 February 1891 **(1)**. Between 1881 and the introduction of the Kilmarnock bonnet in 1904, two types of officers' helmet plate were in use, the first having the silver title scroll reading 'The Lothian Regt.' We can see this in illustration **(2)**, a highly detailed image which also shows the thistle collar badges, and examples of the button and waist-belt clasp. In the same year that Richard Simkin's colour plate was issued, the wording on the scroll changed to 'The Royal Scots' **(3)**.

In illustration **(4)** we see the original artwork produced by artist Edgar A Holloway for a series of postcards published by the Aldershot

firm of Gale & Polden. The Royal Scots in 1881 had taken to wearing the doublet with thistle collar badges. Tartan trews were also worn, the sett similar to that in use by the Black Watch. The helmet continued as the full dress headdress, but as this was not considered to be very Scottish in nature permission was given in 1904 for the adoption of a dark blue Kilmarnock bonnet with diced band and scarlet toorie. The badge of St Andrew's Star was worn on the left side together with black cockade and ornamental black cock's feather. Thistle collar badges and curved brass shoulder titles with the wording Royal Scots can also be seen. We can place the period the artist had in mind by the medals being worn by both the sergeant and private—the Queen's and King's Medals for South Africa. It would be the 1st Battalion that left their home station late in the summer of 1899 for active service against the Boers.

The Kilmarnock bonnet can be seen in a photograph taken of

Lieutenant-General George Hay Moncrieff **(5)** who was appointed colonel of the regiment in 1903. The general had seen action in the Crimean War and wears both the British and Turkish medals for that campaign (second and third medals). He went on to serve as an officer with the Victorian Volunteer Force and for that was awarded (first medal) the Volunteer Decoration.

Images of two musicians now, **(6)** being a sergeant clarinettist (note arm badge above the chevrons), while **(7)** provides a fine study of a piper as photographed by Gregory & Co of the Strand, London and reproduced in Volume 1 of *The British Army and Auxiliary Forces* by Colonel C Cooper-King (published by Cassell & Co, 1893).

Militia Battalion

3rd Battalion In this original artwork by Edgar Holloway for one of Gale & Polden's regimental postcard sets featuring ceremonial and active service scenes **(8)** we see two soldiers talking at a railway station, the condition of their clothing suggesting that they have just returned from France or Belgium. Note also how the mechanism of one man's rifle has been bound around with cloth so as to protect it from the mud and slime of the trenches. The artist has marked the kitbag resting in the right hand corner with the owner's regimental number and unit details, 'B' Company, 3rd Battalion Royal Scots. As a battalion, the 3rd did not join others of the regiment overseas but would have supplied reservists to both regular battalions from the very beginning of the war. It was the former Edinburgh or Queen's Regiment of Light Infantry Militia, headquarters at Glencorse, which provided the 3rd Battalion.

Territorial Battalions

4th and 5th (Queen's Edinburgh Rifles) Battalions Formed from the Queen's Edinburgh Rifle Volunteer Brigade with headquarters at 28 Forrest Road, moving to Forrest Hill in 1910. A painting by Richard Caton Woodville representing both the 4th and 5th Battalions was published in *His Majesty's Territorial Army* by Walter Richards **(9)**. As can be seen, dark grey uniforms with rifle-style fur caps are worn, the image featuring a sergeant, bugler and mounted officer. Unseen in the picture are the battalion's blackened brass shoulder titles **(10)**, which are quite clear in a camp photograph taken in 1913 **(11)**.

6th Battalion From the former 4th Volunteer Battalion, an Edinburgh battalion which occupied headquarters at 33 Gilmore Place. In **(12)** we see a party from the 6th photographed against a backdrop of Edinburgh Castle. Clearly seen on the Territorial far right is the brass shoulder title, T over 6 over Royal Scots.

7th Battalion Headquarters at Dalmeny Street in Leith, the companies in 1914 being located: 'A' to 'G' (at Leith) and 'H' (Musselburgh). This was the former 5th Volunteer Battalion.

8th Battalion Headquarters in 1914 were at Haddington and the several companies located: 'A' (Haddington, Aberlady, Gifford and Pencaitland), 'B' (Tranent, Ormiston, Elphinstone and Macmerry), 'C' (Prestonpans and Cockenzie), 'D' (North Berwick, East Linton, Dunbar and Gullane), 'E' (Dalkeith, Bonnyrigg, Pathhead and Gorebridge), 'F' (Loanhead and Penicuick), 'G' (Peebles) and 'H' (Innerleithen and Walkerburn). The battalion was made up from companies of the former 6th and 7th Volunteer Battalions. The following cadet corps were also affiliated to the battalion: the Haddington Cadet Corps at the Knox Institute in Haddington, the North Berwick Cadet Corps at the High School, North Berwick, the Tranent Industrial School Cadet Corps and Prestonpans Cadet Corps.

9th (Highlanders) Battalion This was the former 9th (Highlanders) Volunteer Battalion at 7 Wemyss Road, Edinburgh, later in 1913 moving to 89 East Claremont Street also in Edinburgh. Illustration **(13)** shows a member of the 9th wearing Hunting Stuart tartan and brown leather equipment. Just visible worn above the right breast pocket is a white metal badge indicating that the wearer had volunteered to serve overseas if required. The brooch has a crown above a bar inscribed 'Imperial Service.'

10th (Cyclist) Battalion Formed from the former 8th Volunteer Battalion with headquarters in 1914 at Linlithgow and the several companies located: 'A' (Linlithgow and Phillipstoun), 'B' (Bo'ness and Carriden), 'C' (Armadale, Whitburn, Pumpherston and Blackridge), 'D' (Bathgate), 'E' (Broxburn and Livingstone), 'F' (Fauldhouse and Harthill), 'G' (West Calder and Addiewell) and 'H' (Kirkliston, Dalmeny, Winchburgh and Newbridge).

Volunteer Battalions

Queen's City of Edinburgh Rifle Volunteer Brigade Although never designated as such, the Queen's City of Edinburgh Rifle Volunteer Brigade constituted the 1st, 2nd and 3rd Volunteer Battalions of the regiment. Originating at the very beginning of the Volunteer Movement in 1859, this corps was to include members from all walks of Edinburgh life, the several companies bearing titles such as 'Advocates', 'Citizens', 'Writers to the Signet', 'Edinburgh University', 'Solicitors before the Supreme Court', 'Accountants', 'Bankers', 'Artisans', 'Civil Service', 'Freemasons', 'Merchants' and 'High Constables'. There was also a company of 'Total Abstainers', and three made up of 'Highlanders' resident in the city. A cadet corps was formed and attached to the brigade by Merchiston Castle School in 1886, followed by another at George Watson's Boys' College in 1905. Transfer to the Territorial Force in 1908 was as 4th and 5th Battalions Royal Scots. 'A' Company of the 3rd Battalion, the old No 4 (Edinburgh University) Company, joined the Senior Division of the OTC as part of its Edinburgh University Contingent. Merchiston Castle and George Watson's both provided contingents of the Junior Division. Illustration **(14)** shows an officer of Queen's City of Edinburgh Rifle Volunteer Brigade, the photograph being from the studio of Alex Asher of 34 Haddington Place, Edinburgh. The uniform is that worn by

the last figure in Lieutenant-General Sir James Moncrieff Grierson's colour image for his book, *Records of the Scottish Volunteer Force 1859-1908* **(15)**. Also seen, from left to right: a private of 1859, a private of the 2nd Highland Company in 1862, private of 1864, corporal for 1881 and a sergeant of 1901 in marching order.

4th Volunteer Battalion This battalion had its origins in a company of the 1st Edinburgh Rifle Volunteer Corps that consisted entirely of total abstainers. Founded by John Hope, a prominent member of the British Temperance League, No 16 Company later provided the nucleus of a new corps of 'teetotallers' which received the title of 3rd Edinburgh Rifle Volunteer Corps. This was re-numbered as 2nd in 1880 and in 1888 became the 4th Volunteer Battalion. The battalion also included a company from Portobello, and another founded by members of the Church of Scotland Teachers' Training College. The British League Cadet Corps comprising four companies of boys (John Hope in command) had been affiliated to No 16 Company since 1861 and this association continued with the 3rd (later 2nd) until 1892 when the corps disappeared from the Army List. Transfer to the Territorial Force in 1908 was as the 6th Battalion. Illustrated **(16)** is a postcard published by W & AK Johnston Ltd of Edinburgh which features the commanding officer of the 4th Volunteer Battalion, Colonel Sir George McCrae. A draper by trade, the colonel also served as member of parliament for Edinburgh East. He is shown wearing his Volunteer Decoration.

5th Volunteer Battalion

Originally the 1st Midlothian Rifle Volunteer Corps which was formed at Leith in 1859 and became the 5th Volunteer Battalion in 1888. Between 1881 and 1908 the establishment of the battalion varied between ten or eleven companies, most of them being recruited at Leith. Transfer to the Territorial Force in 1908 was as the 7th Battalion.

6th Volunteer Battalion The 6th Volunteer Battalion was recruited both in Midlothian and Peebleshire and was, prior to 1888, when it received its Volunteer Battalion designation, the 2nd Midlothian Rifle Volunteer Corps. Battalion headquarters moved from Penicuik to Peebles in 1907 and the original company locations were: Dalkeith (4), Penicuik, Valleyfield, Musselburgh, Loanhead, Peebles (2) and Inverleithen. In 1885 one of the Dalkeith Companies ('D') was moved to Bonnyrigg. Part of the 8th Battalion was provided upon transfer to the Territorial Force in 1908.

7th Volunteer Battalion Formerly the 1st Haddingtonshire Rifle Volunteer Corps which was re-designated as 7th Volunteer Battalion in 1888. Headquarters were at Haddington and the several companies located at Haddington, Aberlady, East Linton, Prestonpans and North Berwick. The North Berwick High School Cadet Corps was formed and affiliated to the battalion in 1901 and the Haddington Cadet Corps in 1906. Four companies of 8th Battalion Royal Scots were provided in 1908.

8th Volunteer Battalion Formerly the 1st Linlithgowshire Rifle Volunteer Corps with headquarters at Linlithgow, receiving its 8th Volunteer Battalion designation in 1888. The original companies were located at Linlithgow, Bo'ness, Torphichen, Bathgate, Uphall, Addiewell and West Calder. 'C' at Torphichen, however, was moved to Armadale in 1881. Two new companies were added in 1900, one at South Queensferry (disbanded in 1906) and the other at Kirkliston, and in the same year 'F' at Addiewell was transferred to Fauldhouse. Transfer to the Territorial Force in 1908 was as the 10th Battalion.

9th Volunteer Battalion (Highlanders) Formed in 1900 at Edinburgh as the Highland Battalion of the Queen's Rifle Volunteer Brigade, being made independent as 9th Volunteer Battalion in the following year. Provided the 9th Battalion in 1908.

1st Berwickshire Rifle Volunteer Corps. Served as a volunteer battalion of the regiment until 1887 when it was transferred to the King's Own Scottish Borderers.

The Galloway Rifle Volunteer Corps Galloway is the district of South West Scotland comprising the counties of Wigtownshire and Kirkcudbrightshire. The several rifle volunteer corps formed within these areas were on 30 June 1860 grouped together under the title of The Galloway Admin Battalion of Rifle Volunteers. In 1880 the battalion was consolidated as the Galloway RVC with headquarters at Newton Stewart and eight companies: 'A' (Kirkcudbright), 'B' (Castle Douglas), 'C' (Stranraer), 'D' (Newton Stewart), 'E' (New Galloway), 'F' and 'G' (Maxwelltown) and 'H' (Dalbeattie). The corps joined the Royal Scots as one of its volunteer battalions (without change in title) in 1881 but transferred to the King's Own Scottish Borders in 1899.

Cadet Battalion

1st (Highland) Cadet Battalion Headquarters at Forrest Road, Edinburgh.

Illustration credits: Alan Seymore (6), Anne SK Brown Military Collection, Brown University Library (4) and (8), Bruce Bassett-Powell and Bob Bennet (2)

QUEEN'S (ROYAL WEST SURREY REGIMENT)

2nd (Queen's Royal) Regiment

The 2nd Regiment was formed in 1661 as garrison troops for Tangier which had been ceded to England as part of the marriage settlement between Donna Catherina of Braganza and King Charles II. It would be first known both as the Tangier Regiment and Queen's Own Regiment, Royal appearing in the title for the first time in 1703. The 2nd (Queen's Royal) Regiment from 1751 would, with its two battalions, provide the Queen's (Royal West Surrey Regiment) in 1881. In addition to the titles held prior to 1751, the regiment was also known by the names of its successive colonels—Henry Mordaunt, Andrew Rutherford (killed at Tangier), Henry Norwood, William O'Brian, Sir Palmes Fairbourne (died of wounds at Tangier), Piercy Kirke (Sr), William Selwyn, Sir Henry Bellasis (cashiered for his part in the looting at Port St Mary), Sir David Colyear, Piercy Kirke (Jr) and Thomas Fowke who was dismissed for failing to reinforce Minorca.

The origins of the regiment's Paschal Lamb badge is, as historians point out, obscure. Regimental tradition associates it, together with the original sea green facings worn, with Catherine of Braganza. But authorities on heraldry have found no connection between the badge and the Portuguese royalty. The device of a Lamb (the 'Lamb of God'), of course, is much used as a religious symbol and thoughts along these lines suggest that it was appropriately adopted by the regiment upon going to fight against infidels in Tangier. Regulations for Clothing and Colours published in 1747, regardless of origin, give a Lamb as the regiment's ancient badge. Indeed, the Colours in 1751 are recorded as having three Lambs on a green ground. Green facings were worn for many years, but blue had appeared by 1768. The Lamb is shown carrying the flag of St George on a staff over its shoulder, which to some suggested a lance. Quite when the regiment acquired its Mutton Lancers nickname is not known. But certainly, Kirke's Lambs would have been in use when the Piercy Kirkes (both father and son) were colonels of the regiment. Certainly, the origins of the Sphinx superscribed with the word Egypt are clear, this badge being authorized 6 July 1802 in recognition of the regiment's service in Egypt the year before.

Regular Battalions

1st and 2nd Battalion Formed from the 1st and 2nd Battalions of the 2nd (Queen's Royal) Regiment of Foot. Bruce Bassett-Powell's illustration **(17)** showing a selection of officers' insignia for the period 1881-1898 includes a queen's crown helmet plate, collar badges, a button and waist-belt clasp. All display the Paschal Lamb, the latter also having *Pristinæ virtutis memor* (Mindful of our former valour), one of the

regiment's mottos. After Queen Victoria's death in 1901, the crown on the helmet plates changed to that shown in **(18)**.

Between 7 January 1888 and 6 September 1902 the *Army and Navy Gazette* published as supplements 177 choropleths by George Berridge & Co of 179 and 180 Upper Thames Street in the City of London featuring the work of Richard Simkin. Each numbered plate measured just under 15 x 10¾ inches and included below the subject the title of the regiment, usually with its pre-1881 numbering. Here we see No 39 in the series which was published 7 March 1891 featuring from left to right a drummer, officer and private **(19)**. Note how the artist has been careful to include (see upper right arm) the drummer's arm badge.

In **(20)**, and from the Anne SK Brown collection, we see the original Harry Payne artwork used by the Aldershot firm of Gale & Polden for one of their postcard series. The scene shows a sentry presenting arms outside the guardroom as a mounted officer returns to barracks ahead of a column. Another delightful painting is that of a drummer by F Stansell from WJ Gordon's book, *Bands of the British Army* **(21)**. On the photographic side, **(22)** offers a clear view of a cloth scouts' badge (lower left arm) and in **(23)** a charming study of a member of the Queen's (Royal West Surrey Regiment) wearing the crossed swords of a gymnastic instructor. In **(24)** we have an unsigned painting from *Her Majesty's Army* by Walter Richards, published by JS Virtue & Co during the 1890s.

Militia Battalion

3rd Battalion Formed by the 2nd Royal Surrey Militia. Two photographs, one **(25)** clearly showing the letter 'M' being worn in this group of officers on the shoulder straps below the rank insignia. In **(26)** NCOs and privates from a company of the battalion are seen with their officers. Just visible on the shoulder straps of some is the number 3 above the W. Surrey shoulder title. Battalion headquarters were at Guildford.

Territorial Battalions

Artist Richard Caton Woodville's watercolour representing the Territorials of the Queen's (Royal West Surrey Regiment) **(27)** includes three officers and a regimental quartermaster sergeant. All wear green uniforms with scarlet facings, black patent leather belts and Pascal Lamb badges. Clearly seen on the pouch of the officer with his back to the viewer is the device of a crown over a bugle-horn. A fourth officer, mounted on the far left, is from the Royal Army Medical Corps. Note how the artist has been careful to show his helmet with a ball in lieu of the usual spike.

4th Battalion Formed from the former 1st Volunteer Battalion. Headquarters in 1914 were at Croydon and the several companies located: 'A', 'B' (Croydon), 'C' (Crystal Palace), 'D' (Croydon), 'E' (Caterham and Godstone), 'F' (Croydon), 'G' (Lingfield and Oxted) and 'H' (Croydon). Affiliated to the 4th Battalion was the West Croydon Cadets at Drummond Road.

The postcard shown in **(28)** represents a scene that must have been commonplace all over Britain during the early months of the First World War. The place is Croydon. The month, August 1914 and the time, if the clock high up on the wall in the distance can be relied upon, is just past quarter-to-four in the afternoon. It is raining. A policeman wears his waterproof cape, several in the crowd sport umbrellas, but most seem content with their bonnets and straw boaters. The occasion which has seen such a large crowd take to the wet street is to see their local Territorials (4th Battalion Queen's) leave for war. The gathering is so vast that a tram is seen in the distance unable to continue on its journey through town. A gathering that would surely contain mothers, fathers, wives, brothers and sisters. Local shop signs appear in the photograph, one for the Domestic Bazar Company, and another for the location of a NTC Public Telephone. Nobody in the crowd will know it, but 'Wilson's Indian Tea' will prove to be poignant, the men, as we now know, finding themselves landing at Bombay on 3 December and in time to celebrate their 1914 Christmas in India.

5th Battalion Previously the 2nd Volunteer Battalion. Headquarters in 1914 were in Guildford and its companies located: 'A' (Reigate, Horley and Brockham), 'B' (Camberley, Bagshot and Frimley), 'C' (Guildford and Albury), 'D' (Guildford and Bramley), 'E' (Farnham and Frensham), 'F' (Godalming, Haslemere, Chiddingfold, Witley, Dunsfold, Alfold and Elstead), 'G' (Dorking, Holmwood and Shere) and 'H' (Woking, Knap Hill, Byfleet and Send). The Frimley and Camberley Cadet Corps at 'Thornhurst' in Camberley and the West Surrey Cadets were affiliated, Army Order 233 of 1912, however, notifying that recognition of the latter had been withdrawn for all except the Farnham portion of the unit which was re-designated as the Farnham Company West Surrey Cadets. Yet another change, this time in 1913 (Army Order 273) saw the corps re-designated as 'G' and 'H' (Surrey) Companies of the 1st Cadet Battalion of Hampshire.

Volunteer Battalions

1st Volunteer Battalion The 2nd Surrey Rifle Volunteer Corps at Croydon was re-designated as 1st Volunteer Battalion in March 1883. There would be ten companies in 1900, reducing to nine in 1903—seven at Croydon, one each at Crystal Palace and Caterham. Transfer to the Territorial Force in 1908 was as 4th Battalion, the Whitgift School Cadet Corps, which was formed and attached to the battalion in 1874, at the same time joining the OTC.

2nd Volunteer Battalion The 4th Surrey Rifle Volunteer Corps with headquarters at Reigate had six companies: 'A' and 'B' (Reigate), 'C' and 'D' (Guildford), 'E' (Farnham) and 'F' (Guildford) and a half-company at Godstone. In 1883, under General Order 37 of March, the corps became the 2nd Volunteer Battalion Queen's (Royal West Surrey Regiment), headquarters moving to Guildford in 1891. Three cadet companies were associated with the battalion: the Charterhouse School Cadet Corps which had been formed in 1873, the Cranleigh School Cadet Corps, formed in 1900, and the Reigate Grammar School Cadet Corps which dates from 1907. Transfer to the Territorial Force in 1908 was as 5th Battalion Queen's, Charterhouse,

Cranleigh and Reigate Schools at the same time joining the OTC.

3rd Volunteer Battalion The 6th Surrey Rifle Volunteer Corps was re-designated as 3rd Volunteer Battalion in March 1883, its headquarters moving from Rotherhithe to Jamaica Road, Bermondsey in 1884. A cadet corps was formed in Bermondsey in 1885, but this disappeared from the Army List after ten years. Another was raised, this time at Streatham Grammar School, in 1899, and transfer to the Territorial Force in 1908 was as 22nd Battalion London Regiment. The Streatham Grammar School Cadets, although the Army Council did approve its transfer to the OTC, was, however, disbanded. Illustrated **(29)** is a member of the 3rd Volunteer Battalion who is identified by his scarlet with blue facings tunic (the 1st, 2nd and 4th wore green uniforms with scarlet facings) and the white embroidered shoulder title, 3 over V over W. Surrey. The photograph was produced by the Tower Bridge Photographic Co of 45 Union Road, Rotherhithe, London.

4th Volunteer Battalion The 8th Surrey Rifle Volunteer Corps at 71 New Street, Kennington was designated 4th Volunteer Battalion in March 1883. The establishment was increased to ten companies in 1890 and a cyclist company was added in 1901. The Mayall College Herne Hill Cadet Corps was formed and affiliated in 1888, but this transferred to the 22nd Middlesex RVC in 1891. Another cadet corps with headquarters at Red Cross Hill in Southwark was added in 1889 and this became the 1st Cadet Battalion Queen's in 1890. Transfer to the Territorial Force in 1908 was as 24th Battalion London Regiment. In the photograph by W Gregory & Co of the Strand in London **(30)**, we see a private and two officers wearing green uniforms with scarlet facings and all badges display the Paschal Lamb. The officer on the right is dressed for

riding and has replaced the spike from his helmet by a ball. This is to protect the horse as the rider leans down to adjust the girth strap.

Cadet Battalions

1st Cadet Battalion Raised at the Red Cross Hall, Southwark in January 1889 as a cadet corps affiliated to the 4th Volunteer Battalion. The idea for this corps was first put forward in January 1889—Captain Salmond of the 3rd Battalion Sherwood Foresters Derbyshire Regiment being asked to take charge of formation. On the following 30 May, at Red Cross Hall, Lord Wolseley made a memorable speech which did much to encourage sufficient boys to come forward to make up two companies. A third followed in 1890, then a fourth, which subsequently led the War Office to grant permission to form the cadets into a battalion. This, the 1st Cadet Battalion, Queen's (Royal West Surrey Regiment), was to be the first independent battalion of its kind in London. There would be six companies by 1891—this was to make the battalion the strongest in England—and by 1904 the establishment stood at eight: 'A' and 'B' at Southwark, 'C' at the Passmore Edward's Settlement in St Pancras and the Marlborough Road Board School in Chelsea,

'D' at the Haileybury Club in Stepney, 'E' at St Andrew's Institute in Westminster, 'F' at St Peter's Institute in Pimlico, 'G at Bethnal Green and 'H' which was at the Eton Mission in Hackney. In 1904 battalion headquarters transferred to 31 Union Street, Southwark. Later re-designated as 1st Cadet Battalion London Regiment (The Queen's).

2nd Cadet Battalion Formed of four companies in November 1890. Headquarters were originally at the Lambeth Polytechnic, but later moves were made to Kirkdale in Clapham, then Brockwell Hall in Herne Hill. The establishment was increased to six companies in 1891 and in 1894 the battalion was re-titled as 1st Cadet Battalion King's Royal Rifle Corps.

A new 2nd Cadet Battalion was formed at Peckham in October 1901 from boys of the 1st Peckham Lads' Brigade which had existed since 1894. Headquarters were at 53 Copeland Road, Peckham and the establishment was six companies.

Illustration credits: Anne SK Brown Military Collection, Brown University Library (20), Alan Seymore (25) and (26), Bruce Bassett-Powell and Bob Bennet (17)

BUFFS (EAST KENT REGIMENT)

3rd (East Kent) Regiment (The Buffs)

The 3rd dates from 1572 when, as the Holland Regiment, it was raised for service in that country. It held the name of Prince George of Denmark's Regiment from 1689 and from 1708 to 1751 was known by the name of its colonel—Robert Sidney, Sir Walter Vane (killed at Seneffe), John Sheffield, Phillip Stanhope, John Sheffield, Sir Theophilus Oglethorpe, Charles Churchill, John Campbell, John Selwyn, Archibald Douglas, Sir Charles Wills, Thomas Pitt, William Tatton, Thomas Howard and Sir George Howard. The first official use of the title The Buffs was in 1747. The regiment's association with Kent was established in 1782 when East Kent was added to its name, the title chosen in 1881 being The Buffs (East Kent) Regiment. As is the case with many ancient regimental badges, the origins of that belonging to the Buffs is obscure. The Green Dragon was mentioned in the Clothing Regulations of 1747 and in the Royal Warrant of 1751 where it is described as the ancient badge. Major HG Parkyn writing in his book *(Military) Shoulder-Belt Plates and Buttons* suggests that the badge probably traces back to the fact that the regiment was raised from the Trained Bands of the City of London. The 'Square Mile', of course, features a dragon in its arms, but it is silver, and the green variety used by the Buffs has no cross of St George on its wings. The beast also has a connection with Ghent and regimental historian Richard Cannon suggests that the dragon was possibly placed on the Colours when the Buffs were stationed at the Belgium city in 1707.

Uniforms in 1667 were noted as being red coats with yellow linings. In later years facings were described as flesh or even ash, but buff soon became closely associated with the regiment so much so that it became, first of all its nickname (for many years in use prior to 1747), then part of its official title. The Rose and Crown was also a badge used from quite early on by the regiment.

Regular Battalions

1st and 2nd Battalions Formed from the two battalions of the 3rd (East Kent) Regiment of Foot (The Buffs). In this superb image by Bruce Bassett-Powell **(31)** we see an officer's gilt and silver helmet plate together with a waist-belt clasp of the same period. Also seen is a pair of White Horse of Kent collar badges,

the old badge of the East Kent Militia inherited by the regiment in 1881. But in this original artwork from the Anne SK Brown Collection **(32)** of an officer and sergeant produced by Harry Payne for a postcard series published by Gale & Polden, we see the later, dragon type, collar badge. The artist has shown the officer wearing both the Queen's and King's Medals for South Africa. It was the 2nd Battalion that on 22 December 1899 had sailed on the *Gaika* for the Cape where it arrived on 13 January 1900. The same medals are seen in the original artwork produced by J McNeill for one of the 'History and Traditions' postcards published by Gale & Polden **(33)**. The collar badges can also be seen in Richards Simkin's colour plate of an officer and two privates, published as a supplement to the *Army and Navy Gazette* on 4 April 1891 as part of the 'Military Types' series **(34)**. In **(35)** we see a trombonist of the regiment as painted by F Stansell for WJ Gordon's book, *Bands of the British Army*. The dragon badge again, complete with a selection of First World War battle honours in this cigarette card published as No 3 in a series of forty-eight by Gallaher's Ltd **(36)**, and from a photograph produced by Gregory & Co of the Strand, London, a study of four NCOs from the regiment **(37)**.

Militia Battalions

3rd Battalion Formed from the East Kent Militia which had its headquarters in Canterbury.

Territorials Battalions

4th Battalion Provided by the former 1st Volunteer Battalion, the 4th in 1914 had its headquarters in Canterbury and its several companies located: 'A' (Ramsgate, Birchington and Broadstairs), 'B' (Canterbury, Chartham and Ash), 'C' (Canterbury, Littlebourne, Wingham and Nonington), 'D' (Folkestone and Hythe), 'E' (Sittingbourne and Sheerness), 'F' (Herne Bay and Whitstable), 'G' (Margate, St Nicholas at Wade and Westgate-on-Sea) and 'H' (Dover). Several cadet companies were affiliated: the Depot Royal Marine Cadets at the RM Depot in Deal, the Herne Bay College Cadet Corps and New College Herne Bay Cadet Corps. The Chatham House College Cadet Corps, which was in Chatham Street, Ramsgate, was formed in 1891 as a cadet corps attached to the 1st Volunteer Battalion and in 1908 became a contingent of the Junior Division of the OTC. Army Order 129 of May 1911, however, notified that the contingent had been disbanded. The school was now represented by a cadet corps which appeared in the Army List as the Chatham House (Ramsgate) Cadet Corps recognised by the Kent Territorial Force Association on 1 May 1911 and affiliated to the 4th Battalion.

5th (The Weald of Kent) Battalion Formed from the former 2nd Volunteer Battalion, with headquarters in 1914 at Ashford and the battalion's eight companies located: 'A' (Cranbrook and Benenden), 'B' (Hawkhurst and Sandhurst), 'C' (Headcorn, Staplehurst, Marden and Sutton Valence), 'D' (Horsmonden, Goudhurst, Lamberhurst, Brenchley, Yalding and Paddock Wood), 'E' (Ashford, Pluckley, Smarden, Bethersden, Aldington, Boughton Aluph and Ham Street), 'F' (Ashford), 'G' (Tenterden, Lydd, Woodchurch, New Romney, Appledore, Wittersham and Rolvenden) and 'H' (Ashford). Illustrated **(38)** are two members, father and son possibly, of the 5th Battalion. The seated Territorial wears the crossed axes badge of a pioneer and two efficiency stars. The standing soldier has the crossed rifles arm badge of marksman.

Volunteer Battalions

1st Volunteer Battalion In 1883 the 2nd Kent Rifle Volunteer Corps under General Order 63 of May, was designated as 1st Volunteer

Battalion. The year 1888 saw 'H' Company at Ashford moving into a new drill hall in Tufton Street, then in 1893, 'I' Company was transferred to Lydd. The headquarters of 'D' Company moved from Hythe to Folkestone in 1896, and those of the battalion from Canterbury to Dover in 1901. Additional personnel were raised at Westgate-on-Sea, Herne Bay, Birchington, Broadstairs, Canterbury and Dover during the war in South Africa which brought the establishment of the battalion up to sixteen companies—two being cyclist formations. A reduction, however, to twelve was made in 1905, these in 1907 being listed as Ramsgate, Canterbury (2), Birchington, Folkestone, Sittingbourne, Herne Bay, Margate, Ashford, Wingham, Dover and Lydd. Transfer to the Territorial Force in 1908 was as 4th Battalion.

Associated with the battalion were several cadet corps, the first of which was formed at Dane Hill School, Margate in 1889. This company was disbanded, however, in 1897. The Chatham House College Cadet Corps at Chatham Street, Ramsgate, was formed in 1891 and in 1908 this became a contingent of the Junior Division Officers' Training Corps. The Chatham House College Company was formed at Ramsgate in 1891 and in 1908 became part of the OTC. Also affiliated, and to join the OTC in 1908, were the South Eastern College Cadets at Ramsgate (formed in 1898 and re-designated St Lawrence College in 1907), Dover College Cadet Corps (formed 1901), the St Edmund's School in Canterbury Cadet Corps and that formed at Sir Roger Manwood's School in Sandwich (both formed 1903). Other cadet units associated with the 1st Volunteer Battalion were at Margate College (formed 1892 and disbanded 1901) and New College Schools Herne Bay (see 4th Volunteer Battalion Queen's Own Royal West Kent Regiment).

In this first aid demonstration by members of the 1st Volunteer Battalion Ambulance Section **(39)** we see how a rifle could be used as a temporary splint. Note also the White Horse of Kent cap badges, the EK embroidered shoulder titles and how two men are wearing circular arm badges on their green with scarlet facings uniforms. These are made up of the intertwined letters 'SB' (Stretcher Bearer) and indicate that the wearer had been issued a certificate of proficiency in ambulance work.

Acting as the patient in (39) is one Albert Ross Ames who we can see featured in illustration **(40).** A native of Folkestone in Kent, Albert served as a part time soldier for twenty-eight years, first with the Kent Rifle Volunteers, and from 1908, the Territorials. After four years and 203 days with the latter, Albert Ross Ames retired with the rank of colour sergeant. During his time he would become recognised as one of his regiment's best shots, winning many shooting medals and cups. Re-enlisting when war was declared in August 1914, he subsequently served some fifteen months in India with the 4th Battalion Buffs. Four of his sons also served, one of them being killed in action. A carpenter by trade, Albert was well known in Folkestone where he died in 1930 aged 69 from an illness contracted during his war service.

2nd (The Weald of Kent) Volunteer Battalion Under General Order 63 of May 1883 the 5th Kent Rifle Volunteer Corps was re-designated as 2nd (The Weald of Kent) Volunteer Battalion the Buffs (East Kent Regiment). The Cranbrook Grammar School Cadet Corps was formed in February 1900 and until the following December, when it transferred to the 2nd Volunteer Battalion, was attached to 1st Cadet Battalion of the Buffs. Transfer to the Territorial Force in 1908 was as 5th Battalion Buffs, Cranbrook Grammar School at the same time becoming part of the OTC.

Cadet Battalion

1st Cadet Battalion Formed on 24 October 1894 with four companies at St George's Hall, Ramsgate. Headquarters were, however, moved to Margate in 1903, the battalion being disbanded in June 1907.

Illustration credits: Alan Seymore (39) and (40), Anne SK Brown Military Collection, Brown University (32) and (33), Bruce Bassett-Brown (31)

KING'S OWN (ROYAL LANCASTER REGIMENT)

4th (The King's Own) Regiment

Raised 13 July 1680 by the 1st Earl of Plymouth, the regiment was originally known as the 2nd Tangier and would later hold the titles Duchess of York and Albany's and the Queen's Own. It would be the King's Own Regiment from 1713, the 4th King's Own after 1751 and the King's Own (Royal Lancaster Regiment) following the reforms of 1881. The regiment was also known by the name of its colonel until 1751—Charles FitzCharles, Piercy Kirke (Sr), Charles Trelawny, Sir Charles Orby, Henry Trelawny, William Seymour, Henry Berkley, Charles Cadogan, William Barrell and Robert Rich.

The Lion of England on its own above or below a crown, is the ancient badge of the regiment. It was given by William III as a reward for its services after his 1688 landing in England. A most comprehensive history of the regiment was written by Colonel L I Cowper in 1939 which provides extensive detail on uniform and badges. Regarding the Lion badge, he notes that it first appeared on the shoulder-belt plates in 1774 and it was then shown without a crown and with the paw raised as in the Royal Standard. In 1822 the paw was depicted lowered and hovering close to the ground. It appears raised again in 1855. The Royal Cypher is listed for the first time in the Army List for 1852, Queen's Regulations, however, mention this as a badge of the regiment in 1844. Uniform historian WY Carman noted that when serving in Africa the regiment could have worn plain red coats, but back in England yellow facings were added. This, he explains, was a colour much favoured by James II and chosen 'in this case for his wife'. When blue facings were introduced is not known, but Mr Carman suggests this would have been early in the eighteenth century.

Regular Battalions

1st and 2nd Battalions Formed by the two battalions of the 4th (King's Own) Regiment. Bruce Bassett-Powell's detailed image of officers' badges **(41)** we see how the Lion of England and the red rose of Lancaster

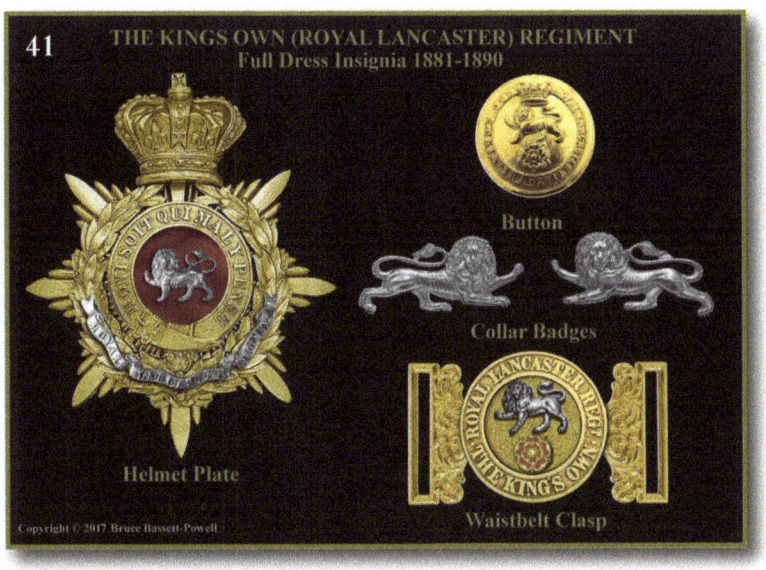

were used for the helmet plates, collar badges, buttons and waist-belt clasps. The rose, according to Major HG Parkyn in his *(Military) Shoulder-Belt Plates and Buttons*, was adopted as a badge by the regular battalions of the regiment in 1881 and was an old badge of the 1st Royal Lancashire Militia. The other ranks' version of the helmet plate is seen in **(42)**.

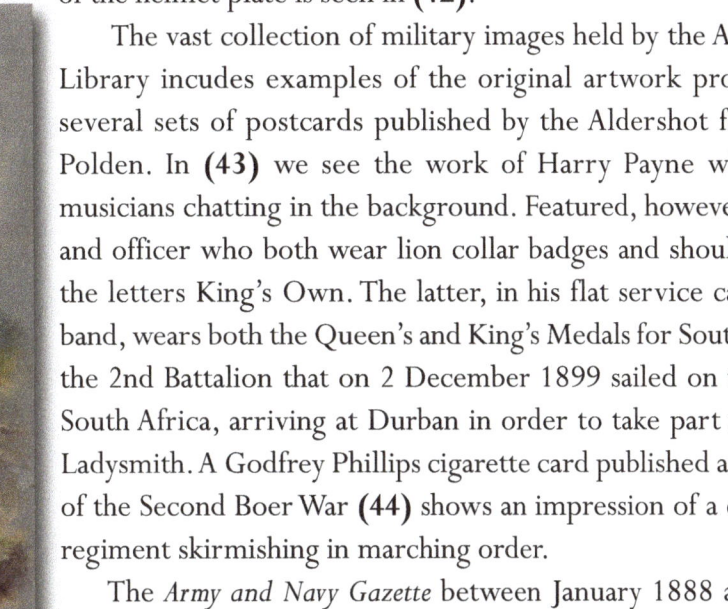

The vast collection of military images held by the Anne SK Brown Library incudes examples of the original artwork produced for the several sets of postcards published by the Aldershot firm of Gale & Polden. In **(43)** we see the work of Harry Payne who shows two musicians chatting in the background. Featured, however, is a sergeant and officer who both wear lion collar badges and shoulder titles with the letters King's Own. The latter, in his flat service cap with scarlet band, wears both the Queen's and King's Medals for South Africa. It was the 2nd Battalion that on 2 December 1899 sailed on the *Dilwara* for South Africa, arriving at Durban in order to take part in the relief of Ladysmith. A Godfrey Phillips cigarette card published around the time of the Second Boer War **(44)** shows an impression of a corporal of the regiment skirmishing in marching order.

The *Army and Navy Gazette* between January 1888 and September 1902 published a series of supplements to their magazine featuring British and Colonial regiments. To represent the King's Own, artist Richard Simkin produced artwork featuring a lance corporal and two officers. The image **(45)** was published on 3 October 1891. The insignia worn of the officer's blue forage cap is made up of a rose over a lion, more clearly seen in **(46)**. About the same time, two photographs **(47)** and **(48)** appeared, the first showing a pioneer of the regiment, the other a private in full marching order and white foreign service helmet.

In full regalia, his decorations including the Victoria Cross won as a young officer during the Indian Rebellion of 1857, we see in **(49)** Field Marshal Frederick Sleigh Roberts inspection a guard of honour provided by the King's Own.

Militia Battalions

3rd and 4th Battalions Formed from the former 1st Royal Lancashire Militia, headquarters of both battalions were in Lancaster.

Territorial Battalions

4th Battalion Formed from the former 1st Volunteer Battalion with headquarters at Ulverston, the eight companies were located: 'A' (Ulverston and Grange-over-Sands), 'B' (Ulverston, Greenodd, Haverthwaite and Lakeside), 'C' to 'F' (Barrow-in-Furness), 'G' (Dalton-in-Furness and Askam-in-Furness) and 'H' (Millom, Broughton-in-Furness, Coniston and Hawkshead). The battalion is clearly identified in this camp photograph **(50)** by the brass shoulder titles, T over 4 over King's Own.

5th Battalion: Formed from the former 2nd Volunteer

Battalion with headquarters at Lancaster, the eight companies were located: 'A' (Lancaster and Galgate), 'B', 'C', 'D' (Lancaster), 'E' (Morecambe), 'F' (Carnforth, Arnside, Silverdale and Caton), 'G' (Fleetwood, Poulton-le-Fylde, Garstang and Blackpool) and 'H' (Fleetwood, Preesall and Thornton). The corporal featured in **(51)** wears on his lower right arm the crossed rifles with star above badge identifying him as having been judged as the best shot in his company. Note also his T over 5 over King's Own brass shoulder titles.

Volunteer Battalions

1st Volunteer Battalion In 1876 the 5th Admin Battalion of Lancashire Rifle Volunteers at Ulverston was consolidated as a new 10th Corps with nine companies: 'A' and 'B' Lancaster, 'C' and 'D' Ulverston, 'E' and 'F' Barrow, 'G' Hawkshead, 'H' Rossall and 'J' Grange. The newly formed 'J' Company also included a detachment at Cartmel. The 10th Corps was then re-designated as 1st Volunteer Battalion King's Own (Royal Lancaster Regiment) in 1883. Two new companies, 'K' and 'L', were added at Dalton in 1887, 'L' moving to Millom, however, in 1889. The Rossall Company was disbanded in 1890, its cadet corps at the same time being transferred to 1st Lancashire Engineer Volunteers. In 1900, the battalion was divided so as to form a new 2nd Volunteer Battalion, the 1st remaining at Ulverston with 'A' and 'B' Companies (Ulverston), 'C' and 'D' (Barrow), 'E' (Hawkshead), 'F' (Barrow) 'G' (Dalton) and 'H' (Millom). The battalion provided the 4th King's Own in 1908. A team from the battalion's 'F' Company won the Tilney Challenge Cup in 1894 and they are seen in **(52)** together with their award. Note the several prize shooting badges being worn on the left arms of three of the men.

2nd Volunteer Battalion Formed in 1900 from the 1st Volunteer Battalion. Headquarters were placed at Lancaster and there were six companies located: 'A' to 'D' (Lancaster), 'E' (Morecambe) and 'F' (Grange). Transfer to the Territorial Force in 1908 was as 5th Battalion King's Own.

Illustration credits: Anne SK Brown Military Collection, Brown University Library (43), Bruce Bassett-Powell and Bob Bennet (41) and (46)

NORTHUMBERLAND FUSILIERS

5th (Northumberland) (Fusiliers) Regiment

An English Brigade was formed in Holland in 1674, one of the four regiments being the predecessor of the 5th (Northumberland) (Fusiliers) Regiment. The regiment was originally part of the Dutch service and known for a while as Viscount Clare's before taking on the title Holland Regiment. On 5 June 1685 the regiment was transferred to the British Line which it joined as the 5th in order of precedence. As with other regiments, the 5th was known by the name of its successive colonels until 1751—Daniel O'Brien, Sir John Fenwick (executed 1697), Henry Wisely, Thomas Monk, Thomas Tollemache, Edward Lloyd, Thomas Fairfax, Thomas Pearce, Sir John Cope and Alexander Irwin. The association with Northumberland was established in 1782 when the place name was added to the title, Fusiliers being included with effect from 4 May 1836. The King had approved this distinction and notice was subsequently given in *The London Gazette* for 13 May. The Northumberland Fusiliers was the title assumed in 1881.

St George and the Dragon, the regiment's ancient badge, appeared on the Colours in 1797. On 17 June 1829 authorization was given for the regiment to include the King's Crest together with red and white roses on its Colours and appointments. A rose slipped with a crown over it was directed in the Royal Warrant of 1751, Chichester and Burgess-Short suggesting that this was a device in use by the Holland Regiments of 1673-4. Certainly, it has always been a badge of the two surviving regiments of that period, the Northumberland Fusiliers and Royal Warwickshire Regiment.

Worn with pride for many years were the white plumes, said, according to uniform authority WY Carman, to be those that the men took from French grenadiers at St Lucia in 1778. Official approval for this tradition was given in 1826. But white plumes were allowed to all infantry regiments except fusiliers and light infantry in 1828, thus removing the distinction enjoyed by the 5th. Permission, however, was later given for a red and white plume to be used, once again placing the 5th apart from the rest of the line. A further distinction came in 1835 in the form of permission to wear grenadier caps 'with the King's Cypher in the front, and the ancient badge of the regiment on the back part.' This would be in recognition of the battle which took place at Wilhelmstahl in June 1762 in which men of the regiment took grenadier caps from the enemy. The battle honour was at the same time authorised to be borne on the Colours for the first time. As fusiliers, of course, a flaming grenade featured on badges.

53

The first uniform noted consisted of a red coat with yellow facings worn with green breeches and linings. Facings are described as yellow-green by 1742, the now familiar gosling-green appearing in regulations from 1751. Cannon in his historical records refers to a Horse Guards letter dated 26 June 1824 in which sanction is given for the facings being changed to a colour described as 'a handsome and lively green.'

Regular Battalions

1st, 2nd, 3rd and 4th Battalions The first two battalions were formed in 1881 from the existing battalions of the former 5th (Northumberland) (Fusiliers) Regiment of Foot. The 3rd and 4th were new creations of 1900, both later to be disbanded in 1907.

Part of the Anne SK Brown Collection includes this

delightful study of a lance corporal, colour sergeant and private of the regiment (53). By Ernest Ibbetson, the painting shows the tall grenade badge worn at the front of the fur caps and the regiment's distinctive red over white plume. Note also the grenade over NF shoulder insignia. The artwork was used by Gale & Polden for one of their 'History and Traditions' postcard series (54).

The 2nd Battalion was stationed at Dover in 1908 and in this photograph (55) we see a holiday crowed enjoying a salute being fired on the occasion of the King's Birthday which took place on 26 June that year. Note how the officer's cap (far right) is much larger than those of the men.

Drums play an important role in all infantry regiments, the drummers also being required to play, in addition, the fife and bugle. We can see all three instruments in this detailed photograph of the 1st Battalion (56), the ages of the group ranging from those of the very young boys in the front row, to that of the stern-looking drum major seated to the left of the drums. Note also the even younger lad, seated far right in the front row, wearing a straw boater and holding one of the regiment's glengarry caps.

A drum major and young drummer again, this time featured on a postcard published by Gale & Polden (57). The artist is Edgar A Holloway who sets the scene as St George's day, 23 April, on which the regiment traditionally decorates the Colours, drums, drum major's staff and the men's headdress with roses.

Joy comes to the collector when he or she finds photographs identifying regiment, battalion, time and place. This vital information sometimes comes in the form of hand written detail on the reverse of the image, but on occasion can be gleaned from comments found accompanying photographs in old family or regimental albums. Such is the case with **(58)** and **(59)**. The occasion is the 'Wiltshire Manoeuvres' of 1890, the place Crookham Camp after a twenty-two mile march from Hazley Heath. A glance at my Army List for 1890 tells me that the 1st Battalion was stationed in England (the 2nd were in India) and from JHF Brabner's *The Comprehensive Gazetteer of England and Wales* I'm informed that Hazley Heath is, 'a tithing in Heckfield parish, Hants, 4¼ miles N of Odiham.' And in **(59)** we see the march referred to, 'D' Company being accompanied by a civilian who manages to keep in step with the leading troops. The mounted officer can be identified as Major Henry Kilgour who had served in the Afghan

war of 1878-80, taking part in two expeditions into the Bazar Valley as transport officer and was also present during the engagement at Deh Sarakh. Unseen, it seems, is 'Ray' who is in fact Second-Lieutenant George Lake Sidney Ray who was commissioned 14 September 1887.

Being able to give names to people in photographs is a delight and this image **(60)** with its attached list represents most of what could be asked for by both the collector and historian. Headed by its commanding officer, Lieutenant-Colonel William FitzAlan Way, here we have a group from the 2nd Battalion at Bengal, India around 1893. Each man is numbered, the accompanying list **(61)**, which I have cropped from the photograph, giving names, place and time.

In **(62)** we see how the regiment's badge of St George and the dragon was used as a device on several items of insignia worn by officers. It also appeared

on the large grenade used to pin back the apron of the pioneer seen in Richard Simkin's chromolith featuring the Northumberland Fusiliers **(63)**. The image appeared as a supplement issued with the *Army and Navy Gazette* on 2 May 1891 and also shows a private and officer. It will be noticed that the facings in the painting are shown as white and not the regiment's famous gosling green. One of the regulations introduced in 1881 was to stipulate that all non-royal English regiments should adopt white facings. The green was, according to uniform historian WY Carman, reintroduced in 1899.

Militia Battalion

3rd, later 5th Battalion The former Northumberland Militia at Alnwick provided the 3rd Battalion in 1881, but owing to the formation in 1900 of the two new regular battalions, the 3rd was re-numbered as 5th. Following their disbandment in 1907, however, the original number was restored.

Territorial Battalions

4th Battalion Formed from part of the 1st Volunteer Battalion, headquarters were at Hexham and the eight companies located: 'A' (Hexham and Acomb), 'B' (Bellingham, Plashetts, Otterburn and Wooburn), 'C' (Haydon Bridge, Allendale, Langley and Newbrough), 'D' (Prudhoe and Mickley), 'E' (Corbridge), 'F' (Haltwhistle), 'G' (Newburn and Whorlton) and 'H' (Prudhoe). The Haltwhistle Territorial Cadets at Scardeburg and Haltwhistle were affiliated to the battalion.

5th Battalion Formed from the former 2nd Volunteer Battalion, headquarters were at Walker, Newcastle-upon-Tyne and the companies located: 'A', 'B', 'C' (Walker), 'D', 'E', 'F' (Wallsend), 'G' (Gosforth, West Moor and Seaton Burn) and 'H' (Gosforth).

6th (City) Battalion Formed from the 3rd Volunteer Battalion with headquarters at St George's Drill Hall, Northumberland Road, Newcastle-upon-Tyne. There were eight companies all at Northumberland Road and an affiliated cadet corps at Allan's School in Northumberland Road.

64

7th Battalion Formed in 1908 from part of the 1st Volunteer Battalion. Headquarters were at Alnwick and the companies located: 'A' (Morpeth), 'B' (Ashington), 'C' (Belford, Ford, Wooler and Chatton). 'D' (Alnwick), 'E' (Amble, Broomhill and Warkworth), 'F' (Alnwick and Rothbury), 'G' (Berwick-upon-Tweed) and 'H' (Berwick-upon-Tweed and Scremerston). The Morpeth Grammar School Cadet Company was also affiliated. Representing the Northumberland Territorial Force Association, Walter Richards included an image by R Caton Woodville showing a parade close by a castle tower in his four-volume work, *His Majesty's Territorial Army*. The tower looking very much like one of those belonging to Alnwick Castle, I have placed the illustration **(64)** with details of the 7th Battalion. Perhaps the onlookers seen in the painting have come up from Alnwick to see their local battalion, relative even, in their smart scarlet uniforms.

8th (Cyclist) Battalion Provisions for a cyclist battalion with this number were made, but by 1910 it had been decided to organise the new unit as an independent body designated as the Northern Cyclist Battalion.

Volunteer Battalions

65

66

1st Volunteer Battalion At Alnwick, the 1st Northumberland Rifle Volunteer Corps in 1881 comprised ten companies: 'A' (Hexham), 'B' (Morpeth), 'C' (Belford), 'D' (Alnwick), 'E' (Bellingham), 'F' (Allendale), 'G' (Berwick-upon-Tweed), 'H' (Lowick), 'I' (Corbridge) and 'K' (Haltwhistle). Under General Order 14 of February 1883 the 1st Corps was re-designated as 1st Volunteer Battalion Northumberland Fusiliers. In 1885 the Lowick Company was disbanded and in its place a new 'K' was formed at Newburn. Nine years later the personnel of this company were transferred to the 2nd Volunteer Battalion and at the same time replaced by a new 'H' at Prudhoe. Headquarters moved to Hexham in 1891 and two new companies were added in 1900. By this time certain reorganisations had taken place within the battalion resulting in the company locations being arranged as: Hexham (2), Belford, Alnwick, Bellingham, Haydon Bridge, Prudhoe, Corbridge, Haltwhistle and Morpeth (2). The two Hexham companies ('A' and 'B') were merged as 'A' in 1903, a replacement 'B' being found by the transfer of No 7 Company of the 2nd Northumberland Royal Garrison Artillery Volunteers at Ashington. Transfer to the Territorial Force in 1908 was as 4th Battalion Northumberland Fusiliers, the Alnwick personnel providing the nucleus of the 7th Battalion.

67

In illustrations **(65)**, **(66)** and **(67)** we see firstly a cigarette card featuring a member of the 1st Volunteer Battalion who wears a green uniform with scarlet collar, cuff ornaments and piping. The helmet worn, with its white metal Maltese Cross plate and fittings, is that shown in (66) and for walking out, a glengarry cap was worn with the badge shown in (67).

2nd Volunteer Battalion The 2nd Northumberland Rifle Volunteer Corps at Walker was re-designated as 2nd Volunteer Battalion Northumberland Fusiliers in 1883, the corps by then consisted of six companies, all at Walker and lettered 'A' to 'F'. In 1894 the Newburn Company of the 1st Volunteer Battalion was transferred to the 2nd as 'G'. The following year 'H' was formed at Wallsend and in 1900 additional personnel raised saw the battalion's companies rearranged as follows: Walker (4), Newburn (2), Wallsend (2) and Gosforth (2). Transfer to the Territorial Force was as the 5th Battalion Northumberland Fusiliers.

3rd Volunteer Battalion Formation of the 1st Newcastle-upon-Tyne Rifle Volunteers began in 1859 when the Newcastle Rifle Club decided to form a corps. By the end of the year sufficient members had been enrolled to form a battalion of nine companies. The first officers were gazetted on 22 February 1860, Sir John Fife becoming commanding officer, Robert Robey Redmayne his second-in-command. The nine companies were made up from all sections of the Newcastle community, each being given names indicating the origins of their members, e.g. Quaysiders, Oddfellows or Temperance. There was even a kilted company recruited from Scotsmen resident in the city and one known as Guards which required its members to be not less than six foot in height. Others came from the Hampton factory, two from Robert Stephenson's locomotive works, another was found at the Elswick Ordnance factory. The battalion had increased to thirteen companies by 1861, but this establishment was later reduced to eight.

Re-designation as 3rd Volunteer Battalion Northumberland Fusiliers was notified in General Order 14 of February 1883 and two new companies were added (one from Durham University) in 1900. Transfer to the Territorial Force in 1908 was as 6th Battalion Northumberland Fusiliers, the University company at the same time becoming a contingent of the Senior Division, OTC.

Illustration credits: Alan Seymore (56), (58), (59) and (60), Anne SK Brown Military Collection, Brown University Library (53), Bruce Bassett-Powell and Bob Bennet (62)

ROYAL WARWICKSHIRE REGIMENT

6th (Royal First Warwickshire) Regiment

The 6th Regiment dates from 1673 when, as the Holland Regiment, it was raised for the Dutch service. From 1688 it was known by the name of its successive colonels—Sir Walter Vane (killed at Seneffe, Luke Lillingston, Thomas Ashley, Sir Henry Bellasis (cashiered for looting at Port St Mary), Philip Babington, George Prince of Hesse Darmstadt (killed at Fort Montjuich), Henry de Caumont, Ventris Columbine, James Rivers, William Southwell, Thomas Harrison, Robert Dormer, James Dormer and John Guise—before being designated as the 6th Regiment of Foot in 1751. The bracketed (1st Warwickshire) was added in 1782, then in 1832, the Royal title. Two battalions strong, the 6th provided the Royal Warwickshire Regiment in 1881.

In a warrant dated 1 July 1751, the facings of the 6th were directed to be deep yellow. The ancient badge of the regiment, the Antelope, was to take its place in the centre of the Second Colour, while the Rose and Crown appeared in the three corners not occupied by the Union flag. The Antelope badge was also in use on caps, breast-belt plates and buttons. Major Parkyn illustrates two oval plates featuring the Antelope, both being surrounded by the name of the regiment. Another, oblong this time, has the animal with a crown above and accompanied by battle honours on scrolls. The Rose and Crown device, complete with stork and leaves, is thought to be in reference to a badge worn by the six Holland Regiments and has always been one of the those in use by the two (5th and 6th) surviving regiments. Upon being made a Royal regiment in 1832, dark blue facings replaced the yellow.

Regular Battalions

1st, 2nd, 3rd and 4th Battalions The 1st and 2nd were formed from the two battalions of the 6th (Royal First Warwickshire) Regiment of Foot. The 3rd was raised in April 1898, the 4th two years later in 1900. Both, however, were disbanded in 1907. Bruce Bassett-Powell's detailed selection of officers' badges **(68)** shows how both the antelope and bear and ragged staff were used on the helmet plates, early collar insignia, the buttons and waist-belt clasp. As can be seen in this Harry Payne artwork **(69)** the bear was later replaced by the antelope. Produced for a Gale & Polden postcard, the image shows the private on the right wearing both the Queen's and King's Medals for South Africa. It was the 2nd Battalion that fought in the Second Boer War, the troops sailing on the *Gaul* towards the end of November 1899 and arriving at the Cap on 16 December.

Drums, double basses, trombones, a French horn, bassoon, cornets and clarinets can be seen in this photograph of a regimental band **(70)**. All members wear foreign service uniform on which such cloth items as rank chevrons and musicians' trade badges are easily removed for laundry purposes. Note also the pouches, which have a device featuring an antelope badge similar to that worn on the officers' forage cap in **(71)**. Curved brass, Warwick, shoulder titles are being worn which dates the photograph sometime prior to 1902.

More musicians in **(72)** and **(73)**. For a postcard produced by Gale & Polden, artist Arthur Chidley depicted a bass drummer (note his leopard skin uniform protector) awaiting orders from his drum major. Less anxious, however, is the cornet player who sits patiently in a photographer's studio somewhere overseas for his picture to be taken. The Gale & Polden postcard sets are extremely popular among collectors. Also highly sought after are examples of the supplements (some 177 were produced) that were issued with copies of the *Army and Navy Gazette* between 7 January 1888 and 6 September 1902. Here in **(74)** we see No 47 in the series which features an officer of the regiment observing the musketry skills of two men. The image was published on 7 November 1891.

Militia Battalions

3rd and 4th, later 5th and 6th The original battalion numbers allotted to the 1st and 2nd Warwick Militia in 1881 were 3rd and 4th. However, with the introduction of two new regular battalions into the regiment as 3rd and 4th, the militia element was re-numbered as 5th and 6th. The regular battalions of the regiment were reduced once again to two in 1907 and with

this reorganisation the former 3rd and 4th numbers were restored. Both battalions had their headquarters in Warwick.

Territorial Battalions

Colours were received from King Edward VII by each of the regiment's Territorial Battalions in 1909, and it is likely that artist R Caton Woodville recalled this event a year later for his Warwickshire Territorial Force Association contribution to Walter Richard's four-volume work, *His Majesty's Territorial Army* **(75)**. The parade over and the Colours in the distance being admired by the men, two officers seemingly pose for the artist while another on horseback looks on.

5th and 6th Battalions Both were provided by the former 1st Volunteer Battalion in 1908. Headquarters and all sixteen companies were to be found in Thorp Street, Birmingham.

7th Battalion Formed from the former 2nd Volunteer Battalion. Headquarters were in Coventry and the battalion's eight companies were located 'A' to 'D' (Coventry), 'E' (Rugby), 'F' (Leamington), 'G' (Warwick and Kenilworth) and 'H' (Nuneaton). The Bablake School Cadet Company in Coventry was affiliated to the battalion.

8th Battalion Historian Walter Richards points out that in 1908 the 8th Battalion was an entirely new unit, but a number of the former Volunteers were members. Richards goes on to say that, 'Of the present officers [1910] five, including the Commanding Officer and senior Field Officer, belonged to the late 1st Volunteer Battalion of the regiment, four to the 2nd, and two to the 1st Volunteer Battalion the South Staffordshire Regiment.' Headquarters of the 8th Battalion were at Aston Manor, Birmingham and the companies located: 'A' (Aston Manor), 'B' (Saltley) and 'C' to 'H' (Aston Manor). Regarding the several companies, Walter Richards notes that 'D' Company was almost entirely composed of employees of the Dunlop Works and that efforts had been made to organise other companies as the 'Drapers', 'Gas workers' and 'Jewellers'.

Volunteer Battalions

1st Volunteer Battalion The 1st (Birmingham) Rifle Volunteer Corps was formed in 1859 and quickly comprised twelve companies recruited from various sources. There was one formed by workers from several newspapers, one made up of gun makers and another of Scots resident in the city. In 1883 1st Warwickshire RVC became 1st Volunteer Battalion Royal Warwickshire Regiment. Four new companies were added in 1891, the battalion then being divided into two: 'A' to 'H' Companies (1st Battalion) and 'I' to 'Q' (2nd Battalion). A cyclist section was formed in 1894, this being increased to a full company in 1900. At Birmingham University in the same year, 'U' Company was formed from staff and students and this, in 1908, became part of the Senior Division OTC. For the rest of the battalion, transfer to the Territorial Force was as both the 5th and 6th Battalions Royal Warwickshire Regiment.

A cadet corps appeared in the Army List as having been affiliated to the battalion in 1883, but this had disappeared by the end of the following year having had no officers appointed to it. Next, in 1904, came the company formed at Solihull Grammar School, then in 1907, that raised by King Edward's School. Both schools became part of the OTC in 1908.

From Colonel Charles J Hart's magnificent history of the 1st Volunteer Battalion (published by the

Midland Counties Herald Ltd, Birmingham in 1906) we have two images, **(76)** showing the uniform of the battalion in 1906, the other **(77)** being a fine portrait photograph of Major AD Fleming who was commissioned on 17 June 1896.

2nd Volunteer Battalion The 1st Admin Battalion of Warwickshire Rife Volunteers was formed with headquarters at Coventry in May 1860 and consolidated in 1880 as the new 2nd Corps. There were twelve companies: 'A', 'B', 'C' and 'D' (Coventry), 'E' and 'F' (Rugby), 'G' (Warwick), 'H' (Stratford-on-Avon), 'I' (Nuneaton), 'K' (Saltley College), 'L' and 'M' (Leamington). The 2nd was re-designated as 2nd Volunteer Battalion Royal Warwickshire Regiment in 1883 and increased to thirteen companies in 1900. There was a reduction to eleven, however, by the end of the following year. The King's Grammar School, Warwick provided a cadet corps in 1885, as did Leamington College in 1900 and King's County School at Warwick in 1905. King's Grammar, which was renamed Warwick School in 1894, was not seen in the Army List after 1906, the Leamington cadets disappearing after a few months having had no officers appointed to it. Rugby School also provided a cadet corps, which, with King's County School, joined the OTC in 1908, the battalion at the same time transferring to the Territorial Force as 7th Battalion Royal Warwickshire Regiment.

Regarding the Rugby School Cadet Corps, much of the old 3rd Warwickshire Rifle Volunteer Corps included staff and senior boys from the town's public school. Regular drills took place within the school grounds (those very playing fields where in 1823 the young William Webb Ellis gave us the game of rugby) and a high standard of drill and musketry was soon achieved. Cadet units, which were to be formed in connection with volunteer corps, were first sanctioned in Volunteer Regulations for 1863, article 279 directing that boys should be twelve years of age and upwards. It would not be until 1873, however, that a cadet corps was formed by the school, the association with the 3rd Corps continuing through to its later affiliation to the Royal Warwickshire Regiment.

One of the cadets is shown in show **(78).** His blue cloth-covered headdress is the Home Service pattern helmet approved for the infantry in 1878. Made of cork, the spike and curbed chin-chain are in white metal, the latter extending from a Tudor Rose and being secured by a hook on the right side when worn as per photograph. Black leather provides the all-around peak and back edging. Die-struck in white metal, the universal-pattern helmet plate has the Queen Victoria crown, the centre circle having the designation 2nd V.B. Royal Warwickshire Regiment. An antelope, the 'ancient badge' of the Royal Warwicks, forms the central device.

A scarlet jacket with blue collar (note the early bear with ragged staff device), cuffs and white piping is being worn. Buttons are the general service, Royal Arms, type in white metal, the white buff waist-belt having a snake-clasp fastening. Trousers would be the usual dark blue with red stripe, but the image reveals that these were not being worn for the purpose of the photograph.

The school arms featuring three griffin heads, a fleur-de-lis and two roses, can be seen worn on the left arm above a scroll bearing the date 1894. Enfield rifle in his hand, the cadet wears the badge as a member of the school shooting team on the occasion of winning the Ashburton Shield that year.

Cadet Battalions

1st Cadet Battalion Two units have been designated as 1st Cadet Battalion, the first being formed of four companies at Birmingham in June 1886 but disbanded in 1893. Next came a battalion recognised by the Warwickshire Territorial Force Association on 15 June 1910, which was located at The Barracks, Aston Manor in Birmingham. There was also a company at Sutton Coldfield.

2nd Cadet Battalion Recognised by the Warwickshire Territorial Force Association on 21 June 1910, headquarters were at Stevens Memorial Hall in Coventry.

3rd Cadet Battalion Recognised by the Warwickshire Territorial Force Association on 4 March 1914 with headquarters at The Drill Hall, Thorp Street, Birmingham.

4th (Schools) Cadet Battalion Recognised by the Warwickshire Territorial Force Association on 4 March 1914 with headquarters at 15-16 Exchange Buildings, Birmingham.

Illustration credits: Alan Seymore (70), Anne SK Brown Military Collection Brown University Library (69), Bruce Bassett-Powell and Bob Bennet (68), (71)

ROYAL FUSILIERS (CITY OF LONDON REGIMENT)

7th (Royal Fusiliers) Regiment

Formed in 1685, the regiment, before being designated as 7th (Royal Fusiliers) in 1751, appeared under several titles: Our Royal Regiment of Fusiliers, Our Ordnance Regiment and by the name of its successive colonels—George Legge, John Churchill, George Hamilton, Edward Fitzpatrick, Sir Charles O'Hara, James O'Hara and William Hargrave. Often the word Fusiliers would be spelt Fuzileers. Raised during the time of the Duke of Monmouth's rebellion, the regiment was intended to guard artillery, its fusil weapon being all the safer around gun powder. With its long association with the 'Square Mile', the title assumed in 1881 was the Royal Fusiliers (City of London Regiment).

When raised, the uniform of the regiment consisted of red coats faced yellow worn with grey breeches and hose. Chichester and Burges-Short refer to a book of military costume held at the British Museum in which a private of the 7th for the period 1742 wears a red coat faced this time with blue. The lace is white and red striped. A tall blue mitre-shaped cap is worn displaying the Rose and Garter and White Horse of Hanover in the front, the authors pointing out that the latter badge was not at the time being worn by other fusilier corps. All badges mentioned would be officially recognised by the Royal Warrant of 1751

Regular Battalions

1st, 2nd, 3rd and 4th Battalions The 1st and 2nd were formed from the two battalions of the 7th

(Royal Fusiliers) Regiment of Foot. The 3rd and 4th were raised in 1898 and 1900 respectively. Possibly one of the best regimental histories ever produced as far as uniform detail is concerned is that written and illustrated for the Royal Fusiliers by Lieutenant-Colonel Percy Groves and published in 1903. The book has fifteen superbly executed watercolours of uniform, included two plates covering the period under consideration here. The 1st **(79)** includes detailed studies of the uniforms worn by a field officer and drummer in 1890. Note how the former is dressed for riding with his spurred boots and sabretache. Colonel Groves provides short notes with his colour plates. For the field officer he reminds his readers how in October 1880 the rank badges on officers' tunics were removed from the collar and placed onto gold cord shoulder straps. Three figures are depicted in the authors plate covering 1895-1903 **(80)**. For the private shown in marching order the accompanying note tells how, 'The tunic was now only worn in review order, and on church parade. The Kersey frock (as shown) was worn on all other occasions.'

The Anne SK Brown Military Collection at Brown University Library in Providence, RI, USA is fortunate in that it holds a superb collection of original artwork produced for postcards. Notable especially are those very collectable sets published by the Aldershot firm of Gale & Polden. For their 'Ceremonial and Active Service' series, artist Ernest Ibbetson painted six watercolours featuring the Royal Fusiliers. For one of the cards he chose to illustrate a privilege enjoyed by the regiment which allowed it to march through the City of London with bayonets fixed, Colours flying and band or drums playing. This is known as the 'City of London Privilege' and reflects an ancient time when recruiting within the City was forbidden. For a comprehensive account of this custom I refer you to that first class reference work, *Military Customs* by Major TJ Edwards (Gale & Polden, 1954). As passengers on an open bus stand for a better view, the Royal Fusiliers march through the City, bayonets firmly fixed and Colours flying. A civilian passes by and, in

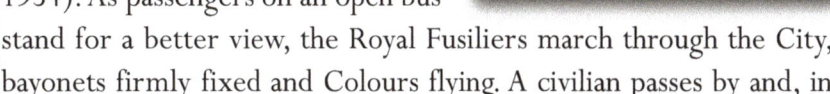

respect, stands to attention by the roadside having removed his hat **(81)**. From the same set, an actual postcard this time **(82)** featuring the fifes and drums.

Postcard expert Geoff White in his useful reference work, *Collecting British Army Postcards,* records how in 1919 Harry Payne was commissioned to paint a number of pictures for Gale & Polden. In **(83)** we see the artist's original artwork used by the Aldershot firm for card No 2089 in a series of uniform studies. As signallers practise their trade in the distance, a sergeant marches by with his rifle at the slope, the weapon just obscuring the NCO's two medals. Clearly seen, however, is a Queen's South Africa Medal which has two bars attached. An educated guess would identify the second medal as that known as the King's Medal for South Africa, this and the Queen's being awarded for service during the Second Boer War of 1899-1902. It was the 2nd Battalion that sailed from Gibraltar on the *Pavonia* during November 1899.

When war was declared in August 1914 the 4th Battalion was stationed at Parkhurst on the Isle of Wight. Here we see the officers **(84)** just prior to the battalion leaving for France on 13 August. Regimental historian HC O'Neill records how the battalion was well received by the French soldiers as they marched past, the fusiliers responding by whistling the 'Marseillaise' followed by 'Hold your hand out, naughty boy.' The French, thinking that the latter tune was the British National Anthem, immediately bowed their heads in respect. The battalion was soon in action, the fighting at Nimy near Mons seeing two members of the 4th awarded the Victoria Cross. These were Lieutenant Maurice James Dease, who we can see standing on the

far right, back row, of the photograph, and Private Sydney Frank Godley. Both were later featured in the same cigarette card set **(85)**, **(86)**.

Neatly chalked on a board is information most useful to the photograph collector. Here in **(87)** we have name of company, and even the section number. But what battalion? A close look at the cloth, white on red RF over 3, shoulder insignia through a magnifying glass reveals that this is the 3rd. The men are wearing leather ammunition bandoliers and slouch hats with the brim held up on the left side by a grenade badge fixing.

From WJ Gordon's *Bands of the British Army* comes F Stansell's illustration of a musician **(88)**. Bandsmen of the regiment could be distinguished by their brass

sword scabbards, a gift from their colonel (1789-1801), HRH Edward Augustus, Duke of Kent, the father of Queen Victoria.

Militia Battalions

3rd, 4th, 5th Battalions, later 5th, 6th and 7th The original 3rd, 4th and 5th Battalions of the regiment were formed respectively by the 3rd Middlesex Royal Westminster Militia with headquarters at Hounslow, the Royal London Militia at Artillery Place in Finsbury, and the 4th Royal South Middlesex Militia, also at Hounslow. The numbers were changed upon the formation of two new regular battalions which were numbered on from 1st and 2nd.

Territorial Battalions

Although the Royal Fusiliers had volunteer battalions between 1881 and 1908, the formation of the Territorial Force saw these separated from the regiment and placed into the newly created London Regiment as its 1st, 2nd, 3rd and 4th Battalions. Although still closely associated with the Royal Fusiliers in its uniform, badges and name, the four battalions are only mentioned in the Army List section dealing with the regiment as being affiliated. All four battalions wore distinctive metal shoulder titles: **(89)** shows the set, with variations.

1st (City of London) Battalion The London Regiment (Royal Fusiliers) From the former 1st Volunteer Battalion. Headquarters were at 33 Fitzroy Square, St Pancras, moving to Handel Street, St Pancras in 1912, and the companies located: 'A', 'B', 'C' (St Pancras), 'D', 'E' (15 Battersea Square, Battersea), 'F', 'G', 'H' (St Pancras). Colours were presented to the battalion by King Edward VII in June 1909 and in the following year, John Player issued a set of fifty cards depicting the Colours and badges of Territorial Force units, **(90)**

being that representing the 1st London Regiment.

2nd (City of London) Battalion The London Regiment (Royal Fusiliers) Formed from the former 2nd Volunteer Battalion. Headquarters and all eight companies were at 9 Tufton Street, Westminster, part of which can be seen in a 1909 photograph featuring the Colours presented that year by King Edward VII **(91)**.

3rd (City of London) Battalion The London Regiment (Royal Fusiliers) Formed from the former 3rd Volunteer Battalion with headquarters at 21 Edward Street, St Pancras. All eight companies were also at Edward Street. There was also, however, a drill station at 207 Harrow Road in Paddington. Affiliated to the battalion was the 1st North Paddington Cadets at Pember Hall, Pember Road, Willesden.

4th (City of London) Battalion The London Regiment (Royal Fusiliers) Formed from the former 4th Volunteer Battalion with headquarters and all companies at 112 Shaftesbury Street, Shoreditch.

Volunteer Battalions

Illustrated are two paintings representing the volunteer battalions of the Royal Fusiliers. The first **(92)** is a watercolour by CA Collins showing a sergeant. In the second painting by Richard Simkin **(93)**, several types of uniform are shown along with examples of a battalion's cyclist and field ambulance sections.

1st Volunteer Battalion The 19th Middlesex Rifle Volunteer Corps was formed at Bloomsbury of three companies on 13 December 1859 from members of the Working Men's College in Great Ormond Street, Holborn. The commanding officer was Thomas Hughes, the author of *Tom Brown's Schooldays*, which led to the corps often being referred to as 'Tom Brown's Corps'. The 19th later comprised ten companies of which three were supplied by the college, others by the St John's Institute in Cleveland Street, the Price Belmont Works at Battersea, the Working Men's College in Paddington Green and the Westminster parishes of St Luke and St. Anne's. Headquarters later moved to 33 Fitzroy Square.

Renumbered 10th in 1880, the corps became a volunteer battalion (without change in title) of the King's Royal Rifle Corps in 1881. General Order 99 of July

1883, however, directed a transfer to the Royal Fusiliers and re-designation as 1st Volunteer Battalion. An eleventh company was added in 1900 and transfer to the Territorial Force in 1908 was as 1st Battalion London Regiment. Illustrated **(94)** is one of the battalion's transport waggons, the men wearing an assortment of uniform and headdress.

2nd Volunteer Battalion It was in January 1861 that the War Office accepted the services of a corps of volunteer riflemen raised within the City and Westminster areas of London. Number 5 Victoria Street, just a short walk down from Westminster Abbey, was its first headquarters, Sir John Villiers Shelley (MP for Westminster) its first Commanding Officer and 46 its allotted number within the fast growing order of battle of Middlesex Rifle Volunteer Corps. Such was the enthusiasm that when the corps, in June 1861, moved just around the corner to new headquarters at 31 Great Smith Street—across the road from the building was the first free public library in London which had been opened four years earlier—eight companies (four in the City, four in Westminster) had been formed. The rank and file, according to one source, was drawn almost entirely from 'the respectable working classes', while the officers were men 'of good social position'. VC hero of the Crimea Lieutenant Colonel Sir Charles Russell was appointed as first honorary colonel in 1877 and he was succeded six years later by Lord Wolsely.

During the next three years the 46th Middlesex RVC was to be subject to two changes in designation: firstly as 23rd Middlesex (this to comply with the general 1880 renumbering of Volunteer Corps throughout the country), then in 1883 as 2nd Volunteer Battalion Royal Fusiliers. The corps had been allotted as one of that regiment's four volunteer battalions two years previously. In 1899 a new headquarters was built just around the corner from Great Smith Street at 9 Tufton Street and transfer to the Territorial Force in 1908 was as 2nd Battalion London Regiment.

3rd Volunteer Battalion On 13 December 1859 the 20th Middlesex Rifle Volunteer Corps of three companies was formed with headquarters at Euston Square, mainly from men employed by the London and North Western Railway Company. Thomas Edward Bigge, who had previously served with the 23rd Royal Welsh Fusiliers, was appointed captain commandant in command. The corps was included in the 4th Admin Battalion until May 1861 and in 1880 re-numbered as 11th. It joined the King's Royal Rifle Corps (without change in title) as one of its volunteer battalions in 1881, transferring to the Middlesex Regiment in 1882 and then the Royal Fusiliers as its 3rd Volunteer Battalion in 1890. Additional personnel were sanctioned in 1900/01 bringing the establishment from eight to thirteen companies. After the war in South Africa, however, a reduction was made to eleven. The battalion occupied several headquarters in the Euston area including No 5 Albany Street near Regent's Park, and in Edward Street, off Hampstead Road. Transfer to the Territorials in 1908 was as 3rd Battalion London Regiment.

4th Volunteer Battalion In 1881 the 1st Tower Hamlets Rifle Volunteer Brigade at 112 Shaftesbury Street in Hoxton appeared in the Army List as one of the volunteer battalions allotted to the Rifle Brigade. There would be no change in title until May 1904 when, having been transferred, the brigade became 4th Volunteer Battalion Royal Fusiliers. A cadet corps was formed in 1885, but this disappeared from the Army List during 1891. The Tower Hamlets Brigade had formed a Machine Gun Battery in 1886 and it was this,

under the command of Captain EV Welby that formed the nucleus of the machine gun section of the City Imperial Volunteers in South Africa. Welby was mentioned in despatches and his sergeant, WJ Park, received the Distinguished Conduct Medal. Dated 1895, illustration **(95)** shows a machine gun mounted on a tandem cycle. Note the 1 over TH shoulder titles and collar badges based on the White Tower at the Tower of London. Transfer to the Territorial Force was as 4th Battalion London Regiment.

5th Middlesex (West Middlesex) Rifle Volunteer Corps Allotted to the Royal Fusiliers as one of its volunteer battalions (without change in title) in 1881, but was transferred to the King's Royal Rifle Corps two years later.

9th Middlesex Rifle Volunteer Corps As a small corps, the 9th Middlesex RVC was attached to the 5th in 1881 and together provided a volunteer battalion (without change in title) of the Royal Fusiliers. Transferred to the King's Royal Rifle Corps in 1883.

22nd Middlesex (Central London Rangers) Rifle Volunteer Corps Served a volunteer battalion (without change in title) of the Royal Fusiliers until transferring to the King's Royal Rifle Corps in 1882.

Cadet Battalion

1st Cadet Battalion Formed with headquarters at St Pancras on 8 May 1901, moving to Pond Street, Hampstead in 1904. Illustration **(96)** shows the whole battalion on parade at their Pond Street headquarters, while **(97)** features a cadet wearing blue cyclist section uniform.

Illustration credits: Anne SK Brown Military Collection Brown University Library (81) and (83)

KING'S (LIVERPOOL REGIMENT)

8th (The King's) Regiment

Robert, Lord Ferrers of Chartley, under a letter of authority dated 19 June 1685, raised the regiment for service during Monmouth's rebellion, his recruits coming in the main from Hertfordshire, Middlesex and Derbyshire. Named Princess Anne of Denmark's at first, the regiment in 1702 would be known as the Queen's after Anne's accession to the throne, then afterwards from 1716 and following the Queen's death in 1714, The King's. George I had been pleased with the regiment's conduct during the recent troubles in Scotland. King's would also accompany the numerical designation from 1751 and in 1881 continue as part of the new King's (Liverpool Regiment) territorial title. In addition to the titles mentioned, the regiment was, until 1751, known by the names of its successive colonels—Robert Shirley, James FitzJames (killed at Phillipsburg 1734), John Beaumont, John Richmond Webb, Henry Morrison, Sir Charles Hotham, John Pocock, Charles Lenoe, Richard Onslow and Edward Wolfe.

Early records show that the original uniform consisted of scarlet coats with bright yellow facings, waistcoats and breeches. White stockings were worn, the broad-brimmed hats being looped with yellow ribbons. A change to dark blue facings accompanied the new King's title in 1716. At the same time the White Horse of Hanover and the motto *Nec aspera terrent* (Difficulties do not daunt) was directed to be worn within the Garter on Colours and appointments. Major Parkyn records that in 1716 the White Horse was peculiar to the 8th, but it later became the badge of several regiments. He also explains that the motto did not appear on the Colours until 1846. For its services during the 1801 campaign in Egypt the regiment was authorised on 6 July 1802 to include the Sphinx superscribed Egypt among its badges. The King's Cypher and Crown was recorded as part of the Second Colour according to the Regulations for Clothing and Colours for 1747.

Regular Battalions

1st, 2nd, 3rd and 4th Battalions The 1st and 2nd were provided by the two battalions of the former 8th (The King's) Regiment. The 3rd and 4th Battalions were formed in 1900; both, however, were disbanded in the following year. In **(98)** Bruce Bassett-Powell has clearly shown how the White Horse was used in the helmet plates, on waist-belt clasps and buttons worn by officers. The Red Rose, seen here used for the collar badges, was an old badge of the 2nd Royal Lancashire Militia and was taken into use by the regiment in 1881. Also from Bruce, **(99)** shows the White Horse badge on an officers' forage cap.

For a set of postcards published by Gale & Polden just after war was declared in August 1914, artist Edgar A Holloway painted six watercolours featuring the King's Liverpool Regiment. One of the cards **(100)** was entitled 'Relieving Sentry' and clearly shows the regiment's blue facings. A parade held for a presentation of

new Colours was also part of the set, the illustration here **(101)** being the original artwork provided by Edgar Holloway. As can be seen in the handwritten instruction at the bottom of the image, this was intended as Card No 1 of the six printed.

A regimental orchestra can be seen in **(102)** which includes most of the woodwind family of instruments. Here are flutes, clarinets, bassoons, an oboe and even in the centre row, fourth from the right, the rarely seen bass clarinet. The brass are not forgotten with their cornets, trombones and euphoniums.

Included in the Edgar A Holloway postcard set mentioned above was a card showing two King's Regiment soldiers and a French cavalry officer. In **(103)** we again have the original artwork provided by the artist who gives his image the title 'Mutual Admiration.' The 1st Battalion from Talavera Barracks in Aldershot had reached Southampton on 12 August from where it embarked for France. The 2nd was stationed at Peshawar, India in August 1914 where it remained.

Militia Battalions

3rd and 4th, later 5th and 6th Battalions The 2nd Royal Lancashire Militia at Warrington comprised two battalions, these in 1881 providing the 3rd and 4th Battalions of the King's Liverpool Regiment. Upon the formation of the two new and short lived regular battalions in 1900, the 3rd and 4th were required to re-number, albeit for just a year.

Territorial Battalions

5th Battalion Formed from the former 1st Volunteer Battalion with headquarters and all eight companies at 65 St Anne Street, Liverpool.

6th (Rifle) Battalion Formed from the former 2nd Volunteer Battalion with headquarters and all eight companies at Prince's Park Barracks, Upper Warwick Street, Liverpool. The battalion was represented in the 1939 John Player set of cigarette cards featuring the uniforms of the Territorial Army **(104)**. Artist

Lance Cattermole depicts an officer set against a backdrop of the Liverpool Town Hall.

7th Battalion Formed from the former 4th Volunteer Battalion with headquarters at 77 Shaw Street, Liverpool. A move was made in 1913, however, to 99 Park Street, Bootle. The eight companies were located as follows: 'A' to 'D' (Bootle), 'E' (Crosby), 'F' (Bootle), 'G' (Southport) and 'H' (Southport and Formby). The Southport Cadet Corps at 60 Scarisbrick New Road in Southport was also affiliated. War having been declared, in **(105)** we see officers of the battalion depositing the Colours for safekeeping at Bootle Town Hall on 15 August 1914. The 7th later moved to Canterbury, reaching France on 8 March 1915.

8th (Irish) Battalion Formed from the former 5th Volunteer Battalion with headquarters and all eight companies at 50-52 Everton Brow, Liverpool, moving to 75 Shaw Street in 1912.

9th Battalion Formed from the former 6th Volunteer Battalion with headquarters at 57-61 Everton Road, Liverpool. The eight companies were located: 'A' to 'E' (Everton Road), 'F' (Ormskirk), 'G' (Everton Road) and 'H' (Ormskirk). Wearing slouch hats and T over 9 over King's brass shoulder titles, the battalion's drums and bugles are seen in **(106)**.

10th (Scottish) Battalion Formed from the former 8th Volunteer Battalion with headquarters and all eight companies at 7 Fraser Street, Liverpool. To represent the West Lancashire Territorial Force Association in Walter Richards's *His Majesty's Territorial Army*, artist Richard Caton Woodville produced a fine study of an officer **(107)**. Clearly seen are the battalion's scarlet facings and Forbes pattern kilts. In **(108)** the band play during a drum head service, the photographer's shot allowing a clear view of the not-too-often seen rear of a baritone saxophone. Note the metal shoulder

108

109

110

title of the musician on the saxophonist's right, better seen in **(109)**.

Volunteer Battalions

1st Volunteer Battalion The 1st Lancashire Rifle Volunteer Corps in Liverpool was re-designation as 1st Volunteer Battalion King's (Liverpool Regiment) via Army Order 81 of March 1888, the establishment of the corps then being ten companies. Two more were sanctioned in 1883, another in 1900 and a cadet corps formed in April 1865 was disbanded in 1884. Transfer to the Territorial Force was as 5th Battalion King's.

2nd Volunteer Battalion With an establishment of ten companies, the 5th Lancashire Rifle Volunteer Corps was re-designated as 2nd Volunteer Battalion King's (Liverpool Regiment) in 1888. Transfer to the Territorial Force was as 6th Battalion King's (Liverpool Regiment).

3rd Volunteer Battalion The 13th Lancashire Rifle Volunteer Corps at Southport of six companies (four at Southport, two, Ormskirk) was designated as 3rd Volunteer Battalion King's (Liverpool Regiment) in 1888. Two more companies were sanctioned in 1899, the personnel being found out of the Mounted Infantry and Cyclist sections. The battalion was disbanded in 1908.

4th Volunteer Battalion The 15th Lancashire Rifle Volunteer Corps was re-designated as 4th Volunteer Battalion King's (Liverpool Regiment) by General Order 81 of March 1888. Transfer to the Territorial Force in 1908 was as 7th Battalion King's (Liverpool Regiment). Illustrated **(110)** is an example of an other ranks' white metal helmet plate.

5th (Irish) Volunteer Battalion The 18th Lancashire Rifle Volunteer Corps at 206 Netherfield Road North was re-designated as the 5th (Irish) Volunteer Battalion King's (Liverpool Regiment) in 1888. In 1900 the battalion was increased to eight companies, but in 1905 one of these was disbanded and replaced by a cyclist company. Transfer to the Territorial Force was as 8th Battalion King's.

6th Volunteer Battalion The 19th Lancashire Rifle Volunteer Corps was designated as 6th Volunteer Battalion King's (Liverpool Regiment) in 1888. A cyclist company was added in 1902, but by 1907 one company had been disbanded. Transfer to the Territorial Force was as 9th Battalion King's (Liverpool Regiment).

7th (Isle of Man) Volunteer Battalion The 1st Isle of Man Rifle Volunteer Corps was designated as 7th (Isle of Man) Volunteer Battalion King's (Liverpool Regiment) under Army Order 81 of March 1888. In 1908 the battalion was not included in the Territorial Force and instead continued service as 7th VB King's under the volunteer system. In *A Military History of the Isle of Man*, author BE Sargeaunt notes that on 28 June 1873 the corps paraded 'at the Drill Shed on the Lake (Douglas)' prior to leaving by rail to form a

Guard of Honour to His Excellency the Lieutenant Governor of the Isle of Man on the occasion of the first railway line being opened on the island from Douglas to Peel. Also recorded is the opening of a new rifle range at Howe Farm, Douglas Head on 10 August 1895. Prior to this the corps had, between 1884 and 1894, used a range at Langness. A new drill hall in Peel Road, Douglas was opened in June 1896.

8th (Scottish) Volunteer Battalion Mr David A Rutter writing in the *Bulletin* of the Military Historical Society in May 1978 noted that the idea of a Scottish Volunteer Corps in Liverpool was suggested in a letter signed 'G Forbes Milne' which appeared in the press on 27 January 1900. Lord Balfour subsequently headed the committee formed to see this through—permission to raise the proposed unit coming from the War Office on 30 April 1900. Enrolment in the 8th (Scottish) Volunteer Battalion King's (Liverpool Regiment) began in the following November. Eight companies were sanctioned, but it would seem that just four were in existence by the end of the year. The strength of the battalion did eventually grow to the required eight. A new drill hall was later opened at 7 Fraser Street and transfer to the Territorial Force in 1908 was as 10th (Scottish) Battalion King's (Liverpool Regiment).

Cadet Battalions

1st Cadet Battalion Formed in January 1890 with headquarters at the Gordon Institute in Stanley Road, Liverpool. Amalgamated with 2nd Cadet Battalion King's in 1904.

1st Territorial Cadet Battalion: Headquarters were at 16 South Castle Street, Liverpool. Recognition by the West Lancashire Territorial Force Association was, however, withdrawn in 1912.

2nd Cadet Battalion Formed in 1902 and amalgamated with the 1st Cadet Battalion King's in 1904.

City of Liverpool Cadet Battalion Headquarters Seaton Buildings, 17 Water Street.

Illustration credits: Alan Seymore (102), Anne SK Brown Military Collection Brown University Library (101) and (103), Bruce Bassett-Powell and Bob Bennet (98) and 99)

NORFOLK REGIMENT

9th (East Norfolk) Regiment

By authority of a letter dated 19 June 1685 the 9th Regiment was raised in Gloucestershire by Captain Henry Cornewall of the Royal Horse Guards and was then known by the names of its successive colonels until 1751—Henry Cornewall, Oliver Nicholas, John Cunningham, William Steuart, Sir James Campbell (killed at Fontenoy), Charles Cathcart, James Otway, Richard Kane, William Hargrave, George Reade, Sir Charles Armand Powlett and John Waldegrave. The Norfolk association came with the East Norfolk title in 1782, the Norfolk Regiment being that assumed with the reorganisations of 1881.

Uniform authority WY Carman records that, in 1733, official permission was given to change the facings from bright green to light orange. This shade would by 1747 be referred to as yellow, a colour that was retained until 1881. Several accounts regarding the use of the figure of Britannia by the 9th Regiment of Foot (later Royal Norfolk Regiment) exist. In 1948 reference to the distinction was made by General Bainbridge upon the occasion of the regiment receiving new Colours, 'This distinguishing badge', he remarked, 'was given to you for your gallantry at the battle of Almanza.' That battle took place in 1707, but Loraine Petre, in his history of the regiment, refers to a letter dated 9 March 1797 which states that the Britannia design had been awarded three years later after the fighting at Saragossa. No authority for its use, however, appeared in the Royal Warrants of 1747, 1751 or 1768. Certainly, the distinction had found its way to the Colours by 1802. There is also a Horse Guards letter dated 3 March 1800 stating that HM the King had granted permission for the badge 'some time ago.' It was, in fact, confirmed as the regiment's ancient badge in 1799. Seeing Britannia during the Peninsular War, a Spanish soldier, thinking it was the Virgin Mary, knelt and crossed himself. This was the origins of the regiment's Holy Boys nickname.

Regular Battalions

1st and 2nd Battalions From the 1st and 2nd Battalions of the 9th (East Norfolk) Regiment of Foot, the regiment's Britannia badge, as used on officers' helmet plates, collar badges, buttons and waist-belt plates,

can be seen in **(111)**. The latter also displays a representation of Norwich Castle, an old badge of the Norfolk Militia. In **(112)** Britannia again, this time on an officer's forage cap, and **(113)** as a collar badge. Note the unusual pattern of bandsman's wings and lace in this photograph. White facings were ordered to be worn from 1881 and we can see this change in Richard Simkin's Norfolk Regiment contribution to the *Army and Navy Gazette's* 'Military Types' series of supplements **(114)**. Harry Payne, on the other hand,

chose to ignore the white and stick with the traditional yellow of the 9th Regiment for the artwork seen in **(115)**. The watercolour was produced for one of Gale & Polden's uniform postcard sets and shows a sergeant and private of the regiment, the former wearing both the Queen's and King's Medals for South Africa, the private having a signallers badge on his lower left arm. It was the 2nd Battalion that saw service during the Second Boer War, sailing for the Cape on 4 January 1900.

In this group of four **(116)** we have a clear view of the curved brass

Norfolk shoulder title. There is also the R in a wreath badge of a rangefinder, and what looks like the HG of a Hotchkiss Gunner.

Stationed in Ireland, the 1st Battalion, having handed its Colours over to Belfast Cathedral for safe keeping, sailed for France on 14 August 1914. Just ten days later, when the men took up positions along the railway line south of the Mons-Condè Canal, an officer was on hand to sketch the scene, his work later being used as a frontispiece to F Loraine Petre's account of the Norfolk Regiment in the 1st World War **(117)**. The attack referred to in the caption would see over 250 from the battalion either killed, wounded or missing.

Militia Battalions

3rd and 4th Battalions Formed from the former 1st Norfolk Militia with headquarters in Norwich, and 2nd Norfolk Militia at Yarmouth.

Territorial Battalions

4th Battalion Formed from part of the former 1st Volunteer Battalion with headquarters at St Giles, Norwich. There were eight companies located as follows: 'A', 'B' (Norwich), 'C' (Long Stratton, Mulbarton and Saxlingham), 'D' (Diss, Harleston and Tivetshall), 'E' (Attleborough, East Harling, Kenninghall, Banham, Old Buckenham, Hingham and Watton), 'F' (Wymondham, Hethersett, Swardeston, Mulbarton, Colney, Saxlingham and Hingham), 'G' (Brandon, Thetford, Methwold and Feltwell) and 'H' (Thorpe St Andrew, Loddon, Blofield, Acle, Burgh St Margaret, Framlingham, Pigot and Coltishall).

5th Battalion Formed after the merger of the former 2nd and 3rd Volunteer Battalions. Headquarters were at East Derham and the eight companies located: 'A' (King's Lynn), 'B' (Downham Market, Hunstanton, Thornham, Hilgay and Stoke Ferry), 'C' (Fakenham, Wells, Syderstone, Aylsham and Corpusty), 'D' (East Derham, Castle Acre, Litcham and Swaffham), 'E' (Sandringham, Dersingham, Wolferton, Hillington and West Newton), 'F' (Cromer, Melton Constable, Holt, Sheringham, North Walsham, Westwick, Gunton and Honing) and 'G', 'H' (Great Yarmouth).

6th (Cyclist) Battalion Created in 1908 with headquarters at York House, Rosary in Norwich, moving to Cattle Market Street in 1911. The companies were: 'A' (Norwich), 'B' (Great Yarmouth), 'C' (King's Lynn and Terrington St Clement), 'D' (Thetford and Attleborough), 'E' (Fakenham, Walsingham, Holkham, Wells and Ryburgh), 'F' (Ditchingham), 'G' (Watton and Swaffham) and 'H' (Norwich and Great Yarmouth).

Volunteer Battalions

1st Volunteer Battalion In the Army List for February 1860 the 1st, 2nd and 3rd Norfolk RVC are shown as having been amalgamated under the title of 1st (City of Norwich) RVC. The new formation comprised six companies under the command of Major Commandant John Davy Brett who had previously served with the 7th Dragoons. The corps was re-designated as 1st Volunteer Battalion Norfolk Regiment in 1883. A cadet corps was formed in 1893, but this was absorbed into the 1st Cadet Battalion Norfolk Regiment in 1895. Transfer to the Territorial Force in 1908 was as part the 4th Battalion Norfolk Regiment.

2nd Volunteer Battalion The 2nd Norfolk Rifle Volunteer Corps, with its nine companies: 'A', 'B', 'C', 'D' Great Yarmouth, 'E' Gorleston, 'F' Bungay, 'G' Beccles, 'H', 'I' Lowestoft, was re-designated as 2nd Volunteer Battalion Norfolk Regiment under General Order 79 of June 1883. A tenth company was added in 1885. The battalion transferred to the Territorial Force in 1908 as part of the 5th Norfolk Regiment.

3rd Volunteer Battalion Under General Order 79 of June 1883, the 3rd Norfolk Rifle Volunteer Corps of ten companies was re-designated as 3rd Volunteer Battalions Norfolk Regiment. A cadet corps had been formed at King's Lynn in 1867, the Army List giving its headquarters as East Dereham from 1883, then as King's Lynn again after 1885. The company finally disappeared from the Army List in February 1888. Another cadet corps was formed at the Norfolk County School, North Elmham in 1888, but this too was disbanded and last seen in 1893. Next came Gresham's School at Holt in 1902 which in 1908 joined the OTC, the battalion at the same time transferring as part of 5th Battalion Norfolk Regiment.

4th Volunteer Battalion The 4th Norfolk Rifle Volunteer Corps with six companies was designated as 4th Volunteer Battalion Norfolk Regiment in 1883. Harleston, Diss, Loddon, Stalham, Blofield and Attleborough were the company locations in 1899, four more being added in 1900. Transfer to the Territorial Force in 1908 was as part of 4th Battalion Norfolk Regiment.

Cadet Battalion

1st Cadet Battalion Formed with headquarters at the Drill Hall, Theatre Street, Norwich as four companies on 23 January 1895. Location is given later as St Peter's Hall, Norwich, and by 1898 as Britannia Barracks. The battalion was last seen in the Army List for March 1900.

Illustration credits: Anne SK Brown Military Collection Brown University Library (115), Bruce Bassett-Powell and Bob Bennet (111) and (112)

LINCOLNSHIRE REGIMENT

10th (North Lincoln) Regiment

Chichester and Burges-Short note how the 10th traces its beginnings back to an independent company of infantry which for many years had been stationed at Plymouth, it being 'expanded into a regiment of ten companies during the troubles of 1685.' John, Earl of Bath's Regiment was the first title held, this being changed according to the names of successive colonels—John Granville, Sir Charles Carney, Sir Beville Granville, William North, Henry Grove, Francis Columbine, James O'Hara and Edward Pole—until 1751. The Lincolnshire Regiment was the title taken in 1881, the county connection appearing in 1782 when North Lincoln was included to the 10th's designation.

WY Carman points out that the regiment was unusual in having blue coats when it was raised, and he shows a fine example of this uniform in Plate 21 of his Richard Simkin book. Chichester and Burges-Short describe this colour a 'butcher's blue' which was faced with red. Also noted by these authors are red breeches and stockings, broad-brimmed hats looped up with red ribbons, Carman adding red waistcoats. Regarding the blue coats: possibly the reason for the adoption of these lies in the fact that the livery of the Earl of Bath at the time was blue with red cuffs and linings. Turing now to the Cannon regimental records, the author confirms

that the 10th was the only infantry regiment to have blue coats at the time and that '…a few years after the revolution of 1688 the 10th were then clothed in red.' Carman puts this date as 1691 and mentions that the red facings were retained until yellow came in during William's reign. The regiment served in the 1801 campaign in Egypt, the badge and honour of a Sphinx superscribed Egypt being authorised 6 July 1802.

Regular Battalions

1st and 2nd Battalions Formed by the two battalions of the 10th (North Lincoln) Regiment of Foot. As can be seen in Bruce Bassett-Powell's detailed image of officers badges **(118)**, the Sphinx superscribed Egypt was featured on the helmet plate, collar badges, buttons and waistbelt clasp. We can also see it as used on the forage cap with a star backing **(119)**. Other ranks wore the Sphinx alone above the title **(120)**. Ernest Ibbetson was commissioned to produce a series of watercolours illustrating the regiment for one of Gale & Polden's 'History and Tradition' uniform sets of postcards. Here in **(121)** we see his original artwork for one of the cards, **(122)** being the finished product which now has text on one side. Note how the facings of the

regiment are shown as white. One of the regulations that came along with the reorganisations of 1881 directed that all non-royal English regiments should change their facing colour to white. Original artwork again, this time from Harry Payne for another of Gale & Polden's postcard sets **(123)**. In **(124)** No 50 in Richard Simkin's 'Military Types' series, published as a supplement to the *Army and Navy Gazette* on 6 February 1892.

Militia Battalions

3rd and 4th Battalions Formed from the Royal North Lincoln Militia and Royal South Lincoln Militia whose headquarters were respectively at Lincoln and Grantham.

Territorial Battalions

4th Battalion Headquarters were in Lincoln and the eight companies located: 'A' (Lincoln), 'B' (Grantham), 'C' (Boston), 'D' (Stamford), 'E' (Lincoln), 'F' (Spalding, Bourne and Sleaford), 'G' (Horncastle and Woodhall Spa) and 'H' (Lincoln).

5th Battalion Headquarters were in Grimsby and the eight companies located: 'A', 'B' (Grimsby), 'C' (Spilsby and Skegness), 'D' (Louth and North Thoresby), 'E' (Barton-upon-Humber), 'F' (Alford), 'G' (Frodingham and Brigg) and 'H' (Gainsborough).

Volunteer Battalions

1st Volunteer Battalion The 1st Lincolnshire Rifle Volunteer Corps at Lincoln had eleven companies: 'A', 'B', 'C' (Lincoln), 'D' (Louth), 'E' (Great Grimsby), 'F' (Spilsby), 'G' (Horncastle), 'H' (Alford), 'I' (Barton), 'J' (Gainsborough) and 'K' (Market Rasen). In 1881 the headquarters of 'K' Company had moved to Frodingham by 1881 then in May 1882, General Order 63 directed a change in designation to 1st Volunteer Battalion Lincolnshire Regiment. In June 1900 the establishment of the battalion was reduced to the following seven companies: 'A' to 'D' (Lincoln), 'E' and 'F' (Gainsborough), 'G' (Horncastle), the remainder of the strength going to form the 3rd Volunteer Battalion Lincolnshire Regiment. Lincoln Grammar School Cadet Corps was formed and affiliated in 1903 and transfer to the Territorial Force in 1908 saw the Lincoln and Horncastle Companies as part of the 4th Battalion Lincolnshire Regiment while the Gainsborough personnel joined the 5th.

2nd Volunteer Battalion The 2nd Lincolnshire Rifle Volunteer Corps at Grantham in 1881 comprised eight companies: 'A', 'B' (Grantham), 'C' (Boston), 'D' (Stamford), 'E' (Sleaford), 'F' (Spalding), 'G' (Gosberton) and 'H' (Billingborough). Re-designation as 2nd Volunteer Battalion Lincolnshire Regiment was notified in General Order 63 of 1883. The King's School, Grantham Cadet Corps was formed and affiliated in 1904 and transfer to the Territorial Force in 1908 was as part of 4th Battalion Lincolnshire Regiment. The King's School cadets at the same time joined the OTC.

3rd Volunteer Battalion Formed with headquarters at Grimsby in June 1900 by the withdrawal from the 1st Volunteer Battalion of its Louth, Grimsby, Spilsby, Alford, Barton and Frodingham companies. The King Edward VI Grammar School Cadet Corps at Louth was formed and affiliated in 1905, followed by the Grimsby

Municipal College Cadet Corps in 1906. Transfer to the Territorial Force was as part of 5th Battalion Lincolnshire Regiment, both the King Edward VI and Grimsby Schools at the same time joining the OTC.

Illustration credits: Anne SK Brown Military Collection (121) an (123), Bruce Bassett-Powell and Bob Bennet (118) and (119)

DEVONSHIRE REGIMENT

11th (North Devon) Regiment

Raised 1685 by Henry, Duke of Beaufort from, according to Cannon, 'men of distinguished loyalty, who resided in the disturbed districts of Devonshire, Somersetshire and Dorsetshire.' The regiment gathered at Bristol and, resigning his commission due to his age, Beaufort handed over command to his son Charles, Marquis of Worcester. After being known by a succession of colonels' names—Henry Somerset, Charles Somerset, William Herbert, Sir John Hanmer, James Stanhope, John Hill, Edward Montague, Stephen Cornwallis, Robinson Sowle, William Graham and Maurice Bocland—the regiment was re-designated as the 11th in 1751, North Devon being added 1782. The Devonshire Regiment was the title assumed in 1881.

The regiment's facing, breeches and stockings colour was first described as tawny, a light brown to brownish-orange. A change was later made to yellow, then to dark green. The 1742 Clothing Book gives this colour, along with red waistcoats and breeches. A star features in the regiment's badges, collar badges being noted as an Imperial crown, later changing to a crowned strap on a star.

Regular Battalions

1st and 2nd Battalions Formed from the two battalions of the 11th (North Devon) Regiment. A representation of Exeter Castle and the motto *Semper fedelis* (Always faithful) had been the badge of the Devon Militia for many years. The Devonshire Regiment took it into use after 1881, and here we see how it was used on the officers' helmet plate, collar badges, buttons and waist-belt clasps **(125)**. Cap badges used the device with a star backing, as seen in the cigarette card illustrated **(126)** and in this example of an officer's forage cap on display at the Bygones Museum in Torquay **(127)**.

Illustration **(128)** is supplement No 51 in the *Army and Navy Gazette* series of colour prints by Richard Simkin.

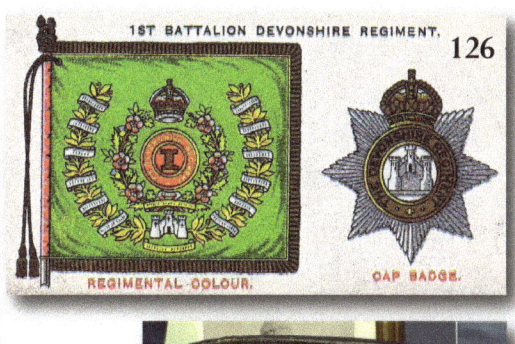

Published on 5 March 1892, the artist shows the officer with the white facings directed to be adopted by English regiments in 1881 while the soldiers wear the all-scarlet frock coat. Harry Payne, in his artwork for one of Gale & Polden's postcard sets however, chose the original green which had been restored to the regiment in 1905 **(129)**. The white facings again, this time in a portrait of Lieutenant Henry Cary who was killed in 1901 during the Second Boar War, which can be seen at the Tore Abbey Museum in Torquay **(130)**. Illustration **(131)** is by F Stansell and shows a drum major.

Militia Battalions

3rd and 4th Battalions The 3rd Battalion was the former 2nd South Devon Militia at Plymouth, the 4th being provided by the 1st Devon Militia whose headquarters were in Exeter.

Territorial Battalions

4th Battalion Formed from the former 1st and 3rd Volunteer Battalions with headquarters at Exeter, the eight companies being located: 'A' (Exeter and Broadclyst). 'B', 'C' (Exeter), 'D' (Exmouth, Budleigh Saltererton and Lympstone), 'E' (Tiverton, Bampton and Dulverton), 'F' (Sidmouth, Ottery St Mary, Newton Poppleford, Honiton and Colyton), 'G' (Cullompton, Whimple, Burlescombe and Uffculme) and 'H' (Axminster, Chardstock and Lyme Regis). The Exeter Cathedral School Cadet Company was affiliated. To represent the Devonshire Territorial Force Association in *His Majesty's Territorial Army* by Walter Richards, artist Richard Caton Woodville chose a portrait of a mounted officer of the 4th Battalion **(132)**.

5th (Prince of Wales's) Battalion Formed from the former 2nd and 5th Volunteer Battalions with headquarters at Plymouth. There were eight companies located as follows: *Companies:* 'A' (Plymouth and Tavistock), 'B' (Plymouth), 'C' (Plymouth, Ivybridge and Kingsbridge), 'D' (Devonport), 'E' (Newton Abbot and Chudleigh), 'F' (Teignmouth, Dawlish and Torquay), 'G' (Moreton Hampstead, Bovey Tracey and Chagford) and 'H' (Totnes, Ashburton and Buckfastleigh). Affiliated to the battalion were the Plymouth Lads' Brigade Cadet Corps at 79 Embankment Road, Plymouth, the Haytor Cadet Corps at Penhurst in Newton Abbot, and the Totnes Cadet Company whose headquarters were at the YMCA in Fore Street, Totnes.

6th Battalion The 6th Battalion at Barnstaple was formed from the 4th Volunteer Battalion and comprised: 'A' Company (Barnstaple and Muddiford), 'B' (Okehampton, Hatherleigh, Bow and Sticklepath), 'C' (Bideford, Appledore, Parkham and Hartland), 'D' (Torrington, St Giles, Holsworthy and Ashwater), 'E' (South Molton, Witheridge, Molland and Chittlehampton), 'F' (Chulmleigh, Winkleigh, King's Nympton, Burrington and Crediton), 'G' (Combe Martin, Berrynarbor, Braunton and Croyde) and 'H' (Barnstaple).

7th (Cyclist) Battalion: With headquarters in Exeter, the 7th Battalion was a new unit in 1908 with companies located: 'A' (Torquay), 'B' (Exeter, Topsham and Woodbury), 'C' (Exeter), 'D' (Cullompton, Bradninch and Silverton), 'E' (Crediton), 'F' (Dartmouth), 'G' (Plymouth) and 'H' (Torquay). The Dartmouth Cadet Company at Crothers Hill, Dartmouth was affiliated.

Volunteer Battalions

1st (Exeter and South Devon) Volunteer Battalion Under General Order 114 of 1885, the 1st Devonshire Rifle Volunteer Corps at Exeter was re-designated as 1st (Exeter and South Devon) Volunteer Battalion Devonshire Regiment. Transfer to the Territorial Force in 1908 was as part of the 4th Battalion Devonshire Regiment. The Exeter School Cadet Corps, which had been affiliated to the battalion since 1897, at the same time became part of the OTC.

In Northernhay Gardens, Exeter there is a small Renaissance pillar commemorating the formation on the 1st Devonshire RVC. The memorial, by local sculptor Harry Hems and erected in 1895, includes plaques recording the names of the first officers to receive commissions, the committee that was responsible for the formation of the corps and a list of places from where the recruits were drawn—'Exeter, Cullompton, Tiverton, Bovey Tracey, Exmouth, Honiton, Brixham, Torquay, Totnes.'

The 1st Devonshire RVC was the senior volunteer unit in the United Kingdom, it being the first to be officially recognised by the Government. It was in January 1852 that Superintendent of the Exminster Lunatic Asylum, Dr John Bucknill of Exeter (through Earl Fortescue, the Lord Lieutenant of Devonshire) submitted a proposal to the Secretary of State (Sir George Grey) that a corps of volunteer riflemen be formed in South Devon for the defence of the coast. Subsequently the services of the Exeter and South Devon Rifle Corps were accepted under the Volunteer Act of 1804, the officers' commissions being signed by Queen Victoria on 4 January 1853. When the Volunteer Force got underway proper in 1859, the corps received the title 1st Devonshire (Exeter and South Devon). A pouch-belt plate worn by the corps on display at the Bygones Museum in Torquay is illustrated **(133)**.

2nd (Prince of Wales's) Volunteer Battalion The 2nd (Prince of Wales's) Rifle Volunteer Corps with eleven companies: 'A' to 'F' (Plymouth), 'G' to 'I' (Devonport), 'K' and 'L' (Tavistock), was designated 2nd (Prince of Wales's) Volunteer Battalion Devonshire Regiment under General Order 114 of 1885. There was an increase to twelve companies in 1900, but there were only eight, however, in 1905. A cadet corps had existed for a while, but this disappeared from the Army List in 1885. Kelly College at Tavistock

also provided a company in 1894 and in 1906 the Army List indicated that the Postal Telegraph Messengers of Plymouth had been formed. This, though, disappeared in July 1907. The Plymouth and Mannamead College Cadet Corps transferred from the 2nd Devonshire RGA (Vols) in 1907. Transfer to the Territorial Force in 1908 was as part of 5th (Prince of Wales's) Battalion Devonshire Regiment, the cadets at Kelly College and Plymouth and Mannamead College at the same time joined the OTC. Illustrated is a portrait of HRH Prince Alfred of Edinburgh in the uniform of the 2nd Volunteer Battalion **(134)**.

3rd Volunteer Battalion The 3rd Devonshire Rifle Volunteer Corps had seven companies: 'A' (Cullompton), 'B' (Buckerell), 'C' (Bampton), 'D' (Honiton), 'E' (Tiverton), 'F' (Ottery St Mary) and 'G' (Colyton). Re-designation as 3rd Volunteer Battalion Devonshire Regiment was notified by General Order 114 of November 1885, the same year seeing a new company ('H') formed at Sidmouth then followed in 1900 by 'I' at Axminster. Cadet corps were formed and affiliated at All Hallows School in Honiton and at Blundell's School, Tiverton in 1900. Transfer to the Territorial Force in 1908 was as part of 4th Battalion Devonshire Regiment, both All Hallows and Blundell's Schools at the same time joining the OTC. Illustrated is an example of the helmet plate worn by officers which can be seen on display at the Bygones Museum in Torquay **(135)**. The battalion's white metal shoulder title is shown in **(136)**.

4th Volunteer Battalion With headquarters in Barnstable, the 4th Devonshire Rifle Volunteer Corps had seven companies: 'A' and 'B' (Barnstaple), 'C' (Hatherleigh), 'D' (Okehampton), 'E' (Bideford), 'F' (Torrington) and 'G' (South Molton). Under General Order 114 of November 1885, the corps was re-

designated as 4th Volunteer Battalion Devonshire Regiment, an additional two companies, one each at Buckfastleigh and Torquay, being sanctioned in 1886. The United Services College Cadet Corps at Westward Ho! was formed and attached in 1900 but, having moved to Harpenden in 1904, its affiliation was transferred to the 2nd Volunteer Battalion Bedfordshire Regiment. Transfer to the Territorial Force in 1908 was as 6th Battalion Devonshire Regiment. With its Exeter Castle central device, an other ranks' helmet plate on display at the Bygones Museum in Torquay is shown at **(137)**.

5th (The Hay Tor) Volunteer Battalion The 5th Devonshire Rifle Volunteer Corps with headquarters in Newton Abbot had six companies—'A' (Ashburton), 'B' (Newton Abbot), 'C' (Totnes), 'D'

(Chudleigh), 'E' (Kingsbridge) and 'F' (Torquay). Re-designation as 5th (The Hay Tor) Volunteer Battalion Devonshire Regiment was notified by General Order 114 of November 1885 and transfer to the Territorial Force in 1908 was as part of 5th Battalion Devonshire Regiment. Two exhibits from Torquay's superb Bygones Museum, an other ranks' helmet with king's crown plate **(138)** and the scarlet tunic of a colour sergeant **(139)**.

Illustration credits: Anne SK Brown Military Collection Brown University Library (129), Bruce Bassett-Powell and Bob Bennet (125)

SUFFOLK REGIMENT

12th (East Suffolk) Regiment

Appointed as colonel of the regiment when raised in 1685 was Henry, Duke of Norfolk, Cannon noting that the Duke had previously raised a company for garrison duty at Windsor and this was to form the nucleus of the new regiment. After being known by the names of its successive colonels—Henry Howard, Sir Edward Henry Lee, Sir Robert Carey, Henry Wharton, Richard Brewer, John Livesay, Richard Philipps, Thomas Stanwix, Thomas Whetham, Scipio Duroure (mortally wounded at Fontenoy) and Henry Skelton—the regiment was designated as 12th. East Suffolk was added in 1782 and the Suffolk Regiment formed in 1881.

Cannon also recorded that, whilst camped on Hounslow Heath in May 1686, the regiment was distinguished by its white colours bearing the red cross of St George. The men at the time were wearing broad-brimmed hats with the brim turned up on one side, and ornamented with white ribands. They had scarlet coats lined white, blue breeches, blue stockings and high shoes with square toes. There were twelve pikemen, each having white sashes round their waists. The white facings were exchanged for yellow by 1742 when the waistcoats and breeches were recorded as red.

For its services during the siege of 1779-83 the 12th was awarded, as a badge, the Castle of Gibraltar, together with Key and motto *Montis insignia calpe* (Badge of the Rock of Gibraltar). An oak wreath also appears as a badge, Colonel Webb's history of the regiment suggesting that this device was connected with the arms of the Durounes. Colonel Scipio Duroune had been appointed as colonel of the 12th in August 1741 and would die of wounds received at Fontenoy in 1745. The Webb history has a number of superb photographic images of badges.

Thomas Carlyle, in his history of Frederick the Great, wrote 'A really splendid victory, this of Minden, August 1st. These unsurpassable Six, in industrious valour, unsurpassable.' The six regiments he was referring to include the 12th which, on Minden Day (1st August), celebrated the victory by wearing roses in their hats and decorating the Colours and drums with the same. The custom recalls how advancing troops during the battle passed among rose briers, snatching up the blossoms and placing them in their headdress and equipment.

Regular Battalions

1st and 2nd Battalions Formed from the two battalions of the 12th (East Suffolk) Regiment of Foot. In Bruce Bassett-Powell's detailed images of officers' insignia **(140)** and **(141)** we see how the Gibraltar device appeared on the helmet plates, collar badges, buttons, waist-belt plates and forage caps. From Colonel Webb's history, artist PW Reynolds illustrates a variety of uniforms and equipment for the year 1913 **(142)**, the officer in the centre wearing both the Queen's and King's Medals for South Africa. It was the 1st Battalion that sailed for the Cape on the *Scott* in November 1899. The same two medals can also be seen in Harry Payne's artwork for one of the Gale & Polden uniform postcard sets **(143)**. Two musicians now, the first being a study of a clarinettist by F Stansell for WJ Gordon's book on British Army bands **(144)**, the second, a photograph of a drummer **(145)**. Note his Gibraltar collar badges, Suffolk brass shoulder titles and three good conduct chevrons.

The other ranks brass helmet plate is shown in **(146)** and the cap badge in **(147)**. Much in the way of regimental insignia, uniform and equipment can be seen at the Suffolk Regiment Museum in Bury St Edmunds, including a fine display of drums **(148)**.

Militia Battalions

3rd and 4th Battalions The 3rd Battalion was provided by the West

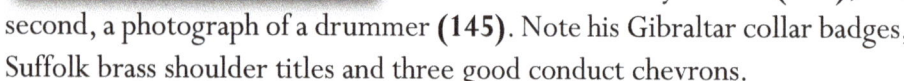

Suffolk Militia at Bury St Edmunds, the 4th at Ely coming from the former Cambridgeshire Militia. The latter was disbanded in 1908.

Territorial Battalions

4th Battalion Formed from the former 1st Volunteer Battalion at Portman Road, Ipswich. There were eight companies located as follows: 'A' to 'D' (Ipswich), 'E' (Lowestoft), 'F' (Halesworth and Saxmundham), 'G' (Framlingham, Woodbridge and Easton) and 'H' (Leiston and East Bridge).

5th Battalion Formed from the former 2nd Volunteer Battalion at Bury St Edmunds with companies located: 'A' (Stowmarket and Eye), 'B' (Beccles and Bungay), 'C' (Hadleigh and Bildeston), 'D' (Sudbury, Long Melford and Bures), 'E' (Bury St Edmunds and Barrow), 'F' (Bury St Edmunds and Lavenham), 'G' (Haverhill and Clare) and 'H' (Newmarket and Mildenhall).

146

147

6th (Cyclist) Battalion A new battalion with headquarters at Ipswich and companies located: 'A', 'B' (Ipswich), 'C' (Ipswich and Brantham), 'D' (Southwold and Aldeburgh), 'E' (Lowestoft), 'F' (Bungay and Beccles), 'G' (Stowmarket) and 'H' (Bury St Edmunds). Originally raised as four companies of the Essex and Suffolk Cyclist Battalion which was divided in 1911 to form 6th Suffolk and 8th Essex Battalions. Extremely scarce are the badges worn by the Essex and Suffolk Cyclists which incorporated both the Gibraltar Castle and arms of Essex **(149)**.

Cambridgeshire Battalion It was originally planned to accommodate the 3rd Volunteer Battalion into the Territorial Force under the title Cambridgeshire Battalion Suffolk Regiment. In 1909, however, the former volunteers were designated as the Cambridgeshire Regiment.

Volunteer Battalions

1st Volunteer Battalion The 1st Suffolk Rifle Volunteer Corps at Woodridge had eight companies: 'A', 'B' and 'C' (Ipswich), 'D' (Framlingham), 'E' (Woodbridge), 'F' (Halesworth), 'G' (Saxmundham) and 'H' (Leiston) and was re-designated as 1st Volunteer Battalion Suffolk Regiment under General Order 181 of December 1887. A new company was added in 1900. The Queen Elizabeth's School at Ipswich formed an affiliated cadet corps in 1889, but this

149

disappeared from the Army List by the end of 1891 only to reappear again in 1900. Framlingham College in 1901 also formed a cadet corps and transfer to the Territorial Force in 1908 was as 4th Battalion Suffolk Regiment. Both Queen Elizabeth's School and Framlingham College at the same time joined the OTC.

2nd Volunteer Battalion The 6th Suffolk Rifle Volunteer Corps had eight companies: 'A' (Stowmarket), 'B' and 'C' (Eye), 'D' (Sudbury), 'E' and 'F' (Bury St Edmunds), 'G' (Hadleigh) and 'H' (Newmarket) and was re-designated as 2nd Volunteer Battalion Suffolk Regiment under General Order 181 of December 1887. Headquarters moved from Sudbury to Bury St Edmunds in 1899 and there was a reduction in establishment to seven companies in 1889, to brought back to eight in 1900. A cadet corps at King Edward's School, Bury St Edmunds was raised and affiliated in 1900, the battalion providing the 5th Battalion Suffolk Regiment in 1908. King Edward School at the same time joined the OTC. The battalion wore grey uniforms with red collars, cuffs, Austrian knots, and piping **(150)**.

3rd (Cambridgeshire) Volunteer Battalion The 1st Cambridgeshire Rifle Volunteer Corps at Cambridge had ten companies: 'A', 'B', 'C' and 'D' (Cambridge), 'E' (Wisbech), 'F' (Whittlesea), 'G' (March), 'H' (Ely), 'I' (Saffron Walden) and 'J' (St Neots). Under General Order 181 of December 1887 the corps was re-designated as 3rd (Cambridgeshire) Volunteer Battalion Suffolk Regiment. In 1889 the Hunts Company ('J') was disbanded. Three cadet corps were affiliated to the 3rd Volunteer Battalion: Leys School in Cambridge formed a company in 1900, followed by the Perse School (also in Cambridge) in 1905. The last formed was by the Cambridge and County School in 1906. On Sunday 29 March 1908 the Colours presented to the original 1st Corps in May 1860 were committed to the keeping of the vicar and churchwardens of Great St Mary. Two days later the Territorial Force came into being and as the 1st Cambridgeshire RVC stood down, the Cambridgeshire Battalion Suffolk Regiment was born, an unpopular title which soon changed to the Cambridgeshire Regiment. At the same time Leys and Cambridge and County Schools became contingents of the Junior Division OTC.

4th (Cambridge University) Volunteer Battalion The 3rd Cambridgeshire Rifle Volunteer Corps was re-numbered as 2nd (Cambridge University) in 1880 and designated as 4th (Cambridge University) Volunteer Battalion Suffolk Regiment under General Order 181 of December 1887. During 1893-94 the company structure was changed to 'A' (Peterhouse, Pembroke, Queens', Corpus Christi and St Catharine's), 'B' (St John's), 'C' (Gonville and Caius), 'D' (Christ's, Emmanuel, Jesus and Magdalene), 'E' (Trinity), 'F' (Clare, Trinity Hall, King's, Sidney Sussex and Selwyn). St John's became part of 'A' Company in 1896 and at the same time Pembroke became 'B' and Downing part of 'A'.

Permission to increase the establishment to eight companies was granted during the early part of 1900, the change requiring the regrouping of the colleges as follows: St John's was removed from 'A' Company to form the new 'G', while at the same time Christ's, Magdalene, Sidney Sussex and Selwyn were taken from 'D' and 'F' to form 'H'. Under Army Order 56 of April 1903 His Majesty the King was graciously pleased to approve the new title of 'The Cambridge University Volunteer Rifle Corps', this being held until transfer to the Senior Division of the OTC in 1908.

Illustration credit: Bruce Bassett-Powell and Bob Bennet (140) and 141)

PRINCE ALBERT'S (SOMERSET LIGHT INFANTRY)

The Prince Albert's (Somersetshire Light Infantry) was the original form of the title, but in 1912 this was shortened by omitting the prefix 'The' and amending 'Somersetshire' to 'Somerset.'

13th (1st Somersetshire) (Prince Albert's Light Infantry) Regiment

Raised 1685 by the Earl of Huntingdon in the southern counties of England and after being known by the names of its successive colonels—Theophilus Hastings, Ferdinando Hastings, Sir John Jacob, James Barry, Stanhope Cotton, Lord Mark Kerr, John Middleton and Harry Pulteney—became the 13th Regiment in 1751. The bracketed 1st Somersetshire was added to the title in 1782, Light Infantry in 1822 and Prince Albert's in 1842. The reorganisations of 1881 saw the 13th designated The Prince Albert's (Somersetshire Light Infantry). Returning to the regiment's second colonel, the military historian JW Fortescue referred to Ferdinando Hastings as 'One of the most unscrupulous scoundrels, even in those days of universal robbery, that ever robbed a regiment.' The author of the classic *A History of the British Army* recalls the cashiering of Hastings for suppling his men with cast-off uniforms.

The early uniform has been described as being long-skirted coats, lined and turned back with yellow, yellow breeches, grey stockings and broad-brimmed hats tied up with yellow ribbons. The tall caps of the grenadiers were of yellow cloth, and the officers and pikemen had white sashes. The yellow facings were sometimes described as light yellow or philemot. Prince Albert brought blue facings along with his name to the regiment in 1842.

Unique to the regiment is the practice of the sergeants being allowed to wear their sashes over the left shoulder instead of the right. The origin of the sash, either worn around the waist or over a shoulder, goes as far back as the seventeenth century when its purpose was to carry a wounded officer from the field of battle. Made of silk (crimson usually), sashes were not only strong but light, their length and width being adequate to carry the human form. But the accessory would later become an indication of rank and the freedom afforded in its wear tightened up by various Clothing Regulations over the years. In short: officers to have the sash tassels falling on the right side, sergeants on the left. Moving now to the Battle of Culloden in 1746 and the final confrontation of the previous year's Jacobite rising. It is said that during the fighting most of the officers from the regiment (that in 1881 would become the Somerset Light Infantry) had become casualties and it would be left to the sergeants to take command. In recognition of this it soon became the custom within the regiment for these NCOs to have the sash terminating on the officers' side. Major-General H J Everett, late of the Somerset Light Infantry, however, would point out in Vol. XIII of the *Journal of the Society for Army Research* that there is no evidence to support this. But on the officers' side it is and in view of the length of time this custom had been observed, be the tradition substantiated or not, Horse Guards gave authorization on 3 April 1865 to this distinction, unique within the British Army.

151

THE PRINCE ALBERT'S SOMERSETSHIRE LIGHT INFANTRY

The badges of the 13th were the Sphinx superscribed Egypt, which was authorized in July 1802 to commemorate the services of the regiment in the campaign of the previous year, and the

Mural Crown which was given with the battle honour Jellalabad in 1842. A light infantry bugle-horn came with the title in 1822, and the cypher of Prince Albert twenty years after that.

Regular Battalions

1st and 2nd Battalions Formed from the two battalions of the former 13th (1st Somersetshire) (Prince Albert's Light Infantry). In **(151)** we see No 43 in the 'Types of the British Army' series published on 4 July 1891 as a supplement to the *Army and Navy Gazette*. The artwork is by Richard Simkin and shows a drummer, colour sergeant and officer. The officer's helmet plate, collar badges, buttons and waist-belt clasp are featured in Bruce Bassett-Powell's detailed image **(152)** and can be seen again being worn by the officer in **(153)** who wears a scarlet tunic with blue facings. The photograph was taken by H Montague Cooper who had studios in both Taunton and Burnham. Quite some way from these Somerset towns were the premises in

Rawalpindi, India of George Dean where the photograph of the officer in **(154)** was taken.

For one of Gale & Polden's uniform postcard sets, artist Harry Payne produced the artwork shown in **(155)**, a study of a sergeant and two bandsmen. The sergeant is shown wearing both the Queen's and King's Medals awarded for service in South Africa during the Second Boar War. It was the 2nd Battalion that sailed for the Cape on 5 December 1899, the splendid Somerset Light Infantry Museum in Taunton including among its exhibits a helmet worn during the campaign **(156)**. Clear in the Harry

Payne image is the bugle collar badge, the brass shoulder title of a bugle over Somerset **(157)** only hinted at.

Also from Bruce Bassett-Powell is this image of an officers' forage cap **(158)**. It can be seen in a photograph taken by G & R Lavis of Major Richard Cooper who was first commissioned into the 13th Regiment in 1869. The studios of G & R Lavis, who also produced miniature painting, could be found at 135 Regent Street in London, or in Eastbourne at 42 Terminus Place **(159)**.

Much overseas service was seen by both battalions. The 2nd Battalion moved to Malta in 1908 where the Grand Studio photographers in Valletta produced a detailed image of the machine gun section **(160)**. Note how the chevrons are detachable on the foreign service uniforms, also the two signallers, with their rolled flags, sitting either side of the officer. In **(161)** we see a Trooping of the Colour ceremony which took place at Valletta on 7 April 1911. Having been placed under orders to proceed to North China, the 2nd Battalion embarked on 17 September 1911 in the HT *Somali*. Chingwangtao was reached on 23 October, the troops then moving by rail to Tientsin and Peking. The two cabinet photographs **(162)** and **(163)**, with their clear photograph's details, show some of the men that were there, and the uniform worn. In 1908 the 1st Battalion was in India **(164)** and **(165)**. The sergeant's foreign service helmet in the second photograph has a green pugaree.

Militia Battalions

3rd and 4th Battalions Formed by the 1st Somerset Militia with headquarters at Taunton, and the 2nd Somerset Militia which had its headquarters in Bath.

Territorial Battalions

The scene is that of Annual Camp. In the background a covered wagon of the Army Service Corps, accompanied by an infantryman in service dress and rifle slopped, passes by on an already mud-drenched road. It had been a dry August, but a slight rain, horses, transport and battalions of marching feet have made their mark. Steady is the line of scarlet-clad Territorials, their sergeant having found them just enough dry ground to prevent the full-dressed detail from the slime. They are being inspected, after all, the blue-frocked officer not so lucky with the mud.

All here is perhaps typical: caps, their badges unclear, uniforms, the shoulder straps giving up nothing in the way of identification. But there can be no doubt as to what regiment this is, the knowledgeable eye falling immediately to the sergeant's sash.

The origin of the sash, either worn around the waist or over a shoulder, goes as far back as the seventeenth century when its purpose was to carry a wounded officer from the field of battle. Made of silk (crimson usually), sashes were not only strong but light, their length and width being adequate to carry the human form. But the accessory would later become an indication of rank and the freedom afforded in its wear tighten up by various Clothing Regulations over the years. In short: officers to have the sash with tassels falling on the right side, sergeants on the left. But the NCO in this picture has his falling to the wrong side; a mistake, surely?

Moving now to the Battle of Culloden in 1746 and the final confrontation of the previous year's Jacobite rising. It is said that during the fighting most of the officers from the regiment (that in 1881 would become the Somerset Light Infantry), had become casualties and it would be left to the sergeants to take command. In recognition of this it soon become the custom within the regiment for these NCOs to have the sash terminating on the officers' side. Major-General H J Everett, late of the Somerset Light Infantry, however,

would point out in Vol XIII of the *Journal of the Society for Army Research* that there is no evidence to support this. But on the officers' side it is and in view of the length of time this custom had been observed, be the tradition substantiated or not, Horse Guards gave authorization on 3 April 1865 to this, unique within the British Army, distinction.

Somerset's response to the 1859 call for volunteer riflemen saw twenty-eight individually numbered corps raised by 1876. Higher organisations saw these merged as three, the Haldane reforms of 1907 demanding yet another consolidation, this time as his 4th and 5th Battalions, Prince Albert's (Somerset Light Infantry) (Territorial Force). Battalion headquarters: Bath (4th), Taunton (5th). The painting **(166)** is by Richard Caton Woodville and from *His Majesty's Territorial Army* by Walter Richards which was published in London by Virtue & Co during 1910 and 1911.

With the towers of Wells Cathedral looking down, the Colour of one of the Territorial battalions is lowered during a royal visit to the city **(167)**.

4th Battalion Formed from elements of all three volunteer battalions with headquarters in Lower Bristol Road, Bath. There were eight companies located: 'A', 'B' (Bath), 'C' (Keynsham, Brislington, Whitchurch and Bitton), 'D' (Frome, Bruton, Mells and Wanstrow), 'E' (Weston-super-Mare, Winscombe and Cheddar), 'F' (Castle Cary, Shepton Mallet and Evercreech), 'G' (Midsomer Norton, Radstock, Bishop Sutton and Peasedown St John) and 'H' (Glastonbury and Wells).

5th Battalion Formed from elements of all three volunteer battalions with headquarters in Taunton at the Old Prison Building, Shuttern then moving in 1914 to the County Territorial Hall. The companies were: 'A' (Taunton), 'B' (Williton, Watchet, Minehead and Washford), 'C' (Bridgwater and North Petherton), D' (Langport, Highbridge and Somerton), 'E' (Yeovil, Martock and Langport), 'F' (Crewkerne and South Petherton), 'G' (Wellington, Milverton and Wiveliscombe) and 'H' (Chard and Ilminster).

Volunteer Battalions

1st Volunteer Battalion The 1st Somersetshire Rifle Volunteer Corps with its seven companies: 'A' (Bath), 'B' (Bathwick), 'C' (Keynsham), 'D' (Warleigh Manor), 'E' (Lyncombe), 'F' (Walcot) and 'G' (Kilmersdon), under General Order 261 of October 1882 became the 1st Volunteer Battalion Somerset Light Infantry making it the first in the land to take on the title of its parent regiment. A new company was added in 1885, followed by two more in 1900. Three school cadet corps were associated with the battalion:

Bath College, becoming affiliated in March 1900, the King Edward's School in Bath during the same year, Monkton Combe School joining in 1904. Transfer to the Territorial Force in 1908 was as parts of both the 4th and 5th Battalions Somerset Light Infantry, Bath College, King Edward's and Monkton Combe at the same time joining the OTC.

2nd Volunteer Battalion The 2nd Somersetshire Rifle Volunteer Corps with its twelve companies: 'A' and 'B' (Taunton), 'C' (Wellington), 'D' (Williton), 'E' (Wiveliscombe), 'F' (Yeovil), 'G' (Crewkerne), 'H' (Langport), 'I' (Bridgewater), 'K' and 'L' (Bridgewater) and 'M' (South Petherton), was re-designated as 2nd Volunteer Battalion Somerset Light Infantry under General Order 261 of October 1882. A new company was added in 1900 and in 1901 and 1903 respectively both the County School at Wellington and King's College in Taunton provided affiliated cadet corps. Transfer to the Territorial Force in 1908 was as parts of both 4th and 5th Battalions Somerset Light Infantry, County School and King's College at the same time joining the OTC. A group of buglers are seen in **(168)** and a young cornet player from one of the cadet corps in **(169)**. The uniforms are grey with black facings and piping.

3rd Volunteer Battalion The 3rd Somersetshire Rifle Volunteer Corps comprised nine companies: 'A' (Burnham), 'B' (Weston-super-Mare), 'C' (Wells), 'D' (Frome), 'E' (Shepton Mallet), 'F' (Glastonbury), 'G' (Castle Cary), 'H' (Keinton) and 'I' (Langford). Headquarters moved to Weston-Super-Mare in 1882 and by General Order 261 of October 1882 re-designation took place as 3rd Volunteer Battalion Somerset Light Infantry. Transfer to the Territorial Force in 1908 was as parts of both 4th and 5th Battalions Somerset Light Infantry.

Illustration credits: Bruce Bassett-Powell and Bob Bennet (152) and (158)

PRINCE OF WALES'S OWN (WEST YORKSHIRE REGIMENT)

14th (Buckinghamshire) (Prince of Wales's Own) Regiment

Regimental historian Richard Cannon's records tell how Sir Edward Hales, Baronet of Woodchurch in Kent raised, in 1685, a company of 100 musketeers and pikemen for the King's service at Canterbury. Other companies were raised and, together with Sir Edward's, formed the regiment that in 1751 would be numbered as 14th. Successive colonels' names used prior to this were: Sir Edward Hales, William Beveridge, John Tidcomb, Jasper Clayton (killed at Dettingen), John Price and William Herbert.

Soon after arriving in Jamaica, the regiment received a letter dated 31 August 1782 directing it to assume the title 14th or Bedfordshire Regiment of Foot, the Bedfordshire association being changed to Buckinghamshire in 1809. This was in consequence of the request made by the regiment's colonel at the time, Sir Harry Calvert, who had large estates in the latter county. The next change was the royal blessing in 1876 which added The Prince of Wales's Own to the title, then to The Prince of Wales's Own (West Yorkshire Regiment) in 1881.

WY Carman points out that apart from the fact that the regiment wore red coats and grey stockings, little more is known regarding dress until 1742 when buff was listed as the facing colour. Cannon's uniform plate shows two officers, Franklin's both buff and red waistcoats. Captain H O'Donnell's history published by AH Swiss in 1893 is generous in its twelve colour plates of uniform and one of Colours. The White Horse and motto *Nec aspera terrent* (Difficulties do not daunt) was authorized to be displayed on the Queen's Colour in February 1873, the Royal Tiger superscribed India on 1 November 1838. This was to commemorate the regiment's services in India 1807-31. The Prince of Wales's Coronet, Plume and motto, *Ich Dien* (I Serve) was authorized along with the change in title in 1876.

Regular Battalions

1st and 2nd Battalions Formed from the 1st and 2nd Battalions of the 14th (Buckinghamshire) (Prince of Wales's Own) Regiment of Foot. In **(170)** we see the ancient badge of the 14th Regiment, the White Horse and motto *Nec Aspera Terrent*, the Royal Tiger, which commemorates the services of the regiment in India between 1807-1831, and the Prince of Wales's coronet, plumes and motto which came with his title in 1876. The officers' forage cap has both the White Horse and plumes **(171)**.

The Aldershot publishing firm of Gale & Polden produced a set of six postcards featuring the West Yorkshire Regiment. In **(172)** we see the original artwork provided by artist Ernest Ibbetson for one of them which in the end carried the title 'A Royal Guard of Honour.' The second illustration **(173)** is a postcard from the same set. The work of another artist always in demand by postcard publishers was Harry Payne whose artwork was used to show a member of the regiment

marching towards the viewer as two bandsman chat in the background **(174)**. Seen in all three postcards are the old buff facings of the 14th Regiment. In 1881, and to comply with new regulations, white was introduced and worn until 1900 when the former colour was once again permitted. White is seen in Richard Simkins No 53 in his 'Military Types' series of supplements produced for the *Army and Navy Gazette* and published on 7 May 1892 **(175)**. The sergeant wears the all scarlet frock coat. In **(176)** we have officers of the regiment on the occasion of a royal visit from King George V and Queen Mary and in **(177)** a regimental orchestra. Illustration **(178)** is a watercolour of two officers by Richard Simkin.

Militia Battalions

3rd and 4th Battalions Formed from the 2nd West York Militia at York and the 4th West York Militia which had its headquarters in Leeds.

Territorial Battalions

5th Battalion Formed from the former 1st Volunteer Battalion with headquarters at York and eight companies located: 'A' (York and Tadcaster), 'B', 'C' (York), 'D' (Selby), 'E' (Harrogate), 'F' (Harrogate and Wetherby), 'G' (Knaresborough, Boroughbridge and Starbeck) and 'H' (Ripon and Pateley Bridge). Richard Caton Woodville's painting representing the Yorkshire (West Riding) Territorial Force Association shows the 5th and 6th Battalions **(179)**.

6th Battalion Formed from the former 2nd Volunteer Battalion with headquarters and all eight companies at Belle Vue Barracks, Bradford. The Bradford Postal Telegraph Messengers' Cadet Corps was affiliated. Illustration **(180)** shows the 6th Battalion mobilizing at Bradford in August 1914.

7th and 8th Battalions (Leeds Rifles) Formed from the 3rd Volunteer Battalion with headquarters at Carlton Barracks, Leeds. There was also a drill station attached to the 8th Battalion at Pudsey. The Leeds Postal Telegraph Messengers Cadet Company was affiliated to the 7th Battalion, Army Order 86 of 1913 however, notified a transfer of affiliated to Northern Command Signal Companies.

Volunteer Battalions

1st Volunteer Battalion The 1st Yorkshire (West Riding) Rifle Volunteer Corps at York had eleven companies: 'A', 'B', 'C', 'D' and 'E' (York), 'F' (Harrogate), 'G' (Knaresborough), 'H' and 'J' (Ripon), 'K' (Tadcaster) and 'L' (Selby). Under General Order 181 of December 1887 the corps was re-designated as 1st Volunteer Battalion West Yorkshire Regiment. A new company was added in 1900 and by 1908 the companies were located: York (5), Harrogate (2), Knaresborough (1), Ripon (2), Pateley Bridge (1) and Selby (1). Transfer to the Territorial Force was as 5th Battalion West Yorkshire Regiment.

2nd Volunteer Battalion The 3rd Yorkshire (West Riding) Rifle Volunteer Corps of eight companies at Bradford in 1887, under General Order 181 of December, was re-designated as 2nd Volunteer Battalion West Yorkshire Regiment. A cyclist company was added in 1900 and transfer to the Territorial Force in 1908 was as 6th Battalion West Yorkshire Regiment. In **(181)** the group from the 2nd Volunteer Battalion

includes bandsmen and a member of the cyclist company who wears the badge shown at **(182)** in his glengarry cap.

3rd Volunteer Battalion On 17 November 1859 the first company of the Leeds Rifle Volunteers was formed within the city. This was numbered as the 11th Yorkshire (West Riding) Rifle Volunteer Corps which by March 1860 consisted of five companies. In May 1860 the 22nd Corps, also in Leeds, was absorbed, but this brought about no increases in establishment. By 1861, however, an additional four companies had been raised. Of these, No 6 was provided by the Monkbridge Steel Company (one of its directors, Frederick W Kitson becoming commanding officer), No 7 by Fairbairn's Wellington Foundry (Andrew Fairburn as captain), No 8 from men at Messrs Greenwood & Bailey (Thomas G Greenwood as captain, George G Greenwood, ensign) and No 9, which was recruited from Messrs Joshua Tetley's Brewery (Francis W Tetley in command). The last company to be formed was in August 1875, this bringing the establishment up to ten companies which remained the strength of the corps until 1908.

As a result of the amalgamation during the early part of 1860 between the Halifax Corps, the 7th position in the West Riding list became vacant. This was filled by the 11th Corps on 3 July 1860. In 1864 the additional title Leeds was added, the next change being as 3rd Volunteer Battalion West Yorkshire Regiment in December 1887. Transfer to the Territorial Force was as 7th and 8th Battalions West Yorkshire Regiment.

Illustration credits: Anne SK Brown Military Collection Brown University Library (174), Bruce Bassett-Powell and Bob Bennet (170) and (172)

EAST YORKSHIRE REGIMENT

15th (York, East Riding) Regiment

The regiment was raised 1685 in Nottinghamshire and adjoining counties, its first colonel being Sir William Clifton. He would retire in the following year, the regiment then being known by the names of its successive colonels—Arthur Herbert, Sackville Tufton, Sir James Leslie, Emmanuel Scrope Howe, Algernon Seymour, Henry Harrison and John Jordan—until designated as 15th Regiment of Foot in 1751. The last title to be held by the regiment, the 15th (York, East Riding), before becoming the East Yorkshire Regiment in 1881 was conferred in 1782, it having just returned to England from the West Indies.

The early uniforms were red, lined red and with white stockings. Yellow facings appeared by 1742. A Simkin watercolour of fifty years later shows a private at the present arms position wearing an oval brass cross-belt plate. Major Parkyn points out that 'there are on record no less than four oval shoulder-belt plates, one having an eight-pointed star with, in its centre, a red cross within a Garter.' He also notes that although the White Rose of York was 'an old badge of the regiment' it did not appear on any belt plates of buttons until after 1881.

Regular Battalions

1st and 2nd Battalions Formed from the two battalions of the 15th (York, East Riding) Regiment of Foot. In **(183)** we see the officers' helmet plate, collar badges, button and waist-belt clasp displaying the regiment's White Rose of York badge within a wreath and superimposed upon an eight-pointed star. The regimental badge is seen here in this card produced from artwork provided by artist J McNeill **(184)**. Dated 1908, the image shows a private wearing two good conduct chevrons and the white facings ordered to be worn by the regiment in 1881. The facings of the old 15th Regiment had been yellow from at least 1742. J McNeill has correctly shown the man's home service helmet with a king's crown plate and given him both the Queen's and King's Medals for South Africa.

Appearing as one of the un-signed colour plates included with Walter Richards's *Her Majesty's Army* (published by JS Virtue & Co during the 1890's) was this image of an officer looking sternly out of the corner of his eye across to a group of three privates enjoying a chat **(185)**. He wears a crimson sash and gold lace decorating the collar and cuffs. The men are in marching order. Illustration **(186)** is supplement No 54 from Richard Simkin's 'Military Types' series, published on 4 June 1892 with the *Army and Navy Gazette*.

Militia Battalions

3rd Battalion Formed from the East York Militia with headquarters at Beverley.

Territorial Battalions

To represent the Yorkshire (East Riding) Territorial Force Association in *His Majesty's Territorial Army* by Walter Richards, artist Richard Caton Woodville chose a study of an East Yorkshire Regiment colour sergeant from one of its two Territorial battalions **(187)**. His rank is identified by the crossed flags above the chevrons. In the background, two officers chat on the right side of the image, while on the left a bugler takes care of an officer's horse. In **(188)** three-tier metal shoulder titles are being worn by the sergeants in this camp photograph, identifying them as from one of the regiment's two Territorial Force battalions. The 4th had T over 4 over E.York, the 5th having the same, but with the relevant number.

4th Battalion Formed from the former 1st Volunteer Battalion with headquarters at Londesborough Barracks in Hull and the following companies: 'A' to 'F' (Hull) and 'G' and 'H' (East Hull).

5th (Cyclist) Battalion Formed in 1908 from four companies of the former 2nd Volunteer Battalion. Headquarters were in Park Street, Hull and the battalion's eight companies located: 'A' to 'D' (Hull), 'E' (Howden, North Cave and Staddlethorpe), 'F' (Beverley, Hessle, Market Weighton and Pocklington), 'G' (Bridlington, Driffield, Hunmanby and Filey) and 'H' (Hornsea, Hedon and Withernsea).

Volunteer Battalions

1st Volunteer Battalion The 1st Yorkshire East Riding Rifle Volunteer Corps at Hull was re-designated as 1st Volunteer Battalion East Yorkshire Regiment under General Order 63 of May 1883. The Hymers College Cadet Corps was formed and affiliated in 1900, the battalion transferring to the Territorial Force in 1908 as 4th Battalion East Yorkshire Regiment, Hymers College at the same time joined the OTC.

2nd Volunteer Battalion Headquarter of the 2nd Yorkshire East Riding Rifle Volunteer Corps were at Beverley and its six companies located: 'A' (Howden), 'B' (Bridlington), 'C' (Beverley), 'D' (Driffield), 'E' (Market Weighton) and 'F' (Pocklington). Re-designation as 2nd Volunteer Battalion East Yorkshire Regiment was notified by General Order 63 of May 1883 and transfer to the Territorial Force in 1908 was as four companies of 5th Battalion East Yorkshire Regiment.

Illustration credit: Bruce Bassett-Powell and Bob Bennet (183)

BEDFORDSHIRE REGIMENT

16th (Bedfordshire) Regiment

Appointed as colonel of the regiment raised in 1688 throughout the southern counties of England was former 1st Regiment officer, Archibald Douglas. His commission was dated 9 October 1688 and he was succeeded by Robert Hodges, James Stanley (killed at Steinkirk), Francis Godfrey, Henry Durell, Hans Hamilton, Richard Ingram, John Cholmley, Henry Scott and Roger Handasyde. The regiment would be titled 16th in 1751, Buckinghamshire being added in 1782. When Sir Henry Calvert became colonel of the 14th (Bedfordshire) Regiment in February 1802 he requested that an exchange of titles be made with the 16th. The Colonel had large estates in Buckinghamshire and his wish was granted in 1809. The 16th (Bedfordshire) Regiment became the Bedfordshire Regiment in 1881.

Regimental historian Richard Cannon noted the first uniform as having round hats ornamented with white ribands, red coats lined and faced with white, white waistcoats and breeches. WY Carman adds that the original linings were red, white being introduced in 1691. Yellow facings, which were worn until 1881, came in some time before 1742. Major Parkyn notes that a star and cross first appeared as a badge of the regiment about 1830. Early versions of this badge suggest that it is a reproduction of the star of the Order of the Bath with its wavy rays and was possibly adopted as a compliment to William Carr, Viscount Beresford, GCB, GCH who had been appointed colonel of the 16th in 1823. From 1874 until 1881 the Arms of Bedford were used as a collar badge.

Regular Battalions

1st and 2nd Battalions Formed from the two battalions of the 16th (Bedfordshire) Regiment of Foot. **(189)** It would not be until 1919 that in recognition of the contribution Hertfordshire had made, the name of the county was added to that of the regiment. From 1881, however, the hart lodged in water from the Borough of Hertford arms would be the main feature of the Bedfordshire Regiment's insignia. Prior to 1881, the 16th

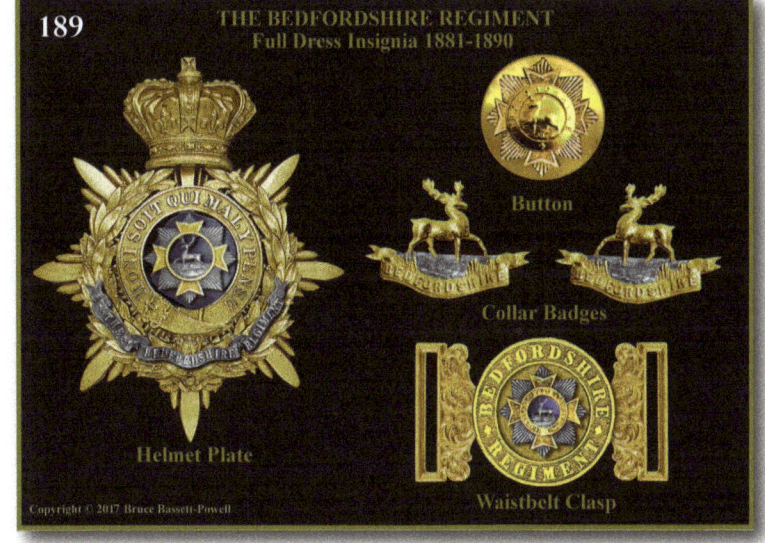

Regiment had used the arms of Bedford. The hart is displayed within a star and cross, Major HG Parkyn in his book *(Military) Shoulder-Belt Plates and Buttons* noting that this was first used as a badge by the 16th Regiment as far back as 1830 and was originally a copy of the star of the Order of the Bath. Major Parkyn suggests that this was perhaps in the form of a compliment to Colonel William Carr who had been appointed as colonel of the regiment in 1823.

The hart device can be clearly seen in the original artwork provided by artist Harry Payne for one of Gale & Polden's uniform postcard sets **(190)**. The facings are white and the officer's lace gold. Officers' helmets (see the two men holding the Colours) had a gilt edging to the peaks while those of other ranks (colour-sergeant in the centre) had leather. Note how the artist has been careful to include this small detail.

Having just attended a church parade at St Michael and St George's Church in Aldershot, the drums lead the 1st Battalion back to barracks along Queen's Avenue in 1913 **(191)**. Illustration **(192)** is an Edwardian postcard showing the Colours, **(193)** being a card from Gale & Polden's 'History and Traditions' series featuring a sergeant and private marching with rifles at the slope down a quiet lane. The artist has shown the private wearing a scout arm badge and both men with Queen's and King's Medals for South Africa. The 2nd Battalion had arrived at the Cape about 8 January 1899 and while there, as the text on the postcard states, '…took a gallant part in some of the toughest fought engagements of the campaign.'

For supplement No 55 in Richard Simkin's 'Types of the Army' series for the *Army and Navy Gazette* **(194)**, the artist chose a scene showing troops in foreign service uniform, either in action or in training. The image was published in 1892, the same year that the 1st Battalion had taken part in the Isazi Expedition on the North West Frontier, India.

Militia Battalions

3rd Battalion From the Bedfordshire Militia with headquarters in Bedford.

4th Battalion From the Hertfordshire Militia with headquarters in Hertford.

Territorial Battalion

5th Battalion Formed by four companies each of the former 3rd and 4th Volunteer Battalions with headquarters at Gwyn Street, Bedford. The companies were located: 'A' (Bedford), 'B' and 'C' (Luton), 'D' (Biggleswade, Sandy, Arlesey and St Neots), 'E' (Ampthill and Olney), 'F' (Luton, Dunstable and Leighton Buzzard), 'G' (Fletton and Yaxley) and 'H' (Huntingdon, St Ives and Ramsey). The Dunstable Grammar School Cadet Corps was affiliated.

Volunteer Battalions

1st (Hertfordshire) Volunteer Battalion The 1st

Hertfordshire Rifle Volunteer Corps at Hertford had eight companies: 'A' and 'B' (Hertford), 'C' (Bishop's Stortford), 'D' (Ware), 'E' (Royston), 'F' (Welwyn), 'G' (Hitchin) and 'H' (Waltham Abbey and Cheshunt). Re-designation as 1st (Hertfordshire) Volunteer Battalion Bedfordshire Regiment was notified by General Order 181 of 1887. A new company ('I') was added at Hoddesdon in 1900. Three cadet corps were affiliated to the battalion: Haileybury College in 1886, Bishop's Stortford Grammar School and Hertford Grammar School both in 1906. Transfer to the Territorial Force was as part of the Hertfordshire Regiment, although portion of the battalion went to form a nucleus of the 1st and 2nd Hertfordshire Batteries Royal Field Artillery. All three cadet corps became contingents of the OTC.

The tent having been successfully erected, with mallets still to hand a party of buglers relax with their bugle major seated centre **(195)**. Note his bugle and chevrons rank insignia. By GH Sills of Berkhamsted, the photograph has a caption on the back which identifies the men as being members of the 1st Volunteer Battalion. This is confirmed by the cloth Bedfordshire over I over V shoulder titles, the Brodrick caps being worn placing the date between 1902 and 1905.

2nd (Hertfordshire) Volunteer Battalion Headquarters of the 2nd Hertfordshire Rifle Volunteer Corps were at Little Gaddesden, its five companies being located: 'A' (Watford), 'B' (St Albans), 'C' (Ashridge), 'D' (Hemel Hempstead and Redbourn) and 'E' (Great Berkhamsted and Tring). Headquarters later moved to Hemel Hempstead. In 1883 a new company ('F') was added at Tring then under General Order 181 of December 1887, the 2nd Corps was re-designated as 2nd (Hertfordshire) Volunteer Battalion Bedfordshire Regiment. 'G' Company was added at Watford in 1892 and cadet corps were formed and affiliated to the battalion at Berkhamsted and St Albans Schools in 1891 and 1903 respectively. Another cadet corps at the United Services College joined the battalion in May 1904 having moved its location from Westward Ho! to Harpenden. Yet another move, this time to Windsor in 1907, saw the company transferred to the 1st London RE (Vols). The battalion transferred to the Territorial Force in 1908 as part of the Hertfordshire Regiment, the cadet corps at the same time becoming contingents of the OTC. Illustration **(196)** shows buglers of the 2nd Volunteer Battalion who wear grey uniforms with green facings.

3rd Volunteer Battalion The 1st Bedfordshire Rifle Volunteer Corps at Woburn had nine companies: 'A' (Bedford), 'B' (Bedford), 'C' (Toddington), 'D' (Dunstable), 'E' (Ampthill), 'F' (Luton), 'G' (Luton), 'H' (Shefford) and 'I' (Woburn). Re-designation as 3rd Volunteer Battalion Bedfordshire Regiment was in 1887 and by July 1894 company locations were: Bedford (2), Dunstable, Ampthill, Luton (3), Shefford and Biggleswade. The Bedford Modern School Cadet Corps was affiliated in 1900 but was transferred to the 1st Bedfordshire Royal Engineers (Volunteers) in 1904. Transfer to the Territorial Force saw the battalion providing four companies of the 5th Battalion Bedfordshire Regiment.

4th (Hunts) Volunteer Battalion Formed on 4 December 1900 with headquarters at Huntingdon. Six companies were authorized, the recruiting for these being carried out in the main from around Huntingdon, St Ives, Fletton and St Neot's. Provided four companies of the

5th Battalion Bedfordshire Regiment were provided in 1908.

Illustration credits: Anne SK Brown Military Collection, Brown University Library (190), Bruce Bassett-Powell and Bob Bennet (189)

LEICESTERSHIRE REGIMENT

17th (Leicestershire) Regiment

Published in 1911, Lieutenant-Colonel EAH Webb's highly detailed and illustrated regimental history tells how the regiment that became the 17th in 1751 was raised in London and its immediate vicinity, its colonelcy being conferred on Solomon Richards by commission dated 27 September 1688. Before 1751, Colonel Richards was succeeded by: Sir George St George, John Courthorpe (killed at Namur), Sir Matthew Bridges, Holcroft Blood, Joseph Wightman, Thomas Ferrers, James Tyrrell and John Wynyard. Leicestershire was added to the title in 1782, the Leicestershire Regiment that assumed in 1881.

Colonel Webb's history contains no less than a thirty-one plate, year-by-year illustrated account of uniform, equipment and Colours. In 1695, he records that the coats and breeches of the sergeants and soldiers were of a grey colour, drummers having purple with grey breeches. The headdress of the period he refers to as being of two types, 'basinet' or 'pott' and the skull cap. 'The pott was a low-crowned helmet painted black, and as a distinction for officers, was ornamented with plumes.' For the year 1742 the author refers to that valuable record kept in the British Museum entitled 'A Representation of the Clothing of His Majesty's Household, &c., in 1742' in which a private of the regiment is depicted wearing greyish facings. Plate 3 of the regimental history shows this, the soldier also having a red waistcoat, white lace with a double zigzag line, white stockings and buff equipment.

The 1751 Royal Warrant directs scarlet coats, faced and lined with greyish white. Nine numbered buttons are illustrated, some also with crowns. Another described as officers' gilt and dated 1840 has no number, but a crowned reversed and intertwined VR cypher. The badge of the Royal Tiger superscribed Hindoostan was conferred by King George IV on 25 June 1825. Other colour plates of uniform included in the history are a grenadier of 1751, grenadier 1768, officers for 1800 and 1814, drum-major and bandsman of 1830, a sergeant, grenadier and bugler 1830, officers 1830 and 1831, officer 1834, officer and private 1846 and seven types of uniform for the period 1861 to 1903. The book also included photographic images of shako and breast ornaments.

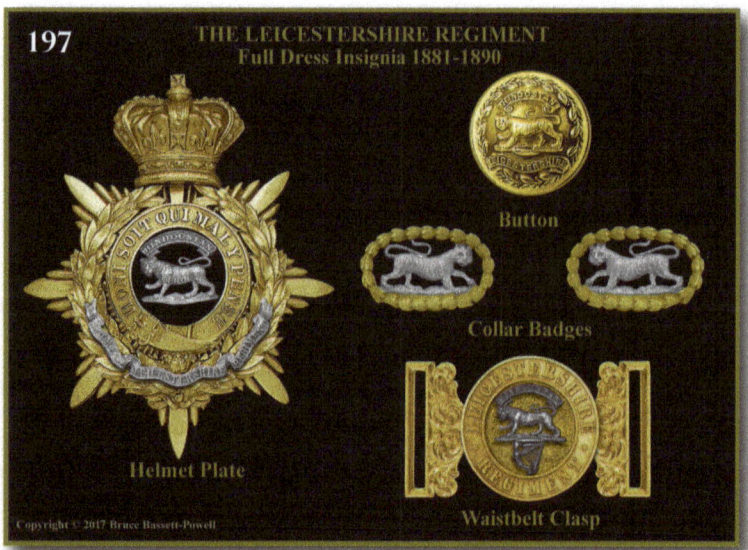

Regular Battalions

1st and 2nd Battalions Formed from the two battalions of the 17th (Leicestershire) Regiment of Foot. For its service in India between 1804 and 1823, the 17th Regiment was awarded the Royal Tiger badge superscribed 'Hindoostan'. Here in **(197)** we see how it was used on the officers' helmet plate, collar badges, buttons and waist-belt clasp. An Irish harp appears on the latter, this being a badge of the former Leicestershire Militia commemorating how, on 13 February 1856, a detachment of fourteen officers and 324 other ranks had proceeded to Ireland in aid of the civil power.

Illustration **(198)** shows one of the original oil on board painting by Harry Payne produced for one of Gale & Polden's uniform postcard sets. The facings are white, and the Royal Tiger collar badge is clearly seen. In **(199)**, more troops rush forward as a kneeling officer with sword drawn observes the firing. The image is No 56 in Richard Simkin's 'Military Types' series of supplements produced for the *Army and Navy Gazette* and published on 6 August 1892. Both helmets and flat service caps are being worn in this photograph **(200)** of the 1st Battalion at Aldershot in 1911, **(201)** showing an Edwardian postcard featuring the Tiger and Hindoostan badge as well and two items in use prior to 1881 by the 17th Regiment.

The new 1st Battalion Colours presented in 1910 are seen in **(202)**. An Army Order issued in March 1910 had announced that the King had been graciously pleased to approve of the Leicestershire Regiment being permitted to bear the battle honour 'Namur 1695' on its Colours.

Militia Battalion

3rd Battalion Formed by the Leicestershire Militia with headquarters in Leicester.

Territorial Battalions

4th Battalion Formed from the Leicester and Wigston Companies of the former 1st Volunteer Battalion. Headquarters were in Oxford Street, Leicester and the eight companies located: 'A' (Leicester), 'B' (Leicester and Anstey), 'C' (Leicester and Syston), 'D' to 'G' (Leicester) and 'H' (Wigston Magna).

5th Battalion Formed from part of the 1st Volunteer Battalion. Headquarters were in Loughborough and the eight companies were located: 'A' (Ashby-de-la-Zouch and Coalville), 'B' (Oakham,

Cottesmore, Whissendine and Uppingham), 'C' (Melton Mowbray, Bottesford, Harby and Wymondham), 'D' (Hinckley), 'E' (Market Harborough, Kibworth and Fleckney), 'F' (Mountsorrel and Woodhouse Eaves), 'G' (Uppingham, Barrowden, Bisbrooke, Shepshed and Ketton), and 'H' (Loughborough).

Volunteer Battalions

1st Volunteer Battalion With headquarters at Leicester, the 1st Leicestershire Rifle Volunteer Corps had eleven companies: 'A' (Leicester), 'B' (Belvoir), 'C' (Melton Mowbray), 'D' to 'G' (Leicester), 'H' (Loughborough), 'J' (Ashby-de-la-Zouch), 'K' (Leicester) and 'L' (Hinckley). A new company was raised at Market Harborough in 1882 and in the following year General Order 14 of February directed that the 1st Corps was to be re-designated as 1st Volunteer Battalion Leicestershire Regiment. Further increases in establishment saw new companies added, two at Leicester and one each at Wigston and Mountsorrel in 1900. Transfer to the Territorial Force in 1908 saw the 4th Battalion formed by the Leicester and Wigston personnel and 5th Battalion by the remainder, less the Belvoir Company which was disbanded. Illustrations **(203) and (204)** show an other ranks helmet plate and button of the 1st Volunteer Battalion. Both are in white metal.

Illustration credit: Anne SK Brown Military Collection, Brown University Library (198), Bruce Bassett-Powell and Bob Bennet (197)

ROYAL IRISH REGIMENT

18th (The Royal Irish) Regiment

Cannon's regimental records note that the 18th existed for many years as independent companies of pikemen and musketeers on the establishment of Ireland previous to its formation in 1684. Arthur Earl of Granard was conferred as colonel by commission dated 1 April 1684 and was succeed prior to 1751 by Arthur Forbes (2nd Earl of Granard), Sir John Edgeworth (cashiered for clothing the regiment in cast-off uniforms), Edward Brabazon, Frederick Hamilton, Richard Ingoldsby, Robert Stearne, William Cosby, Sir Charles Hotham, John Armstrong, Sir John Mordaunt and John Folliott. The title Royal Regiment of Ireland was conferred in 1685, the 18th (The Royal Irish) Regiment of Foot in 1751 and The Royal Irish regiment in 1881.

On 20 August 1695, the regiment took part in the assault on the castle at Namur, a heroic attack after which King William was graciously pleased to confer the right to display the badge of the Harp and Crown and that of the Lion of Nassau together with the motto *Virtutis Namurcensis Præmium* (Reward for valour at Namur). With this distinction came the change in title to Royal Regiment of Ireland. The King was present at the battle and Captain Parker wrote that 'The King saw this action from rising ground at the back of Salsine Abbey and took particular notice of the behaviour of our regiment; for ours, only mounted the top of the breach, and we planted our colours thereon.' It is of interest that the battle honour Namur was not at the time approved and it would not be until February 1910 that permission was granted for its inclusion on the Colours. WY Carman notes that even before becoming royal, the regiment had red coats lined blue.

The Sphinx superscribed Egypt was authorized in July 1802 for services during the previous year's campaign, and the Dragon superscribed China (authorized January 1843) for that of 1840-42. Major Parkyn illustrates an oval pouch-belt plate which he places as an officer's of about 1800. It has the motto on a crowned strap in the centre of which is a harp with a shamrock below.

Regular Battalions

1st and 2nd Battalion Formed by the 1st and 2nd Battalions of the 18th (The Royal Irish) Regiment of Foot. Bruce-Bassett-Powell in **(205)** illustrates an officer's helmet plate, a pair of silver collar badges, a button and waist-belt clasp. The harp and crown, notes Major HG Parkyn in his *(Military) Shoulder-Belt Plates and Buttons,* are said to have been conferred on the regiment together with the arms of Nassau by King William III. The arms, together with the motto *Virtutis Namurcensis Præmium,* were given as a reward for the gallantry shown by the then Royal Regiment of Ireland during the siege and assault of Namur in 1695. Interestingly, 'Namur' as a battle honour was not approved for the Colours until 1910.

The two men in this Gale & Polden postcard by artist Harry Payne **(206)** can be identified as signallers, both by the blue and white flags that they carry and their arm badges. The facings are dark blue, the collar badges being the arms of Nassau type. In this 'History and Traditions' postcard from Gale & Polden **(207)**, artist J McNeill has shown the sergeant and private wearing Queen's and King's Medals for South Africa. It was the 1st Battalion that sailed on the *Goscon* on 14 December 1899 for South Africa. Both men have the crossed rifles of a marksman, the private also wearing two good conduct chevrons on his left lower arm.

Illustrations **(208)**, **(209)** and **(210)** show respectively an all brass cap badge with Victorian crown, an Edwardian postcard featuring the badges of the regiment and a brass detachable other ranks helmet plate centre. In **(211)** the scene chosen for this supplement issued by the *Army and Navy Gazette* on 3 September 1892, is obviously Egypt. Ten years before, in 1882,

the 2nd Battalion had taken part in the Egyptian Campaign, including the engagements at Kassassin and Tel-el-Kebir. The artist is Richard Simkin. Illustration **(212)** is from WJ Gordon's book, *Bands of the British Army* and shows a bandsman wearing a sprig of shamrock in his helmet of St Patrick's Day. The artwork is by F Stansell.

Militia Battalions

3rd Battalion Formed by the Wexford Militia and disbanded in 1908.

4th, later 3rd Battalion Formed by the North Tipperary Militia with headquarters at Clonmel and re-numbered as 3rd Battalion upon the disbandment of the original 3rd in 1908.

5th, later 4th Battalion Formed by the Kilkenny Militia as 5th Battalion, being re-numbered as 4th in 1908.

Illustration credit: Bruce Bassett-Powell and Bob Bennet (205)

ALEXANDRA, PRINCESS OF WALES'S OWN (YORKSHIRE REGIMENT)

Until 1902 the title of the regiment appeared as The Princess of Wales's Own (Yorkshire Regiment),

19th (1st York, North Riding) Princess of Wales's Own Regiment

In addition to his duties as Member of Parliament for Minehead in Surrey, Francis Lutterell found time to raise several companies of pikemen and musketeers for the King's service. It was these that provided Lutterell's Regiment in 1688. Successive colonels prior to 1751 were: Thomas Erle, George Freke, Richard Sutton, George Grove, Sir Charles Howard and Lord George Beauclerk. The 19th's Yorkshire connection was established in 1782, and that with the Princess of Wales in 1875. Both battalions of the Princess of Wales's Own (Yorkshire Regiment) were found in 1881.

WY Carman notes that as officers' coats in the seventeenth century were blue, it may be that the men were clothed the same, 'possibly with yellow facings.' Certainly, yellow was the facing colour in 1709. When

green was introduced is uncertain, but during the period when General Sir Charles Howard was its colonel (1738-48) the regiment was known as the Green Howards. This nickname would stand the test of time and, from 1920, even form part of the official title. The White Rose of York is considered an ancient badge of the regiment, the Princess of Wales's Cypher and Coronet being granted when the 19th took on her name in 1875.

Regular Battalions

1st and 2nd Battalions Formed by the 1st and 2nd Battalions of the 19th Regiment of Foot. Princess, later Queen, Alexandra was from Denmark and in reference to this the cross from the Order of Dannebrog was taken into use by the regiment as a badge. The device also incorporated the cypher and coronet of the princess. Here we see it displayed in the centre of an officer's helmet plate, as the collar badge, on the buttons and waist-belt clasp **(213)**. The date '1875' referes to the year that Alexandra's name was first added to the title of the old 19th Regiment.

The facings of the 19th Regiment had been green since the early part of the eighteenth century, but they was ordered to change to white in 1881. Green, however, was restored in 1899. White is seen here in Richard Simkin's suppliant No 58 in his 'Types of the Army' series produced for the *Army and Navy Gazette* **(214)**. The image was published on 1 October 1892.

Illustrations **(215)** and **(216)** show the original artwork produced by artist Ernest Ibbetson for two cards in one of Gale & Polden's postcard sets. The collars and cuffs are green now, as is the Regimental Colour on the right in (215). The bayonets are fixed as the battalion marches past, (216) showing the drill procedure (the rifles firmly gripped between the knees) for unfixing.

In this photograph of officers **(217)**, one of those lying down in the front wears a glengarry cap and seems to have injured his right arm. See how the jacket is being worn over the offending limb, the sleeve being draped across the body. Besides him, and looking quite uncomfortable, another officer wears the forage cap seen in **(218)**. The facings are white which should date the image between 1881 and 1899.

Nine bandsmen pose for their photograph (note the bugle arm badges) who wear the white facings of 1881 to 1899 and white stitched York shoulder titles **(219)**. All but one man wears Indian General Service Medals with their red-dark blue-red-dark blue-red striped ribbons. Note also the soldier second from the left in the front who has a crossed rifles badge indicating him as the best shot in the band.

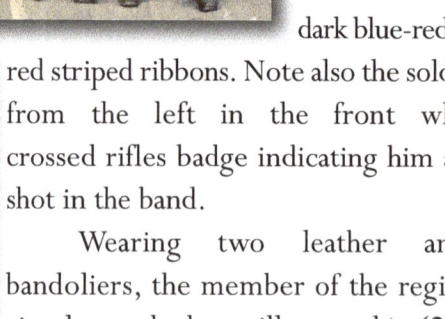

Wearing two leather ammunition bandoliers, the member of the regiment in **(220)** sports the pre-1908 circular cap badge as illustrated in **(221)**. The first cap badge, this pattern was worn until replaced by **(222)** in 1908.

Militia Battalions

3rd Battalion Formed by the 5th West Yorkshire Militia with headquarters at Knaresborough.

4th Battalion Formed by the North York Militia with headquarters at Richmond and disbanded in 1908. Having volunteered for war service, the 4th Battalion embarked for South Africa with a strength of twenty-nine officers and 564 other ranks. Just prior to their departure, the officers were photographed for the *Navy and Army Illustrated* **(223)**.

Territorial Battalions

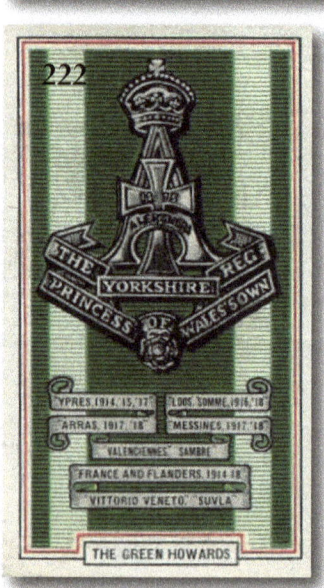

4th Battalion Formed from the former 1st Volunteer Battalion with headquarters at Northallerton and companies located at: 'A', 'B' (Middlesbrough), 'C' (Yarm-on-Tees, Great Ayton, Stokesley and Hutton

Rudby), 'D' (Guisborough, Eston, South Bank and Grangetown), 'E' (Richmond, Catterick, Eppleby and Reeth), 'F' (Redcar and Marske-by-the-Sea), 'G' (Skelton, Carlin How, Lingdale and Loftus) and 'H' (Northallerton, Bedale, Thirsk, Easingwold, Brompton and Helperby).

5th Battalion Formed from the former 2nd Volunteer Battalion with headquarters at Scarborough and companies located: 'A' (Market Weighton,

223 MORE MILITIA FOR THE FRONT.

THE "GREEN HOWARDS" MILITIA.

Pocklington, Newbald and Stamford Bridge), 'B' (Bridlington, Filey, Hunmanby and Flamborough), 'C' (Beverley and Cottingham), 'D' (Driffield and Sledmere), 'E', 'F' (Scarborough), 'G' (Pickering, Helmsley, Kirby Moorside, Grosmont, Ebberston and Thornton Dale) and 'H' (Malton, Sand Hutton, Sheriff Hutton and Hovingham).

Volunteer Battalions

1st Volunteer Battalion The 1st Yorkshire (North Riding) Rifle Volunteer Corps at Richmond had nine companies: 'A' (Thornton Rust), 'B' (Bedale), 'C' (Stokesley), 'D' (Catterick), 'E' (Richmond), 'F' (Reeth), 'G' (Skelton), 'H' (Northallerton) and 'K' (Guisborough). Headquarters moved to Northallerton in 1883 and in the same year General Order 14 of February notified re-designation as 1st Volunteer Battalion Yorkshire Regiment. After a number of relocations, amalgamations, disbandments, and in 1884 the formation of a new company, by 1893 company locations were: Leyburn, Bedale, Stokesley, Catterick, Richmond, Skelton, Northallerton, Thirst, Guisborough and Wensleydale. The coming years saw further of the same, the companies by 1898 being at: Middleham, Bedale, Stokesley, Catterick, Richmond, Redcar, Skelton, Northallerton, Thirsk and Guisborough, and by 1908: Bedale, Eston, Stokesley, Catterick, Richmond, Redcar, Skelton, Northallerton, Thirsk and Guisborough. Transfer to the Territorial Force in 1908 was as 4th Battalion Yorkshire Regiment.

2nd Volunteer Battalion The 2nd Yorkshire (North Riding) Rifle Volunteer Corps at Scarborough had seven companies: 'A' (Malton), 'B' and 'C' (Hovingham), 'D' and 'E' (Scarborough), 'F' (Helmsley-in-Ryedale) and 'G' (Pickering). Under General Order 14 of February 1883 the 2nd Corps was re-designated as 2nd Volunteer Battalion Yorkshire Regiment, the battalion providing four companies of 5th Yorkshire Regiment in 1908.

Illustration credits: Alan Seymore (217) and (219), Anne SK Brown Military Collection (215) and (216), Bruce Bassett-Powell and Bob Bennet (213) and (218)

LANCASHIRE FUSILIERS

20th (East Devonshire) Regiment

Chichester and Burgess-Short record how, when William of Orange arrived at Exeter after landing at Torbay on 5 November 1688, he was met by a number of noblemen and gentlemen to whom he later gave commissions for the raising of new regiments. One of these was Sir Robert Peyton who had then under his command thirteen companies coated in red with yellow facings. WY Carman agrees with the red but suggests the facing and linings were white. By 1740, however, yellow was certainly the colour in use. Succeeding Sir Robert Peyton, the colonels were prior to 1751: Gustavus Hamilton, John Newton, Thomas Meredith, William Egerton, Francis Howard, Richard St George, Alexander Rose, Thomas Bligh, George Germain (dismissed for his conduct at Minden) and George Keppel. Having been designated 20th Regiment of Foot in 1751, East Devonshire was added to the title thirty-one years later. The 20th provided the two regular battalions of the Lancashire Fusiliers in 1881. The Sphinx superscribed Egypt featured on the regiment's badges and appointments after 1801.

Thomas Carlyle, in his history of Frederick the Great, wrote 'A really splendid victory, this of Minden, August 1st. These unsurpassable Six, in industrious valour, unsurpassable.' The six regiments he was referring to include the 20th which, on Minden Day (1st August) celebrated the victory by wearing roses in their hats and decorating the Colours and drums with the same. The custom recalls how advancing troops during the battle passed among rose briers, snatching up the blossoms and placing them in their headdress and equipment.

Regular Battalions

1st, 2nd, 3rd and 4th Battalions

The first two were provided by the 1st and 2nd Battalions of the 20th (East Devonshire) Regiment of Foot. The 3rd and 4th Battalions were formed in 1898 and 1900 respectively, both being disbanded in 1906. Illustration **(224)** show several items bearing the Sphinx superscribed 'Egypt' within a wreath, this honour having been awarded to the 20th Regiment for its services during the campaign of 1801. The sketch in **(225)** shows how this device was incorporated into the regimental cap badge. The 2nd Battalion had moved to India in 1881, this group being photographed wearing all white uniform in 1893 **(226)**.

For a set of postcards published by the Aldershot firm of Gale & Polden featuring the Lancashire Fusiliers, artist Ernest Ibbetson produced six watercolours.

The set was part of a series which postcard authority Geoff White refers to as the 'Alphabet Series' due to the cards produced for each regimental set of six being identified on the reverse by a letter and number. Illustrated are five from the Lancashire Fusiliers set, the missing one, 'B55', having the caption 'The Landing at Gallipoli.' 'The Commanding Officer' was the caption given to card 'A55' **(227)**, the illustration here being the original artwork supplied by Ernest Ibbetson and used by Gale & Polden. Mounted and leading his troops, the CO wears the Distinguished Service Order and both the Queen's and King's Medals for South Africa. This leads me to suggest that this is in fact Lieutenant-Colonel George Henry Bail Freeth who had served with the 2nd Battalion during the Boer War from 1899 to 1902, receiving his DSO in April 1901. Also one of Ernest Ibbetson's originals is

that captioned 'Trooping the King's Colour' which appeared as card No 'C 55' and is seen here in **(228)**. The next three Illustrations, **(229)**, **(230)** and **(231)**, show the remaining cards, 'D55', 'E55' and 'F55', as published. All images show the regiment's white facings and distinctive yellow plume.

Illustrations **(232)**, **(233)** and **(234)** are all by Richard Simkin, the first two being originals from the Anne SK Brown Military Collection held at Brown University Library. The third image is supplement No 44 from the 'Types of the British Army' series published with the *Army and Navy Gazette* between 7 January 1888 and 6 September 1902.

Four cyclists are shown in **(235)**, and from left to right in **(236)** a sergeant, colour sergeant, officer and private in full and service dress. Illustration **(237)** is an original watercolour by Harry Payne, produced for one of Gale & Polden's uniform postcard sets, **(238)** being one of that company's 'Soldiers' Pay' series.

Militia Battalions

3rd, later 5th Battalion Formed from the 7th Royal Lancashire Militia as 3rd Battalion in 1881 with headquarters in Bury, but re-numbered as 5th upon the formation in 1898 of the new 3rd Regular Battalion. Became 3rd again in 1908.

4th, later 6th Battalion Formed in 1891 out of the 3rd Battalion with headquarters in Bury. Became 6th upon the formation of the new 4th Regular Battalion, then 4th again in 1908.

Territorial Battalions

5th Battalion Formed from the former 1st Volunteer Battalion with headquarters at the Castle Armoury, Bury. The eight companies were located: 'A', 'B' (Bury), 'C', 'D' (Heywood), 'E', 'F' (Bury), 'G' (Bury and Radcliffe) and 'H' (Bury).

6th Battalion Formed from the former 2nd Volunteer Battalion with headquarters in Rochdale. The eight companies were located: 'A' (Middleton), 'B', 'C', 'D' (Rochdale), 'E' (Middleton), 'F' (Rochdale) and 'G' and 'H' (Todmorden).

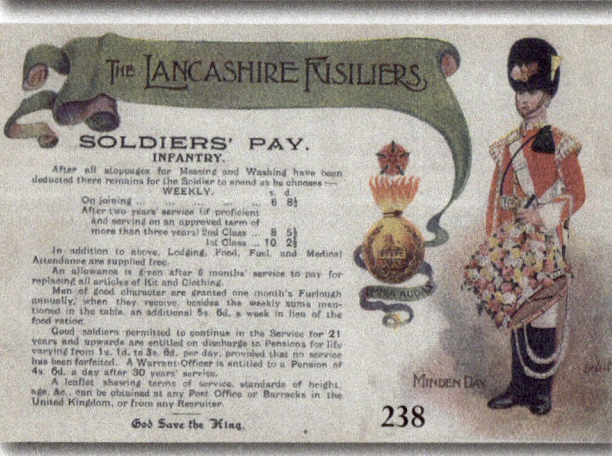

7th Battalion Formed from the former 3rd Volunteer Battalion with headquarters and all eight companies in Cross Lane, Salford.

8th Battalion Formed from the former 3rd Volunteer Battalion with headquarters and all eight companies in Cross Lane, Salford. The Broughton Lads' Brigade was affiliated, being re-designated as 1st Cadet Company 8th Battalion in 1914.

Volunteer Battalions

1st Volunteer Battalion The 8th Lancashire Rifle Volunteer Corps at Bury was re-designated as 1st Volunteer Battalion Lancashire Fusiliers under General Order 14 of 1883 and in the same year two more companies were added. The Bury Grammar School Cadet Corps was formed and affiliated in 1892. Transfer to the Territorial Force in 1908 was as 5th Battalion Lancashire Fusiliers, Bury Grammar School at the same time joining the OTC.

2nd Volunteer Battalion The 12th Lancashire Rifle Volunteer Corps at Rochdale was re-designated as 2nd Volunteer Battalion Lancashire Fusiliers under General Order 14 of February 1883. Transfer to the Territorial Force was as 6th Battalion Lancashire Fusiliers.

3rd Volunteer Battalion In 1881 the 17th Lancashire Rifle Volunteer Corps at Salford joined the Manchester Regiment as one of its Volunteer battalions, transferring in March 1886 as the 3rd Volunteer Battalion Lancashire Fusiliers. The Salford Cadet Corps was formed and affiliated to the battalion in 1888 but disbanded in 1891. Transfer to the Territorial Force was as 7th and 8th Battalions Lancashire Fusiliers.

Illustration credits: Alan Seymore (226), Anne SK Brown Military Collection (227), (228), (232) and (233), Bruce Bassett-Powell and Bob Bennet (224)

ROYAL SCOTS FUSILIERS

21st (Royal Scots Fusiliers) Regiment

The 21st derives its origin from 1678 and the formation that year of the Earl of Mar's Regiment which had been raised for what Cannon describes as the 'commotions' in Scotland. These were the sectarian troubles in the reign of Charles II. Early uniforms included grey breeches which would lead to the regiment's unofficial title of 'Earl of Mar's Greybreeks'. In July 1691 a list of regiments then serving in Flanders was published which referred to 'O'Farrell's Fusiliers', its uniform being 'red, faced and lined with the same colour.' Brigadier-General Fergus O'Farrell had been appointed colonel of the regiment on 1 March 1689 and was to be cashiered for surrendering Diense in Holland in 1695. Others to give their name to the regiment prior to 1751 were: Thomas Buchan (he was later deprived of his commission by William III), Robert Mackay, Archibald Row (killed at Blenheim), John Mordaunt, Sampson de Lalo (killed at Malplaquet), Thomas Meredith, Charles Boyle, George Maccartney, Sir James Wood and John Campbell. It was quite early in the regiment's history that the style Fusiliers was used, one of its first duties being as a guard and escort to the artillery. The title Scots Fusiliers Regiment came in around 1707, Chichester and Burgess-Short noting that in an official document of 1713 the regiment was referred to as the Royal North British Fusiliers. When the Royal title was conferred is not clear, but along with it came blue facings. With its two battalions, the regiment provided the Royal Scots Fusiliers in 1881.

Recorded in the regulations for 1747, and also displayed on the Colours that year, was the Thistle within

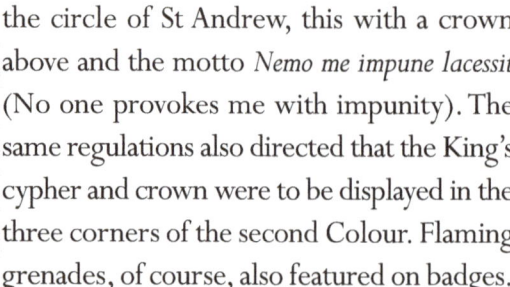

the circle of St Andrew, this with a crown above and the motto *Nemo me impune lacessit* (No one provokes me with impunity). The same regulations also directed that the King's cypher and crown were to be displayed in the three corners of the second Colour. Flaming grenades, of course, also featured on badges.

Regular Battalions

1st and 2nd Battalions Formed from the 1st and 2nd Battalions of the 21st (Royal Scots Fusiliers) Regiment of Foot. The thistle and figure of St Andrew have been badges of the 21st Regiment since at least 1747 when both appeared on the Colours. The Royal Arms, as seen on the ball of the fur cap grenade, was introduced in 1881 **(239)**.

Chirat had been a hill station occupied by British troops since the 1860s, the years that followed seeing several regiments leaving a reminder of their stay there by carving a badge into the chalk soil. Here in the photograph **(240)** we see, besides that of the Royal Scots Fusiliers (far left), those of the King's Royal Rifle Corps, the 2nd Wiltshire Regiment and 1st Royal Irish Fusiliers. The 2nd Battalion Royal Scots Fusiliers had arrived in India in 1887, the photograph showing the regimental band in 1892. Clear are the grenade over SF shoulder titles, Glengarry caps being worn by most save for the bandmaster and a sergeant seated in the second row from the front. They wear forage caps as in **(241)**.

From James Clark's *Historical Record and Regimental Memoir of the Royal Scots Fusiliers*, illustration **(242)** shows a colour sergeant, officer and piper in the uniform of 1885. Once a sergeant in the regiment, James Clark' history has five colour plates of uniform and one of colours. The two colour plates shown in **(243)** and **(244)** are from the highly detailed, *History of The 21st Royal Scots Fusiliers* by Lieutenant-Colonel Percy Groves which was published by W & AK Johnston in 1895. The artist was Harry Payne who shows a piper and bandsman (note the grenade badge on the pouch) a captain and mounted field officer for 1894. Harry Payne's postcard work can also be seen in **(245)**, the artist on this occasion providing a

detailed view of a drummer as he talks to one of the pipers. The background shows a sergeant and mounted officer. In a friendly way, drummers are often referred to in Scottish regiments as 'pipers' labourers.'

Showing the regiment forming square, illustration **(246)** is from *Our Armies* by Richard Simkin and published by Day & Son in 1890. In the following year, the artist also produced No 45 in a series of supplements by the *Army and Navy Gazette* **(247)**.

Militia Battalions

3rdBattalion Formed by the Scottish Borderers Militia with headquarters at Dumfries and transferred to the King's Own Scottish Borderers as it 3rd Battalion in 1887.

4th, later 3rd Battalion Formed as 4th Battalion from the Royal Ayr and Wigtown Militia in 1881 with headquarters at Ayr. Re-numbered as 3rd in 1887.

Territorial Battalions

4th Battalion Formed by the former 1st Volunteer Battalion at Kilmarnock. The eight companies were located: 'A' (Kilmarnock), 'B' (Irvine and Kilwinning), 'C' (Stewarton and Kilmaurs), 'D' (Beith, Glengarnock and Lochwinnoch), 'E' (Saltcoats), 'F' (Dalry and Kilbirnie), 'G' (Darvel, Galston and Newmilns) and 'H' (Kilmarnock).

5th Battalion Formed by the former 2nd Volunteer Battalion with headquarters at Ayr. The companies were located at: 'A' (Ayr), 'B' (Catrine and Darnconnar), 'C' (Maybole and Girvan), 'D' (Stranraer, Portpatrick and Castle Kennedy), 'E' (Cumnock and New Cumnock), 'F' (Troon), 'G' (Muirkirk and Glenbuck) and 'H' (Dalmellington, Waterside and Rankinston).

A number of photographs were produced in 1914 by AC Bruce of Newhaven Leith showing Scottish battalions shortly after mobilization. Here we see a group of cyclists from the 5th Battalion which in May 1915 would sail from Liverpool bound for Gallipoli **(248)**.

Ardeer Company An independent company attached to the 4th Battalion and formed in 1912 from workers employed at Nobel's Explosives Factory in Ardeer. The men came from nearby Kilwinning, Stevenston and Saltcoats. Younger employees provided two companies of 1st Cadet Battalion RSF.

Volunteer Battalions

Plate XV from *Records of the Scottish Volunteer Force 1859-1908* by Lieutenant-General Sir James Moncrieff Grierson features both the 1st and 2nd Volunteer Battalions **(249)**.

1st Volunteer Battalion The 1st Ayrshire Rifle Volunteer Corps ad eight companies: 'A' (Kilmarnock), 'B' (Irvine), 'C' (Largs), 'D' (Beith), 'E' (Saltcoats), 'F' (Dalry), 'G' (Darvel) and 'H' (Galston). Headquarters were at Kilmarnock. Under General Order 181 of December 1887 the corps was re-designated as 1st Volunteer Battalion Royal Scots Fusiliers. Two new companies, one a cyclist, were added at Kilmarnock in 1900, 'C' Company moving to Stewarton and 'H' to Kilmarnock during the same year. The Kilmarnock Academy Cadet Corps was affiliated in 1901. Transfer to the Territorial Force was as 4th Battalion Royal Scots Fusiliers.

2nd Volunteer Battalion The 2nd Ayrshire Rifle Volunteer Corps had seven companies: 'A' and 'B' (Ayr), 'C' (Maybole), 'D' (Girvan), 'E' (Cumnock), 'F' (Sorn) and 'G' (Newmilns). Headquarters were at Ayr. In 1883 'H' Company was added at Troon and in the same year 'F' Company moved from Sorn to Catrine. Under General Order 181 of December 1887, 2nd Ayrshire RVC was re-designated as 2nd Volunteer Battalion Royal Scots Fusiliers. A Cyclist company ('I') was formed at Ayr in 1900 and transfer to the Territorial Force eight years later was as 5th Battalion Royal Scots Fusiliers.

1st Dumfriesshire Rife Volunteer Corps This corps served as a volunteer battalion of the Royal Scots Fusiliers until 1887 when it was transferred to the King's Own Scottish Borderers.

The Galloway Rifle Volunteer Corps Served as a volunteer battalion of the regiment until transfer to the King's Own Scottish Borderers in 1899.

1st Roxburgh and Selkirk (The Border) Rifle Volunteer Corps Served as a volunteer battalion of the regiment until transfer to the King's Own Scottish Borderers in 1887.

Cadet Battalion

1st Cadet Battalion Headquarters were at The Academy, Ayr and the several companies located: 'A' (Ayr Academy), 'B' (Girvan High School), 'C' (Kilmarnock Academy), 'D' (Royal Academy, Irvine) and 'E', 'F' (Nobel's Explosive Works, Ardeer). The companies were affiliated: 'A' and 'D' to 5th Battalion, 'B' and 'C'

4th Battalion, 'E' and 'F', the Ardeer Company.

Illustration credits: Alan Seymore (240), Bruce Bassett-Powell and Bob Bennet (239) and (241)

CHESHIRE REGIMENT

22nd (Cheshire) Regiment

WY Carman states that the Acorn badge was not introduced until 1881 and the formation that year of the Cheshire Regiment by the 22nd (Cheshire) Regiment of Foot. Certainly there was no mention of it in the Royal Warrant of 1751 regarding uniform and colours which gives the facings as pale buff. The Army List is also silent of the matter of badges, showing none for the 22nd. Of interest, however, is the fact that a sprig of acorn featured in the arms of the Duke of Norfolk, the regiment's first colonel, and also those of its second, Sir Henry Bellasis. Henry, Duke of Norfolk had been responsible for the raising of the regiment in 1689. A survivor of the West Indian climate was Captain R Timpson of the 22nd who was, in 1767, granted a coat of arms that included as its crest a sprig of oak almost identical to a post 1881 collar badge of the Cheshire Regiment.

Also, as a source for the Acorn, and its possible use prior to 1881, is the story of how at Dettingen a detachment of the 22nd closely guarded the King as he observed the fighting from under an oak tree. Several times the enemy were fought off, the grateful monarch afterwards plucking a leaf from the tree, handing it to an officer with a request that in memory of the detachment's gallant conduct an oakleaf could be worn in the caps, and placed on the Colours. Tim Carew mentions this event in his book *How The Regiments Got Their Nicknames*. The author also explains the reason behind one of the regiment's nicknames, the Red Knights referring to the early uniform of red coats, waistcoats and breeches.

As mention above, the 22nd had also served in the West Indies and it was after returning from there, much depleted in its ranks due to disease in 1795, that it was ordered to recruit 1,000 'poor boys' between the ages of twelve and sixteen. These were to come from the parish poor houses of Chelmsford, among them being the famous John Shipp who went on to win two commissions during his service. Shipp's autobiography provides much information regarding his time with the 22nd.

Returning to regimental titles, the following colonels' names were used prior to 1751: William Selwyn, Thomas Handasyde, Robert Handasyde, William Burrell, James Sinclair, John Moyle, Thomas Pager and Richard O'Farrell.

Regular Battalions

1st and 2nd Battalions Formed by the 1st and 2nd battalions of the 22nd (Cheshire) Regiment of Foot. In **(250)** we see the 22nd Regiment's acorn badge, the Prince of Wales's plume, coronet and motto being a former badge of the Royal Cheshire Militia. In Edgar A Holloway's original artwork for one of Gale & Polden's postcard sets, the artist has shown the Colours and helmets decorated with sprigs

of oakleaves **(251)**. The acorn collar badges can be seen clearly in Harry Payne's study of a private **(252)** as are the regiment's buff facings. In 1881, English regiments with no royal connection title were required to change the colour of their facings to white. Buff, however, was restored to the Cheshire Regiment in 1904. Both Queen's and King's Medals for South Africa are being worn in (252) and in the 'History and Traditions' postcard at **(253)**.

Militia Battalions

3rd Battalion Formed from the 1st Royal Cheshire Militia with headquarters at Chester.

4th Battalion Formed from the 2nd Royal Cheshire Militia with headquarters at Macclesfield. The battalion was disbanded in 1908.

Territorial Battalions

4th Battalion Formed from the former 1st Volunteer Battalion with headquarters at Grange Road, Birkenhead. The eight companies were located: 'A' to 'D' (Birkenhead), 'E' (Tranmere), 'F', 'G' (Liscard) and 'H' (Heswall, Parkgate, West Kirby and Hoylake). The 1st Birkenhead Cadet Corps was at St Catherine's Institute, Tranmere, the 1st New Brighton Cadet Corps at Mona House, the 2nd New Brighton Cadet Corps with headquarters at 65 and 67 Rowson Street, the 3rd New Brighton Cadet Corps at Oarside Farm, Mount Pleasant Road, the 1st Egremont St John with Columbus Cadet Company (the affiliation was cancelled when the unit became part of the Church Lads Brigade in 1914), the Liscard High School Cadet Corps, the 1st Oxton Cadet Corps in Birkenhead and 1st

Poulton Cadet Company which could be found at St Luke's Parish Hall were all attached to the battalion. A variety of dress is being worn in this camp photograph, including the battalion's grey with scarlet facings full dress uniform **(254)**.

5th (Earl of Chester's) Battalion Formed from the former 2nd and 3rd Volunteer Battalions with headquarters at 8 Black Friars, Chester. A move was made, however, to Volunteer Street, Chester in 1912. The eight companies were located: 'A' (Altrincham and Knutsford), 'B' (Chester and Kelsall), 'C' (Sale and Cheadle), 'D' (Hartford), 'E' (Chester), 'F' (Frodsham and Lymm), 'G' (Runcorn) and 'H' (Hartford).

6th Battalion Formed from the former 4th Volunteer Battalion with headquarters at The Armoury, Stockport. The companies were located: 'A', 'B' (Stalybridge), 'C' (Hyde), 'D' (Glossop and Hadfield) and 'E' to 'H' (Stockport).

7th Battalion Formed from the former 5th Volunteer Battalion with headquarters at Congleton. A move was, however, made to Macclesfield in 1910. The companies were located: 'A' (Congleton), 'B' (Congleton and Bollington), 'C' and 'D' (Macclesfield), 'E' (Macclesfield and Winsford), 'F' (Nantwich and Crewe), 'G' (Sandbach, Middlewich and Winsford) and 'H' (Wilmslow, Winsford and Middlewich). The Macclesfield Industrial School Cadet Corps and Macclesfield Grammar School Cadet Corps were affiliated.

Volunteer Battalions

1st Volunteer Battalion Headquarters of the 1st Cheshire Rifle Volunteer Corps were Oxton and the battalion's eight companies were located: 'A' (Birkenhead), 'B' (Oxton), 'C' (Egremont), 'D' (Bebington), 'E' (Neston), 'F' (Hooton), 'G' (Tranmere) and 'H' (Bromborough). General Order 181 of December 1887 directed the change in designation from 1st Cheshire RVC to 1st Volunteer Battalion Cheshire Regiment. New companies were formed at Birkenhead, Liscard and Heswall by 1900. Called the 'Greys', from the colour of its uniform, the 1st Volunteer Battalion transfer to the Territorial Force in 1908 as 4th Battalion Cheshire Regiment.

Several cadet units were formed and affiliated to the battalion, the first to appear in the Army List being that raised by Wirral College in 1892. Both Mostyn House School at Parkgate and the West Kirby School provided companies the following year, the Wirral College Corps, however, being disbanded in 1884 followed by West Kirby in 1900. In 1903 Liscard High School, Wallasey Grammar, and the New Brighton High School all appear in the Army List as having formed units. But by April 1904 all three had disappeared having had no officers appointed.

The grey helmet shown in **(255)** can be seen at the Cheshire Regiment Museum in Chester. An officers' pattern, the headdress has silver plate and fittings, the central badge being the three garbs from the arms of Cheshire.

2nd (Earl of Chester's) Volunteer Battalion Chester was the headquarters of the 2nd Cheshire (Earl of Chester's) Rifle Volunteer Corps, its nine companies being located: 'A' to 'E' (Chester), 'F' and 'G' (Runcorn), 'H' (Weaverham) and 'I' (Frodsham). General Order 181 of December 1887 directed the change in designation from 2nd Cheshire RVC to 2nd (Earl of Chester's) Volunteer Battalion Cheshire Regiment. Two new companies were formed in 1900. Just prior to transfer to the Territorial Force in 1908 as headquarters and four companies of 5th Battalion Cheshire Regiment, the returned strength of the 2nd Volunteer Battalion stood at 1,081 all ranks.

On display at the Cheshire Regimental Museum in Chester is this fine example of a colour sergeant's scarlet jacket. The battalion title is stitched into the shoulder straps, the collar badges being the Prince of Wales's plumes, coronet and motto. The right arm is adorned with a rifle badge for musketry and a lozenge and several stars awarded for having been passed as efficient over more than twenty years **(256)**.

3rd Volunteer Battalion Headquarters of the 3rd Cheshire Rifle Volunteer Corps were at Knutsford, its eight companies being located: 'A' and

'B' (Altrincham), 'C' (Knutsford), 'D' (Northwich), 'E' (Winsford), 'F' (Cheadle), 'G' (Sale Moor) and 'H' (Lymm). The 3rd Corps was designated as 3rd Volunteer Battalion Cheshire Regiment in 1887, the change being notified in General Order 181 of December, and at the closing of the Volunteer Force its total strength stood at 736 all ranks. Transfer to the Territorial Formed was as four companies of the 5th Battalion Cheshire Regiment. The photograph of a sergeant **(257)** was taken at the studio of A Debenham & Sons in Cowes, Isle of Wight. The embroidered shoulder title is 3 over V over CHESHIRE, the jacket scarlet with white facings.

4th Volunteer Battalion Headquarters of the 4th Cheshire Rifle Volunteer Corps were at Stockport, its several companies being located: 'A' to 'C' (Stalybridge), 'D' to 'I' (Stockport), 'K' (Hyde), 'L', 'M' and 'N' (Glossop). General Order 181 of December 1887 directed the change in designation from 4th Cheshire RVC to 4th Volunteer Battalion Cheshire Regiment and at the close of the Volunteer Movement the last return of the battalion gave a combined strength of 1,066 all ranks. Transfer to the Territorial Force in 1908 was as 6th Battalion Cheshire Regiment. In **(258)** we have a cyclist wearing a leather ammunition bandolier, **(259)** being one of the uniform exhibits at the Cheshire Regimental Museum.

5th Volunteer Battalion Headquarters of the 5th Cheshire Rifle Volunteer Corps were at Congleton, nine companies being located: 'A' and 'B' (Congleton), 'C', 'D', 'E' and 'F' (Macclesfield), 'G' (Sandbach), 'H' (Wilmslow) and 'I' (Nantwich). By October 1880 the Army List indicated a ten-company establishment, the addition being commanded by a former lieutenant of the 27th Wilmslow Corps. General Order 181 of December 1887 directed the change in designation from 5th Cheshire RVC to 5th Volunteer Battalion Cheshire Regiment. The strength of the battalion just prior to transfer to the Territorial Force in 1908 as 7th Battalion Cheshire Regiment was returned as 868 all ranks.

Cadet Battalion

1st Cadet Battalion Formed with an establishment of four companies at Northenden, the first officer being commissioned on 2 December 1901. The battalion transferred to the Territorial Force in 1908, gaining recognition on 29 June 1910. Headquarters were at 12 St Peter's Square, Stockport and affiliated was to the 6th Battalion.

Illustration credits: Anne SK Brown Military Collection, Brown University Library (251) and (252), Bruce Bassett-Powell and Bob Bennet (250)

ROYAL WELSH FUSILIERS

23rd (Royal Welsh Fusiliers) Regiment

The first colonelcy of the regiment that would become the Royal Welsh Fusiliers in 1881 was conferred on Henry Herbert on 8 March 1689. The uniform worn at this time consisted of blue coats with white facings and linings. Regimental titles followed the names of successive colonels—Charles Herbert (killed at Aughrim), Toby Purcell, Sir John Morgan, Richard Ingoldsby and Joseph Sabine—until 1714 when, while stationed in Ireland, the name The Prince of Wales's Own Royal Regiment of Welsh Fusiliers was conferred. By this time red coats were being worn, the new Royal title bringing with it blue facings. The year 1727 saw the title changed to The Royal Welsh Fusiliers, 23rd being added in 1751.

The Royal Warrant dated 1 July 1751 concerning uniformity in clothing and colours of the army directed that the 23rd Regiment should have 'In the centre of their colours, the device of the Prince of Wales, namely three feathers issuing out of the Prince's Coronet; in the three corners of the second colour, the badges of Edward the Black Prince, namely, the Rising Sun, Red Dragon, and the THREE FEATHERS in the CORONET; with the motto *Ich Dien* [I Serve]' To commemorate the services of the regiment during the Egyptian campaign of 1801, the Sphinx superscribed Egypt was authorized in July 1802.

Regular Battalions

1st and 2nd Battalions Formed by the 1st and 2nd Battalions of the 23rd (Royal Welsh Fusiliers) Regiment of Foot. The Prince of Wales's plumes, coronet and motto featured on the badges of the regiment, the title often appearing with two spellings—'Welsh' and 'Welch.' As we see in **(260)** 'S' appears on the waist-belt clasp, 'C' on the button. This irregularity was dealt with in 1920 when an Army Order came down in favour of the 'C'.

In 1834 the then Colonel of the 23rd Regiment, Lieutenant-General Sir J Gordon, received the following letter dated 28 November from Horse Guards: 'Sir, By desire of the General Commanding-in-Chief, I have the honour to notify to you that in consequence of your letter and Lord Hill's Recommendation, the King has been graciously pleased to approve of the 'Flashes' now worn by Officers of the Twenty-Third Foot, or Royal Welch Fusiliers, being henceforth worn and established as a peculiarity whereby to mark the dress of that distinguished regiment. John MacDonald, Adjutant-General.'

The letter referred to by the Adjutant-General had been written in response to an inspection carried out of the regiment's Depot Companies at Portsmouth in 1834. The Flashes seen here being worn, they would not be at all to the liking of the Inspecting General Officer who noted them as being 'superfluous decoration' and ordered them to be done away with. Possible one of the best dress distinctions within the British Army is the set of black ribbons (the 'Flash') worn by the Royal Welsh Fusiliers. When wigs were abolished in the army, the fashion developed of tying-up the hair in a queue, or tail at the back of the head. In 1808 this custom too was done away with, as hair at that time was ordered to be cut short. News of this seems not to have reached the 23rd who were then stationed in Canada, the black ribbons continuing to be

worn for many years after that. Here then is the Flash as seen in one of Harry Payne's postcards **(261)**.

An unusual brass shoulder title exists, the currency of which has yet to be determined, showing a grenade joined by three bars to the letters RW FUS **(262)**. The more usual pattern of the grenade over RWF can be seen in this photograph from the George Craddock Co of India **(263)**. The corporal also wears the Indian General Service Medal with two bars.

From *Bands of the British Army* by WJ Gordon, artist F Stansell's artwork showing the drum major and regimental mascot **(264)**. Also from a first class reference work, *Her Majesty's Army* by Walter Richards, is **(265)** which features an officer by Frank Feller.

Militia Battalions

3rd Battalion Formed by the former Royal Denbigh and Flint Militia with headquarters at Wrexham.

4th Battalion Formed by the former Royal Carnarvon and Merioneth Militia with headquarters at Carnarvon. Disbanded in 1908.

Territorial Battalions

4th (Denbighshire) Battalion Formed from the former 1st Volunteer Battalion with headquarters at Wrexham. The companies were located: 'A' (Wrexham), 'B' (Gresford and Wrexham), 'C' (Ruabon), 'D' (Denbigh and Ruthin), 'E' (Coedpoeth), 'F' (Gwersyllt), 'G' (Rhosllanerchrugog) and 'H' (Llangollen and Chirk).

5th (Flintshire) Battalion Formed from the former 2nd Volunteer Battalion with headquarters at Hawarden, moving to Flint in 1911. The companies were: 'A' (Mold), 'B' (Hawarden and Buckley),

'C' (Rhyl and St Asaph), 'D' (Holywell and Mostyn), 'E' (Flint and Bagillt), 'F' (Caergwle), 'G' (Colwyn Bay and Llanddulas) and 'H' (Connah's Quay). Card No 21 in the 1939 John Player series of cigarette cards dedicated to the Territorial Army shows a pioneer of the 5th Battalion against a background of Rhuddlan Castle **(266)**.

6th (Carnarvonshire & Anglesey) Battalion Carnarvon. *Companies:* 'A' (Carnarvon), 'B' (Portmadoc), 'C' (Penygroes and Nantlle), 'D' (Llanberis and Ebenezer), 'E' (Conway and Llandudno), 'F' (Penmaenmawr), 'G' (Pwllheli and Criccieth), 'H' (Holyhead and Menai Bridge). To represent the Carnarvon Territorial Force Association in Walter Richards's *His Majesty's Territorial Army,* artist R Caton Woodville chose a study of a sergeant talking to a private in the grounds of Carnarvon Castle **(267)**.

7th (Merioneth & Montgomery) Battalion Formed from the former 5th Volunteer Battalion South Wales Borderers with headquarters at Newtown, Montgomeryshire. The companies were located: 'A' (Llanidloes, Montgomery, Caersws and Carno), 'B' (Newtown), 'C' (Welshpool, Llanfair Caereinion, Llanfyllin, Llanwddyn, Llansaintffraid and Llanfechain), 'D' (Machynlleth, Llanbrynmair, Cemmaes and Corris), 'E' (Dolgelly, Barmouth and Harlech), 'F' (Towyn, Aberdovey, Abergwynolwyn and Llwyngwril), 'G' (Blaenau Festiniog, Festiniog and Penrhyndeudraeth) and 'H' (Bala, Corwen and Glyndyfrdwy).

Volunteer Battalions

1st Volunteer Battalion The 1st Denbighshire Rifle Volunteer Corps at Wynnstay had eight companies: 'A' and 'B' (Wrexham), 'C' (Ruabon), 'D' (Denbigh), 'E' (Gresford and Chirk), 'F' (Gwersyllt), 'G' (Ruthin) and 'H' (Llangollen). General Order 78 of June 1884 notified a change in designation from 1st Denbighshire RVC to 1st Volunteer Battalion Royal Welsh Fusiliers and in the following year headquarters moved to Wrexham. Three new companies were added in 1900 and transfer to the Territorial Force in 1908 was as 4th (Denbighshire) Battalion Royal Welsh Fusiliers.

2nd Volunteer Battalion The 1st Flintshire and Carnarvonshire Rifle Volunteer Corps had ten companies: 'A' (Mold), 'B' (Hawarden), 'C' (Rhyl), 'D' (Holywell), 'E' (Flint), 'F' (Caergwle), 'G' and 'H' (Carnarvon), 'I' (Portmadoc) and 'K' (Llanberis). Headquarters were at Rhyl. Under General Order 78 of June 1884 the corps was re-designated as 2nd Volunteer Battalion Royal Welsh Fusiliers, the establishment of which by 1896 had reached sixteen companies. On 26 May 1897, however, this was reduced to eight when the Carnarvonshire personnel were withdrawn to form the new 3rd Volunteer Battalion RWF. That same year headquarters of the 2nd Volunteer Battalion, now exclusively in Flintshire, moved to Hawarden. Three years later an additional three companies were sanctioned then, in 1904, a reduction was made to ten. Transfer to the Territorial Force was as headquarters and seven companies of the 5th Battalion Royal Welsh Fusiliers.

3rd Volunteer Battalion Formed on 26 May 1897 by the removal of the eight Carnarvonshire companies then forming part of the 2nd Volunteer Battalion, RWF. Headquarters were placed at Carnarvon and in 1900 Anglesey, without volunteers since the disbandment of its last corps in 1863, provided a new company at Holyhead. In the last year of the Volunteer System the strength of the battalion stood at 836 all ranks, its nine companies being located Carnarvon (2), Portmadoc, Penygroes, Llanberis, Conwy, Penmaenmawr, Pwllheli and Holyhead. In 1908 provided headquarters and seven companies of the 6th Battalion Royal Welsh Fusiliers.

Illustration credit: Bruce Bassett-Powell and Bob Bennet (260)

SOUTH WALES BORDERERS

24th (2nd Warwickshire) Regiment

Raised 1689 in Ireland by Sir Edward Dering, the regiment, having been numbered as 24th in 1751, took on its Warwickshire association in 1782. With two battalions, it would become the South Wales Borderers in 1881. The following colonels' names were in use prior to 1751: Sr Edward Dering, Daniel Dering, Samuel Venner, Louis James le Vasseur, William Seymour, John Churchill, William Tatton, Gilbert Primrose, Thomas Howard, Thomas Wentworth, Daniel Houghton and William Henry Kerr. Battle honours authorized prior to 1881 were: Egypt, Cape of Good Hope, Talavera, Fuentes n' Onor, Salamanca, Vittoria, Pyrenees, Nivelle, Orthes, Peninsula, Punjaub, Chillianwallah and Goojerat.

Green facings are the first on record, the skirt linings noted as white by 1742. In earlier years willow green appeared in official records, grass green being a later description. In commemoration of the regiment's service during the Egyptian campaign of 1801, the Sphinx superscribed Egypt was authorized as a badge in July of the following year. Well known are the 24th's encounters with the Zulu nation in 1879, the disaster at Isandlwana which was followed by the heroic stand at Rorke's Drift. After Isandlwana both Lieutenant's Melville and Coghill would sacrifice their lives in an attempt to save the Queen's Colour from the enemy. At first, the Colour was lost in the Buffalo River, but when found a few days later it was taken back to England where Queen Victoria asked to see it. Touched by the gallantry of the officers (both posthumously awarded Victoria Crosses), and the regiment's heroic stand at Rorke's Drift she placed a silver wreath of immortelles on the staff. A representation of the wreath would later become a feature of regimental badges.

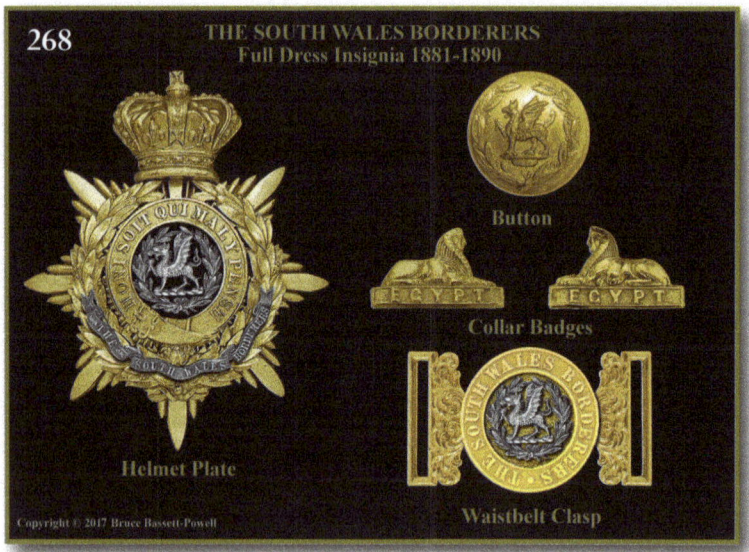

Regular Battalions

1st and 2nd Battalions Formed by the 1st and 2nd Battalions of the 24th (2nd Royal Warwickshire) Regiment of Foot. In **(268)** we see both the dragon and Sphinx badges of the regiment, **(269)** being the post-1902 King's crown version of the officers' gilt and silver helmet plate. The dragon of Wales had been a badge of the Royal South Wales Borderers Militia and was adopted by the regiment in 1881. The Sphinx commemorates the services of the former 24th Regiment in Egypt in 1801.

In Harry Payne's artwork for one of Gale & Polden's uniform postcards **(270)** we see the regiment's green facings and Sphinx collar badges. A sergeant is seen chatting to a private who wears both the Queen's and King's Medals for South Africa. It had been the 2nd Battalion that sailed for South Africa on the *Bavarian* in January 1900. Another fine set of postcards from Gale & Polden featured the work of Ernest Ibbetson **(271)** showing a scene at Brecon Barracks in which the Colours were paraded. Here we have the green of the Regimental Colour, the head of the King's Colour pike having a silver wreath of immortelles. It was Queen Victoria who in 1880 had asked to see the Queen's Colour which had been lost in

the Buffalo River after the 24th Regiment's tragic disaster at Isandhlwana in 1879. Later found, it was brought home to Osborne House on the Isle of Wight where the queen, having heard a first-hand account of Isandhlwana and Rorke's Drift, placed the wreath in the Colour. One of the many Victoria Crosses awarded for the action at Rorke's Drift went to Lieutenant Gonville Bromhead (famously played by Michael Caine in the film 'Zulu') who is seen in **(272)**. He served with the South Wales Borderers until his death in India from typhoid fever on 9 February 1891.

Returning with the 2nd Battalion after the Boer War were the two wildebeest seen in this image by Edgar Holloway **(273)**. The mascots were also photographed with their handler this time wearing the Broderick cap **(274)**. Another rarely seen form of headdress is the fur caps seen in **(275)** being worn by the 2nd Battalion at Tientsin, North China in 1914.

Two items of artwork now, **(276)** by Orlando Norie and showing a maxim gun detachment about 1890, **(277)** being the title page to Volume 2 of *Her Majesty's Army* by Walter Richards. Note how the artist

(unknown) has shown the sentry in white facings. This was the colour taken into use in 1881, the former grass green returning in 1905.

Militia Battalions

3rd Battalion Formed from the Royal South Wales Borderers Militia with headquarters at Brecon.

4th Battalion Formed from the Royal Montgomeryshire Militia with headquarters at Welshpool. Disbanded in 1908.

Territorial Battalion

Brecknockshire Battalion Un-numbered, the Brecknockshire Battalion was formed by the former 1st Volunteer Battalion. Headquarters were at Brecon and the eight companies located: 'A' (Brecon), 'B' (Brynmawr), 'C' (Crickhowell), 'D' (Hay-on-Wye), 'E' (Builth Wells and Llanwrtyd Wells), 'F' (Talgarth), 'G' (Cefn Coed) and 'H' (Ystradgynlais, Brynamman and Seven Sisters).

Volunteer Battalions

1st Volunteer Battalion The 1st Brecknockshire Rifle Volunteer Corps at Brecon had eight companies: 'A' (Brecon), 'B' (Brynmawr), 'C' (Crickhowell), 'D' (Hay-on-Wye), 'E' (Builth Wells), 'F' (Talgarth), 'G' (Cefn Coed) and 'H' (Brecon). A Mounted Infantry Company was formed at Glosbury in 1884, this being disbanded in 1898, and in 1894 a new company was raised at Ystradgynlais. In 1894 and 1901 respectively, cadet units were formed and attached to the battalion at Christ College, Brecon and Brecon Intermediate School. The corps was designated 1st Volunteer Battalion South Wales Borderers in 1885 and joined the

Territorial Force in 1908 as The Brecknockshire Battalion South Wales Borderers.

Brecon photographer Charles S Bell's photograph of the Diamond Jubilee Procession in 1897 conveniently names all those that represented the battalion on the day **(278)**. A fine specimen of an officer's helmet, with its silver helmet plate and fittings, is shown in **(279)**, and three members of the battalion in **(280)**.

2nd Volunteer The 1st Monmouthshire Rifle Volunteer Corps had seven companies: 'A' (Chepstow), 'B' and 'C' (Newport), 'D' and 'E' (Pontymister), 'F' (Tredegar) and 'G' (Bassaleg). The corps was re-designated as 2nd Volunteer Battalion South Wales Borderers in 1885. By 1900 the establishment of the battalion stood at eleven companies—Chepstow, Newport (4), Tredegar, Pontymister, Blackwood, Rogerstone, Rhymney and Caerleon. Provided the 1st Battalion Monmouthshire Regiment in 1908.

3rd Volunteer Battalion Formed as one company at Pontypool towards the end of 1859 and shown as 3rd Corps until April 1860 when renumbered as 2nd. Colonel Thomas Mitchell in *History of the Volunteer Movement in Monmouthshire,* notes that the 2nd Corps had

its headquarters at 'Pontypool Works'. During the later months of 1859 companies were formed near to Pontypool which, towards the end of 1860, were drawn into the 2nd Corps to form a battalion of six companies located: No 1 (Pontypool), No 2 (Ebbw Vale), No 3 (Abersychan), No 4 (Ebbw Vale), No 5 (Sirhowy) and No 6 (Abercarn). Headquarters about this time were transferred to Bank Chambers, Pontypool—where the Post Office now stands. Absorbed the 11th Corps in May 1861 and the companies were later lettered 'A' to 'F'.

The Abercarn Company was removed from the records after 1866, but Regimental Orders dated 14 May 1868 make mention of a six-company establishment carrying out drills at Cwmbran. GA Brett in his 1933 history of the 2nd Monmouthshire Regiment suggests that a new company was formed in 1867 in the district between Pontypool and Cwmbran—references, he notes, were made in later years to a company described variously at Panteg, Upper Pontnewydd and Cwmbran.

In 1877 'G' Company was added at Garndiffaith, with 'H' following in 1884 at Victoria. This, records GA Bret, necessitated the reorganisation of the 2nd Corps as 'A' Company (Pontypool), 'B' (Abersychan), 'C' and 'D' (Ebbw Vale), 'E' (Garndiffaith) 'F' (Sirhowy), 'G' (Panteg) and 'H' (Victoria). The corps was re-designated as 3rd Volunteer Battalion South Wales Borderers in 1885.

A further change in company organisation took place in 1897 when 'A' was to be found at Pontypool, 'B' Abersychan, 'C' Upper Pontnewydd, 'D' and 'E' Ebbw Vale, 'F' Sirhowy, 'G' Abersychan and 'H' Abertillery. This would remain the order of battle of the battalion until 1900 when 'C' Company is recorded as being located at Cwmbran and 'E' at Newbridge—the move from Ebbw Vale was in December 1898. Two new companies were added in 1900, 'I' at Abercarn and 'K' (Cyclist), Ebbw Vale. In 1903 the Ebbw Vale Iron and Coal Company presented a building for use as a Drill Hall for the Abercarn Company.

On 20 December 1902 a new headquarters building in Osborne Road, Pontypool was opened by Honorary Colonel JC Hanbury and transfer to the Territorial Force in 1908 was as 2nd Battalion Monmouthshire Regiment.

4th Volunteer Battalion The 3rd Monmouthshire Rifle Volunteer Corps had eight companies located: 'A' (Blaenavon), 'B' (Pontypool), 'C' (Monmouth), 'D', 'E' and 'F' (Newport), 'G' (Usk) and 'H' (Abergavenny). Re-designated as 4th Volunteer Battalion South Wales Borderers in 1885. The establishment was increased to ten companies in 1900 and in 1904 a cadet corps was raised and affiliated to the battalion at Monmouth Grammar School. Headquarters moved from Pontypool to Newport in 1901 and transfer to the Territorial Force in 1908 was as 3rd Battalion Monmouthshire Regiment.

5th Volunteer Battalion Formed with headquarters at Newtown on 1 April 1897 with Major E Pryce-Jones in command. The original establishment was four companies, two more being added later—one according to the *Territorial Yearbook* for 1909, being raised by Aberystwyth University College on 17 March 1900. Transfer to the Territorial Force in 1908 was as headquarters and four companies of 7th Battalion Royal Welsh Fusiliers. The University personnel became part of the OTC.

Illustration credits: Anne SK Brown Military Collection, Brown University Library (271), Bruce Bassett-Powell and Bob Bennet (268)

KING'S OWN SCOTTISH BORDERERS

The original title allotted in 1881 was the King's Own Borderers, this being changed to the above in 1887.

25th (King's Own Borderers) Regiment

A plaque situated at the Edinburgh Castle Esplanade tells how 'Hereabouts on the 19th of March in 1689 David Leslie - Earl of Leven – raised a Regiment of Foot in the space of two hours for the defence of the City.' As well as bearing the names of its colonels—James Maitland, William Breton, Richard Boyle, John Middleton, John Leslie, Hugh Sempill, John Lindsay and William Maule—the Edinburgh Regiment became the 25th (Edinburgh) Regiment in 1751 but would lose its Scottish title connection in 1782 when Sussex replaced the name of the Scottish capital. A website dedicated to the history of the regiment includes a fine study of an officer for the period 1689. He wears a red coat with yellow lining and gold lace. Blue facings, however, replaced the yellow when in 1805 the Sussex subtitle was dropped and replaced by The King's Own Borderers. This alone would be the title assumed in 1881.

Along with the King's Own title in 1805 came the regiment's Royal Crest badge and the motto *In veritate religious confide* (I put my trust in the truth of religion). Featured also on the badges, and authorized 8 March 1832, is the Castle of Edinburgh together with the city's motto *Nisi Dominus frustra* (Without the Lord everything is in vein). The White Horse of Hanover had been displayed on the Colours previous to 1805, the Sphinx superscribed Egypt, authorized in 1802, commemorating the campaign of the previous year. All four badges, Royal Crest, Edinburgh Castle, the White Horse of Hanover and Sphinx, can be seen of a splendid Rococo-style, pre-1855, shoulder-belt plate illustrated by Major Parkyn (see item 220 in his book *(Military) Shoulder-Belt Plates and Buttons*). Franklin's plate shows, with their yellow facings, various uniforms dated 1755-85 and also includes an illustration of an oval cross-belt plate, c1779, displaying a thistle below a crown. Two patterns of lace are shown, both with red, yellow and black lines.

The National Army Museum are in possession of a painting depicting the 25th Regiment at Menorca. Oil on canvas and attributed to Giuseppe Chiesa, the image shows the regiment on the march and carries the title Lord George Lennox, Colonel of the 25th Regiment of Foot, 1771. But, as the museum's notes point out, the painting does not seem to depict Lennox at all—'the officer who appears to the right of the drummer carries a spontoon and is unlikely to be a Colonel.' Grenadiers are shown wearing the new fur caps issued in 1768, but no plates are in evidence.

Thomas Carlyle, in his history of Frederick the Great, wrote 'A really splendid victory, this of Minden, August 1st. These unsurpassable Six, in industrious valour, unsurpassable.' The six regiments he was referring to include the 25th which, on Minden Day (1st August) celebrated the victory by wearing roses in their hats and decorating the Colours and drums with the same. The custom recalls how advancing troops during the battle passed among rose briers, snatching up the blossoms and placing them in their headdress and equipment.

Regular Battalions

1st and 2nd Battalions Formed by the 25th (King's Own Borderers) Regiment of Foot. Uniform historian WY Carman records that the King's Own Borderers had become a Lowland Regiment in 1882, its dress at the same time to include doublets and trews. Helmets were worn until the introduction of the Kilmarnock bonnet in 1903. Illustration **(281)** is by Richard Simkin and shows a group of nine men standing behind an officer. A piper is to the right and in the distance can be seen a mounted officer. The image is No 62 in the 'Military Types' series of supplement that were issued with the *Army and Navy Gazette*. This particular one was published on 4 February 1893.

In Bruce Bassett-Powell's detailed image of an officer's helmet plate, collar badges, button and waist-belt clasp **(282)** we see two of the regiment's badges: the Royal Crest, which had been conferred by King George III together with the 'King's Own' title in 1805, and a representation of Edinburgh Castle together with the motto *Nisi dominus frustra*. This dates from 1832, the motto being that of the City of Edinburgh. Introduced in 1903, the Kilmarnock bonnet can be seen in two postcards **(283)** and **(284)**. Clearly shown by artist Harry Payne are the white metal cap badges, KOSB shoulder titles and Edinburgh Castle on the collars. Both the Queen's and King's Medals for South Africa are being worn in both images, the 1st Battalion having arrived at the Cape on two transports, the *Braemar Castle* and *Goorkha*, around 26 January 1900.

The 2nd Battalion in 1909 were stationed at Maryhill Barracks in Glasgow, a Colours inspection parade by General Sir E Leach taking place there which was photographed. In **(285)** we see Captain Patrick Alexander Vansittart Stewart in front of his company, **(286)** and **(287)** providing views of the troops as they line up on what looks like a dismal day. Also of the 2nd Battalion is illustration **(288)** which shows the quartermaster on the left, and regimental quartermaster sergeant on the right. Note the latter's KOSB over 2 cloth white on red shoulder title.

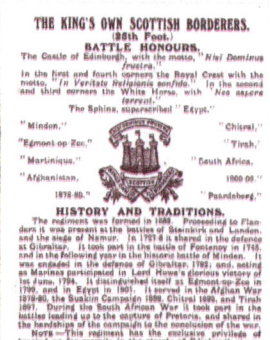

Militia Battalion

3rd Battalion The regiment was without a militia battalion until 1887 when the 3rd Battalion Royal Scots Fusiliers (the former Scottish Borderers Militia) was transferred. Headquarters were at Dumfries.

Territorial Battalions

4th (The Border) Battalion Formed by both the 1st Roxburgh and Selkirk Volunteer Rifle Corps and the 2nd Volunteer Battalion. Headquarters were at Melrose, moving to Galashiels in 1910, and the companies were located: 'A' (Kelso and Jedburgh), 'B' (Hawick), 'C' (Hawick, Melrose, St Boswells and Newcastleton), 'D' (Duns, Greenlaw, Lauder and Earlston), 'E' (Coldstream, Ayton, Eyemouth, Chirnside, Swinton and Coldingham), 'F', 'G' (Galashiels) and 'H' (Selkirk, Melrose and, transferred from 'C' Company in 1914, St Boswells). The pipers on the 4th Battalion wore Buccleugh tartan **(289)**.

5th (Dumfries & Galloway) Battalion Formed by the former 3rd Volunteer Battalion and Galloway Rifle. Headquarters were at Dumfries and the companies located: 'A' (Dumfries and Moniaive), 'B' (Annan, Langholm and Canonbie), 'C' (Lockerbie, Ecclefechan and Moffat), 'D' (Sanquhar, Thornhill and Kirkconnel), 'E' (Maxwelltown), 'F' (Dalbeattie), 'G' (Castle Douglas, Corsock, Gatehouse and Kirkcudbright) and 'H' (Newton Stewart, Wigtown, Creetown, Kirkcowan, Whithorn and Garlieston).

Volunteer Battalions

1st Roxburgh and Selkirk (The Border) Rifle Volunteer Corps Headquarters of this corps were at Newtown St Boswells, its nine companies being located: 'A' (Jedburgh), 'B' (Kelso), 'C' (Melrose), 'D' and 'E' (Hawick), 'F' and 'G' (Galashiels) and 'H' and 'I' (Selkirk). The corps became one of the volunteer battalions allotted to the Royal Scots Fusiliers in 1881, but General Order 61 of May 1887 notified a transferred (without change in title) to the King's Own Scottish Borderers. At the same time 'H' Company moved to Galashiels. A new company ('K') was added at Hawick in 1892, followed by 'L' and 'M', also at Hawick, in 1901. The latter two, however, were disbanded in 1903. Battalion headquarters were transferred to Melrose, 'L' (Cyclist) Company was formed at Newcastleton, and Kelso High School Cadet Corps was affiliated in 1901. Transfer to the Territorial Force in 1908 was as six companies of 4th Battalion King's Own Scottish Borderers.

2nd (Berwickshire) Volunteer Battalion With headquarters at Coldstream, the 1st Berwickshire Rifle Volunteer Corps comprised seven companies: 'A' (Duns), 'B' (Coldstream), 'C' (Ayton), 'D' (Greenlaw), 'E'(Lauderdale), 'F'(Earlston) and 'G' (Chirnside). The corps became a volunteer battalion (without change in title) of the Royal Scots in 1881, but General Order 61 of May 1887 notified the transfer to the King's Own Scottish Borderers. The new designation of 2nd (Berwickshire) Volunteer Battalion was authorized in the following December by General Order 181. Headquarters had moved from Coldstream to Duns in 1885. On 1 April 1891 'H' Company was formed at Duns, followed by 'I' Company at Ladykirk in May 1900. But the latter was re-lettered as 'H' upon disbandment of the new Duns personnel in 1905. In 1908 provided two companies of the 4th Battalion King's Own Scottish Borderers.

In this camp photograph **(290)** we see four members of the battalion wearing bandsman arm badges. Also clearly seen, and identifying the battalion, are white embroidered 2 over V over KOSB shoulder titles.

3rd (Dumfries) Volunteer Battalion Headquarters of the 1st Dumfriesshire Rifle Volunteer Corps were at Dumfries and its ten companies located: 'A' and 'B' (Dumfries), 'C' (Thornhill), 'D' (Sanquhar), 'E' (Penpont), 'F' (Annan), 'G' (Moffat), 'H' (Langholm), 'I' (Lockerbie) and 'K' (Lochmaben). The corps became a volunteer battalion (without change of title) of the Royal Scots Fusiliers in 1881 but transferred to King's Own Scottish Borderers with title 3rd (Dumfries) Volunteer Battalion in 1887. The change being notified in General Order 181 of December. In March 1885 'E' Company was absorbed into 'C' as a section and at the same time a new 'E' was formed at Ecclefechan. 'K' Company moved to Canonbie in December 1888. Transfer to the Territorial Force in 1908 was as headquarters and four companies of the 5th (Dumfries and Galloway) Battalion KOSB.

The Galloway Rifle Volunteer Corps Galloway is the district of South West Scotland comprising the counties of Wigtownshire and Kirkcudbrightshire. The several rifle volunteer corps formed within these areas were on 30 June 1860 grouped together under the title of The Galloway Admin Battalion of Rifle Volunteers. In 1880 the battalion was consolidated as the Galloway RVC with headquarters at Newton Stewart and eight companies: 'A' (Kirkcudbright), 'B' (Castle Douglas), 'C' (Stranraer), 'D' (Newton Stewart), 'E' (New Galloway), 'F' and 'G' (Maxwelltown) and 'H' (Dalbeattie). The corps joined the Royal Scots as one of its volunteer battalions (without change in title) in 1881 but transferred to the King's Own Scottish Borders in 1899. Again, no change in designation was assumed. Headquarters moved to Castle Douglas in 1885, then to Maxwelltown in 1904. Four companies of 5th King's Own Scottish Borderers and one company of the 5th Royal Scots Fusiliers was formed in 1908.

Illustration credit: Bruce Bassett-Powell (282)

CAMERONIANS (SCOTTISH RIFLES)

26th (Cameronians) Regiment

Just as the 25th Regiment was raised in a very short time, the next in line sprang from twenty companies recruited within twenty-four hours: the Cameronians, the name coming from the religious reformer Richard Cameron. Just one day (14 May 1689) would see the men mustered on the banks of Douglas Water in South Lanarkshire, their first commanding officer being William Cleland, their colonel the nineteen-year-old James Douglas, Earl of Angus who would later be killed at Steinkirk. He has a statue that today overlooks the spot where the regiment began. From a succession of colonels' names—Andrew Monro, James Ferguson, William Borthwick (killed at Ramillies), John Dalrymple, George Preston and Phillip Anstruther—the regiment took on the number 26th in 1751, Cameronians making its way into the Army List from 1786. With just one battalion, the 26th went to form the 1st Battalion Cameronians (Scottish Rifles) in 1881.

WY Carman notes that possibly the regiment's early red coats were faced with white, but evidence is lacking on this point. Certainly, pale yellow facings were being worn by 1742. Badges featured a Dragon superscribed China and, from the crest of the Grahams (the 26th was raised by Thomas Graham), a mullet star.

90th (Perthshire Volunteers) (Light Infantry) Regiment

The origins of this regiment are unusual. In 1792, the Laird of Balgowan, Thomas Graham, was on holiday in the Mediterranean when his wife Mary died of tuberculosis. She was subsequently buried in Toulouse where later her coffin was desecrated by some drunken revolutionaries. It would be this outrage that prompted Thomas Graham to return home and raise a regiment to fight the French.

Thomas Graham had gained permission to raise his regiment, his request records Chichester and Burges-Short, 'was conceded with some reluctance, as the King had a dislike to giving military commands to persons with no previous army training.' He was, however, commissioned on 10 February 1794 and was, by the following 13 May, able to front a regiment comprising seven officers and 746 men. Records note these numbers were made up of ninety-five Scottish Highlanders, 430 Scottish Lowlanders, 165 English and fifty-six Irish. One source notes that many of the recruits had come from Perthshire prisons. The 90th (Perthshire Volunteers) received its Light Infantry title in 1815 and was to provide the 2nd Battalion Cameronians (Scottish Rifles) in 1881. The regiment's scarlet coats had buff facings. It's nickname, The Perthshire Grey-breeks referring possible to the colour of the trousers but, it is thought, possibly to the regiment's prison origins. Convict's breeches were at the time of a drab grey colour. Bugle-horn badges were worn, the Sphinx superscribed Egypt being authorised in July 1802. The Arms of Perth was also worn. Captain Alex M Delavoye's 1880 history also includes a roll of officers from 1795 to 1880. Volume 1 of the Cameronians records by S H F Johnston covers the period 1689-1910.

Regular Battalions

1st and 2nd Battalions The 1st Battalion was formed by the 26th (Cameronians) Regiment, the 2nd from the 90th (Perthshire Volunteers) (Light

Infantry). The regiment's silver mullet star and bugle horn badges are seen in Bruce Bassett-Powell's detailed image **(291)** of a helmet plate, waist-belt clasp and pouch-belt ornaments. Illustration **(292)** shows the officers of the 1st Battalion, the photograph being taken at Glasgow in 1914 shortly before landing in France on 15 August. The colour of the uniform can be seen in Richard Simkin's supplement No 63 which was produced for the *Army and Navy Gazette* and published 4 March 1893 **(293)**.

In both (292) and (293) green cloth shakos are being worn, **(294)** providing a more detailed view of this headdress which had replaced the earlier helmet. The image is from the 1900 edition of *Dress Regulations for the Offices of the Army* which gives the following description: 'Rifle green cloth, 4½ inches high in front and 7¾ at the back, the crown 6 inches long and 5¾ inches cross. Bands of black lace, thistle pattern, 1¾ inches wide round the base, and 5/8 inch round the top. At the sides two small bronze thistle ornaments for ventilation and with hook attachments. Black silk square cord plait in front carried up to the hooks at each side, and a double cord carried round the back aver ring at rear, with black egg moulds and slider at left side. Black silk doubled square body line, 76 inches long, with swivel to attach to the ring behind, with black egg moulds and sliders. Horizontal peak, black leather chin strap.'

Details of the tall plumes are also provided: 'Black ostrich feathers, a black vulture feather bottom in a bronze corded ball socket with three upright leaves. The height of the plume from the top of the shako is 7 inches.' The shako had been introduced in 1892, the headdress previous to this being the green cloth helmet as seen in Orlando Norie's 1882 watercolour showing three officers, a bugler and private **(295)**.

The photograph shown in illustration **(296)** comes with a handwritten caption stating how the doublet had been introduced in October 1891 and the shako just over a year later in November 1892. Featuring all ranks of the 1st Battalion, the image seems to have been created with the purpose of illustrating the several recent changes in dress. Note how one man at the back has a black cover to his shako. Here it is again (fourth man from the right)

in this photograph which seems to have been taken at the same time **(297)**. All in **(298)** wear the glengarry and foreign service dress and carry rifles. The man second from right at the front, however, seems to be armed only with a bassoon.

In J McNeill's original artwork for one of Gale & Polden's postcard sets **(299)**, one man carries a signal flag, both having medals for the South African war of 1899-1902. The 2nd Battalion had sailed on the *City of Cambridge* on 23 October 1899, arriving at Durban around 21 November.

Militia Battalions

3rd and 4th Battalions Formed by the 2nd Royal Lanarkshire Militia with headquarters at Hamilton.

Territorial Battalions

5th Battalion Formed from the former 1st Lanarkshire Volunteer Rifle Corps with headquarters at and all eight companies at 261 West Princes Street, Glasgow.

6th Battalion Formed from the former 2nd Volunteer Battalion, headquarters were at Muir Hall, Hamilton and the companies located: 'A', 'B' (Hamilton), 'C' (Uddingston), 'D' (Larkhall and Strathaven), 'E' (Bothwell and Palace Colliery), 'F' (Blantyre) and 'G', 'H' (Motherwell).

7th Battalion Formed from the former 3rd Volunteer Battalion with headquarters and all eight companies at Victoria Road, Glasgow. The Hutcheson's Grammar School Cadet Corps at Crown Street in Glasgow was affiliated.

8th Battalion Formed by the former 4th Volunteer Battalion with headquarters and

all eight companies at 149 Cathedral Street, Glasgow. The 8th Battalion embarked for Gallipoli in May 1915, the photograph shown in **(300)** of the Machine Gun Section having been taken in December of the previous year.

Volunteer Battalions

1st Lanarkshire Volunteer Rifle Corps This corps in Glasgow served, without change in title, as the regiment's 1st Volunteer Battalion and in 1908 provided its 5th Battalion. Associated with the 1st Corps since its formation in 1902 was the High School Glasgow Cadet Corps which, in 1908, became a contingent of the Junior Division OTC. The battalion was represented in Major-General Sir James Moncrieff Grierson's book, *Records of the Scottish Volunteer Force 1859-1908,* by the painting shown in **(301)** which shows the grey uniforms with blue facings of the 1st Lanarkshire Rifle Volunteers.

2nd Volunteer Battalion The 2nd Lanarkshire Rifle Volunteer Corps at Hamilton had ten companies: 'A' and 'B' (Hamilton), 'C' (Uddingston), 'D' (Strathaven), 'E' (Bothwell), 'F' and 'G' (Wishaw), 'H' (Motherwell), 'I' (Blantyre) and 'K' (Motherwell). Re-designation as 2nd Volunteer Battalion Cameronians (Scottish Rifles) was notified in General Order 181 of December 1887. In 1892 'D' Company was absorbed into 'K' (with headquarters at Strathaven) and at the same time a new 'D' formed at Larkhall. 'L' (Cyclist) Company was added at Hamilton in 1899. In 1904 the headquarters of 'K' Company were transferred to Motherwell. Transfer to the Territorial Force was as 6th Battalion Cameronians.

3rd Lanarkshire Rifle Volunteer Corps Glasgow's 3rd Lanarkshire Rifle Volunteer Corps had its headquarters in Victoria Road, its twelve company establishment being raised to thirteen when a cyclist company was formed in 1902. The corps became a volunteer battalion of the Cameronians (without change in title) in 1881, providing the regiment's 7th Battalion in 1908.

4th Volunteer Battalion The 4th Lanarkshire (Glasgow 1st Northern) Rifle Volunteer Corps was re-designated as 4th Volunteer Battalion Cameronians (Scottish Rifles) by General Order 181 of December 1887. Headquarters were at 149 Cathedral Street Glasgow and a rifle range was used at Flemington. Transfer to the Territorial Force in 1908 was as 8th Battalion Cameronians, the Kelvinside Academy Cadet Corps which had been formed and attached in September 1893, at the same time became a contingent of the OTC. The battalion was represented in Major-General Sir James Moncrieff Grierson's book, *Records of the Scottish Volunteer Force 1859-1908,* by the painting shown in **(302)** which shows the several uniforms worn.

5th Volunteer Battalion When the 7th Lanarkshire Rifle Volunteer Corps was re-designated as 5th Volunteer Battalion in 1887 it comprised eight companies: 'A' (Coatbridge), 'B' (Airdrie), 'C' (Shotts), 'D' (Airdrie), 'E' (Coatbridge), 'F' (Cheyston), 'G' (Caldecruix) and 'H' (Newarthill). On 1 April 1897 the battalion was disbanded as a result of severe criticism regarding discipline by the officer commanding the 26th Regimental District.

Illustration credits: Alan Seymore (286 and 287), Anne SK Brown Military Collection (285 and 289), Bruce Bassett-Powell and Bob Bennet (281)

ROYAL INNISKILLING FUSILIERS

27th (Inniskilling) Regiment

The 27th first entered the Army List as Brigadier-General Zachariah Tiffin's Regiment of Foot. Raised from independent companies in 1689, it became the 27th (Inniskilling) Regiment in 1751 and provided the 1st Battalion Royal Inniskilling Fusiliers in 1881. Until 1751 the regiment was known by the names of its successive colonels: Thomas Whetham, Richard Molesworth, Archibald Hamilton and William Blakeney. For many years it was thought that the regiment had grey uniforms, but later research has established that red coats with blue breeches were worn. The breeches are on record as having been purchased from London in 1689. WY Carman notes that in the following year a quantity of red shalloon was sent in a list of 1690 and that this may have been used as a lining to the scarlet cloth sent at the same time for officers. By 1742, facings were buff. There exists a watercolour by Richard Simkin showing a musketeer of Colonel Tiffin's Regiment in 1689 and this shows a long scarlet coat with buff facings. The breeches and hose are black. Detailed are the sixteen colour plates of uniform included in the regimental history published by Constable in 1928.

Thomas Carlyle, in his history of Frederick the Great, wrote 'A really splendid victory, this of Minden, August 1st. These unsurpassable Six, in industrious valour, unsurpassable. The six regiments he was referring to include the 27th which, on Minden Day (1st August) celebrated the victory by wearing roses in their hats and decorating the Colours and drums with the same. The custom recalls how advancing troops during the battle passed among rose briers, snatching up the blossoms and placing them in their headdress and equipment.

The badge of the Castle of Inniskilling with St George's flag flying from its central tower is mentioned in the Royal Warrant of 1751, and for its services during the rebellion of 1715, the device of the White Horse of Hanover was authorized to be displayed on the Colours. Authorized in July 1802 was the badge of the Sphinx superscribed Egypt.

108th (Madras Infantry) Regiment

Raised 1854 in India as the Honourable East India Company's 3rd (Madras European Infantry). It became the 108th in 1862 and in 1881 provided the 2nd Battalion Royal Inniskilling Fusiliers. The regiment served in Central India during the Mutiny, coming home from Bombay to England in 1874. Facings were deep yellow.

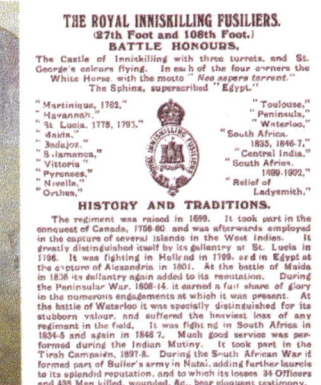

Regular Battalions

1st and 2nd Battalions 1st Battalion formed from the former 27th (Inniskilling) Regiment of Foot, the 2nd from the 108th (Madras Infantry) Regiment. In illustration **(303)** we see the regiment's Inniskilling Castle badge being displayed on the fur cap grenade, button and collar badges. It also appears on the officers' waist-belt clasp along with the White Horse of Hanover and Sphinx superscribed 'Egypt.' Richard Simkin's supplement No 64 in the 'Types of the Army' series for the *Army and Navy Gazette* shows two officers, a private and drummer **(304)**. Two bandsman are shown in this cigarette card from Phillips **(305)** and a corporal and officer in this Harry Payne watercolour produced for one of Gale & Polden's postcards **(306)**. Also appearing as a postcard in the 'History and Traditions' series was a study of two members of the regiment, one wearing a scouts arm badge, the other both the Queen's and King's Medals for South Africa **(307)**.

Militia Battalion

3rd Battalion The original 3rd Battalion was formed in 1881 from the former Fermanagh Light Infantry Militia at Enniskilling. Re-numbered as 4th Battalion in 1908. At this time the then 4th Battalion was re-numbered as 3rd.

   4th Battalion The original 4th Battalion was formed in 1881 from the former Londonderry Light Infantry Militia. In 1882, however, it was converted as 9th Brigade North Irish Division Royal Artillery. The original 5th Battalion was re-numbered as 4th in 1882, then designated as 3rd Battalion in 1908.

   5th Battalion The regiment's 5th Battalion was originally supplied in 1881 by the Royal Tyrone Fusiliers Militia at Omagh, but upon the conversion of the 4th to artillery in 1882 it was re-numbered as 4th. When the 3rd was re-numbered as 4th in 1908, the battalion was re-designated as 3rd.

   6th Battalion Formed in 1881 from the former Donegal Militia at Lifford. The battalion was re-numbered as 5th in 1882, then disbanded in 1908.

Illustration credits: Anne SK Brown Military Collection, Brown University Library (306), Bruce Bassett-Powell and Bob Bennet (303)

GLOUCESTERSHIRE REGIMENT

28th (North Gloucestershire) Regiment

The 28th Regiment, later in 1881 the 1st Battalion Gloucestershire Regiment, had its origins in Colonel Sir John Gibson's Regiment of Foot which was raised by him at Portsmouth in 1694, the Gloucestershire association appearing as part of the title in 1782. Successive colonels until 1751 were: Sampson de Lalo, John Mordaunt, Andrew Windsor, William Burrell, Nicholas Price and Philip Bragg.

Bright yellow facings were worn. The Royal Crest as a badge was recorded quite early and can be seen on buttons dated around 1780. But most famous of all is the regiment's 'Back Badge' which commemorates the 28th's gallantry during the Battle of Alexandria in 1801 when it fought back-to-back as the French came on from both the front and rear. From this came the tradition of wearing a Sphinx badge both at the front and back of the headdress and nicknames such as Brass before and brass behind, and the Fore and Afts.

61st (South Gloucestershire) Regiment

Raised 1756 at Chatham as 2nd Battalion of the 3rd Regiment and regimented as 61st in 1758. Buff facings and linings were worn, the lace being white with a blue stripe. South Gloucestershire was added to the numerical designation in 1782, the 61st providing the 2nd Battalion Gloucestershire Regiment in 1881. For its services in 1801, the regiment was authorized to adopt their Sphinx superscribed Egypt badge in July 1802.

Regular Battalions

1st and 2nd Battalions The 1st Battalion was provided by the former 28th (North Gloucestershire) Regiment, the 2nd from the 61st (South Gloucestershire). The Sphinx superscribed Egypt was a badge awarded to both the 28th and 61st Regiments, the same device within a wreath being worn at the back of the headdress as a distinction gained by the

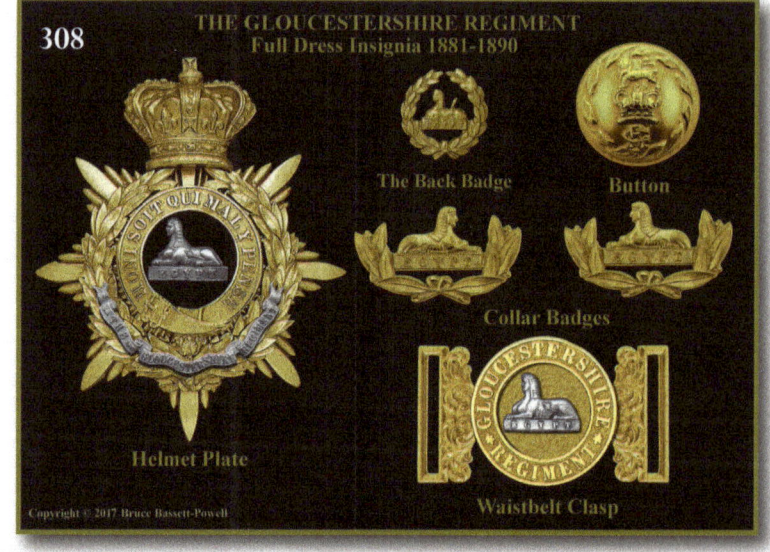

former for its gallantry at Alexandria. Both are shown in **(308)**, the button having the royal crest above GR. Artist Ernest Ibbetson illustrates how the back badges were worn in his Gale & Polden postcards featuring a sergeant major with three sergeants, and a bandsman with several drummers **(309)** and **(310)**. Illustrations **(311)** and **(312)** show the Sphinx as used in the other ranks helmet plate and glengarry badge. Also worn was the arms of the City of Gloucester which was an old badge of the Gloucestershire Militia. Here we see it as used on the front of the officers' forage caps **(313)**. Illustration **(314)** is No 65 in the 'Military Types' series of supplements published for the *Army and Navy Gazette* between 7 January 1888 and 6 September 1902.

Militia Battalions

3rd and 4th Battalions The 3rd Battalion was the former Royal South Gloucestershire Light Infantry Militia with headquarters at Bristol, the 4th being the old Royal North Gloucestershire Militia at Cirencester which would be disbanded in 1908. Illustration **(315)** is a detailed photograph taken in 1898 showing members of the 3rd Battalion as winners of the Permanent Staff Challenge Shield. The award was for a shooting competition and not surprisingly crossed rifles marksman badges are much in evidence. Most wear glengarry caps with the usual Sphinx cap badge, four senior NCOs, however, having forage caps with the City of Gloucester arms badge as seen in illustration (313).

Territorial Battalions

4th (City of Bristol) Battalion Formed by the former 1st Volunteer Battalion at Queen's Road, Clifton, Bristol. The eight companies were located as follows: 'A' to 'E' (Clifton), 'F' (Mangotsfield, moving to St George, Bristol in 1913) and 'G', 'H' (Bristol). Territorial battalions, although permitted to use the Sphinx on its insignia, were not allowed to include the word Egypt. The tablet would, therefore, have to be left blank as shown in this John Player cigarette card of 1910 **(316)**.

Although only required to service as home defence, officers and men of the peacetime Territorial Force could also offer to serve outside of the United Kingdom in time of national emergency. Under the conditions set out for the Imperial Service Section, a Territorial could undertake to serve abroad, but only with his own unit, or part of his own unit. He could not be drafted as an individual to any other regiment or corps, except at his own request. Upon 90% of a unit's strength having volunteered, the words 'Imperial

316

317

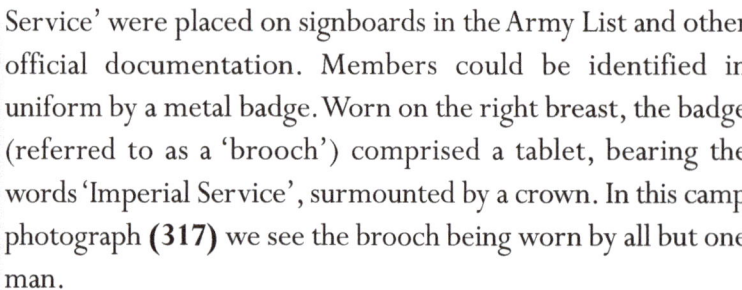

'Service' were placed on signboards in the Army List and other official documentation. Members could be identified in uniform by a metal badge. Worn on the right breast, the badge (referred to as a 'brooch') comprised a tablet, bearing the words 'Imperial Service', surmounted by a crown. In this camp photograph **(317)** we see the brooch being worn by all but one man.

5th Battalion From the former 2nd Volunteer Battalion with headquarters at The Barracks, Gloucester. The companies were: 'A', 'B' (Gloucester), 'C' (Stroud and Cirencester), 'D' (Tewkesbury, Forthampton and Kemerton), 'E', 'F' (Cheltenham), 'G' (Dursley and Wotton-under-Edge) and 'H' (Campden, Blockley, Willersey, Shipston-on-Stour, Moreton-in-the-March, Mickleton and Stow-on-the-Wold). The 5th Battalion wore green, rifle style, uniforms with scarlet facings, Illustration **(318)** showing a fine example of the headdress worn. Note the blank tablet cap insignia. Some of the battalion's cyclist in service dress are shown in **(319)**.

318

6th Battalion: From the former 3rd Volunteer Battalion at St Michael's Hill, Bristol. The 1st and 2nd Cadet Companies at Bristol were affiliated.

The photograph in **(320)** shows Drummer Robert Harper of the 6th Territorial Battalion.

As was the case with their volunteer predecessors, Territorial Force units choosing to adopt the badges of their parent regiment could do so only if any wording included in battle honours was omitted. It followed therefore that the Sphinx superscribed EGYPT awarded to the Gloucestershire Regiment and worn as a cap badge would be amended. Fully complying with regulations, this is the cap badge seen being worn by Robert Harper.

Although only required to act in a home defence role, Territorials could also offer to serve outside the United Kingdom. So volunteered, members could be identified in uniform by a metal badge worn on the

319

320

right breast. Usually referred to as a brooch, the distinction which was unique to the Territorial Force comprised a white metal tablet bearing the words IMPERIAL SERVICE surmounted by a crown.

Shoulder titles for the Territorial Force in most cases were made up of the letter T over a battalion number and the name of the regiment, in this case T over 6 over GLOSTER. Note the alternative way of spelling the name of this South West England county. The title here, again according to regulations, is in brass.

Drummer Harper wears the full-dress uniform of his regiment: scarlet jacket with white collar, cuffs and piping. But as a drummer he has in addition decorative white lace adorning his arms, shoulder wings, collar and shoulder straps. Clearly seen in the photograph are the red crowns that embellish the distinction. Seen also are green bugle cords worn around the neck and passing over the left shoulder to the front. Buttons are of the general service, Royal Arms, type. In thick brown leather, the waist-belt is fastened by a general service pattern (lion over crown and motto DIEU ET MON DROIT) brass locket-type clasp.

Just visible on Robert Harper's right arm is the outer edge of his drummers' arm badge: a heavily padded and embroidered side drum complete with tension ropes. But clearer are his two shooting awards, the left arm displaying the crossed rifles and star of best shot in band (top) and best junior ranks shot in battalion which has the addition of a wreath (bottom). Both badges are in gold wire embroidery on a scarlet backing.

Volunteer Battalions

321

1st (City of Bristol) Volunteer Battalion The battalion comprised ten companies by June 1860 and was permitted to include City of Bristol as part of its official title. Under General Order 63 of May 1883 1st Gloucestershire was re-designated as 1st (City of Bristol) Volunteer Battalion Gloucestershire Regiment, the Bristol Grammar School Cadet Corps being affiliated in 1900. An eleventh company was authorized in 1902. Transfer to the Territorial Force in 1908 was as 4th Battalion Gloucestershire Regiment. Bristol Grammar School became a contingent of the OTC. The battalion wore the pouch-belt plate shown in **(321)**, the Maltese Cross design having in its centre crossed rifles over the arms of the City of Bristol.

2nd Volunteer Battalion The 2nd Gloucestershire Rifle Volunteer Corps at Gloucester had ten companies: 'A' (Gloucester Dock), 'B' (Gloucester), 'C' (Stroud), 'D' (Cirencester), 'E' (Cheltenham), 'F' (Dursley), 'G' (Coleford), 'H' (Newnham), 'I' (Stow-on-the-Wold) and 'K' (Chipping Campden). Re-designation as 2nd Volunteer Battalion Gloucestershire Regiment was notified in General Order 63 of 1883. A cadet corps is shown as affiliated in 1867 and in 1883 this same unit is given as being formed by Cheltenham College. The college transferred its affiliation to the 1st Gloucestershire Engineer Volunteers in 1889 but returned to the 2nd Volunteer Battalion in 1904. Gloucester County School at Hempstead provided a company of cadets in 1889, as did Cirencester in 1896. Both, however, were disbanded in 1891 and 1897 respectively. Transfer to the Territorial Force in 1908 was as 5th Battalion Gloucestershire Regiment, Cheltenham College at the same time joining the OTC.

3rd Volunteer Battalion Eight companies formed with headquarters at Bristol on 24 July 1900. Transfer to the Territorial Force was as 6th Battalion.

Illustration credits: Alan Seymore (315), Bruce Bassett-Powell and Bob Bennet (308) and (313)

WORCESTERSHIRE REGIMENT

29th (Worcestershire) Regiment

The 29th was raised in 1694 and was at first known as Lieutenant-General Thomas Farrington's Regiment of Foot. Successive colonels were: Lord Mark Kerr, Henry Disney, William Anne Kepple, George Reade, Francis Fuller and Peregrine Thomas Hopson. Worcestershire was added to the number in 1782, this county association continuing in 1881 when the 28th became 1st Battalion Worcestershire Regiment.

WY Carman records that the regiment was supplied with coats of white kersey faced with yellow and blue breeches in 1694. Two years later, however, red coats with yellow facings were being worn. A watercolour by Richard Simkin of an officer c1842 shows a jacket being adorned with gold lace and an oblong silver and gilt shoulder-belt plate which features in its centre a lion. This is the ancient badge of the regiment, its star device only originating from 1784 when pouch badges were discontinued. Through the influence of Queen Charlotte, the 29th were permitted to continue wearing star plates on their valises. Official authority was obtained in May 1838. Major TJ Edwards, in his book *Military Customs,* relates the star badge to the fact that founder of the regiment, Thomas Farrington, was a colonel of the Coldstream Guards and that this was also the origin of the nickname Guards of the Line.

36th (Herefordshire) Regiment

The regiment was known by the names of twelve of its colonels before designated 36th in 1751. First, when raised in Ireland in 1701, was William Caulfeild (2nd Viscount Charlemont) who in turn was replaced by Thomas Alnutt in 1706, Archibald Campbell (3rd Duke of Argyll) in 1709, Henry Disney, who was appointed in 1710, the Hon William Egerton in 1715, Sir Charles Hotham in 1719, John Pocock 1720, Charles Lenoe 1721, John Moyle 1732, Humphrey Bland 1737, James Fleming 1741 and Lord Robert Manners 1751. Herefordshire was added to the title in 1782, the 36th providing the 2nd Battalion Worcestershire Regiment in 1881. The first mention of the regiment's green facings was in 1742. Later records refer to the colour as gosling or grass green. A nickname of the regiment was The Saucy Greens, one nineteenth century historian suggesting that the first word referred to the regiment's apparent energetic attraction to women. Seen on many badges and devices, the motto *Firm* certainly dates from 1773, if not before.

Regular Battalions

1st, 2nd, 3rd and 4th Battalions The 1st Battalion was provided by the 29th (Worcestershire) Regiment, the 2nd by the 36th (Herefordshire) Regiment. Formed early in 1900 were the 3rd and 4th Battalions. In **(322)** we see the lion badge and eight-pointed star of the former 29th Regiment. The motto 'Firm' is from the 36th and the round tower of Worcester Castle an old badge of the Worcestershire Militia. Here in **(323)** we can see worn on the flap of the valise an elongated eight-pointed brass star. Unseen in the centre, however, are the initials WR. Major Roger Bennett points out in his book *Badges of the Worcestershire Regiment,* how at

some time in the first half of the nineteenth century the 29th had taken into use star badges on their packs. Turning now to Major T J Edwards and his *Military Customs*, we learn how the valise star was 'A much prized distinction' of the Worcestershire Regiment. The practice of wearing an ornament on the equipment had, indeed, been discontinued for line infantry regiments. Guards regiments were, however, permitted valise badges and it is suggested by several authorities that the 29th had assumed the distinction on the basis of its historical connections with the Coldstream, a fact recalled in one of the regiment's several nicknames—'The Guards of the Line.'

No 66 in Richard Simkin's 'Military Types' series is shown in **(324)**. Published as a supplement to the *Army and Navy Gazette*, the image appeared on 3 June 1893. For their several postcard sets of six featuring both ceremonial and active service images, Gale & Polden employed several well-known military artists. The cards included images set around the early months of the First World War, Edgar Holloway in **(325)** reminding all of the time by the banner headline carried by the newsboy. For the same set, Edgar Holloway chose a busy railway platform scene in which we see troops from the regiment about to begin their journey to the front **(326)**. The battalion is uncertain, but the markings on the kitbags leaves no doubt as to Regiment. Both (325) and (326) are the original watercolour paintings supplied by the artist to the publisher. Also an artist's original produced for postcard production is the Harry Payne scene of a corporal saluting his officer as two bandsmen chat in the distance **(327)**.

Militia Battalions

3rd and 4th Battalions, later 5th and 6th Battalions From the Worcestershire Militia at Worcester. The battalions were numbered as 3rd and 4th until 1900 when the two new Regular battalions took those numbers.

Territorial Battalions

7th Battalion Formed with headquarters at Kidderminster from the former 1st Volunteer Battalion. The companies were located: 'A' (Kidderminster), 'B' (Tenbury, Kidderminster and Bockleton), 'C' (Stourport and Bewdley), 'D' (Stourport and Kinver), 'E' (Oldbury), 'F' (Halesowen) and 'G', 'H' (Dudley). Illustration **(328)** shows a two-piece version of the battalion's brass shoulder title. Titles of this type, as opposed

to a one-piece broken version, can be recognised by the T and number having two (north and south) lugs on the back.

8th Battalion Formed with headquarters at Silver Street, Worcester from the former 2nd Volunteer Battalion. The companies were located: *Companies:* 'A', 'B' (Worcester), 'C' (Pershore, Great Malvern, Upton-upon-Severn, Elmley Castle and Fladbury), 'D' (Evesham and Badsey), 'E' (Droitwich and Stoke Works), 'F' (King's Norton and Rubery), 'G' (Bromsgrove) and 'H' (Redditch).

Volunteer Battalions

329

1st Volunteer Battalion The 1st Worcestershire Rifle Volunteer Corps at Hagley had eleven companies: 'A' (Wolverley), 'B' (Tenbury), 'C' and 'D' (Kidderminster), 'E' (Bewdley), 'F' (Halesowen), 'G' (Dudley), 'H' (Stourport), 'I' (Stourbridge), 'K' (Oldbury) and 'L' (Kidderminster). In 1882 a new company was added at Dudley and in the following year the corps was designated as 1st Volunteer Battalion Worcestershire Regiment. Headquarters were transferred to Stourbridge between 1885-1886, then to Kidderminster in 1891, 'A' Company moving to Dudley sometime before 1908. Transfer to the Territorial Force was as 7th Battalion Worcestershire Regiment. The Worcestershire Rifle Volunteers from the early days of their formation in 1859 took into use a representation of a pear tree from the arms of the county. Here in **(329)** we see a post 1901 officers' pouch-belt plate.

2nd Volunteer Battalion The 2nd Worcestershire Rifle Volunteer Corps at Worcester had eight companies: 'A' and 'B' (Worcester), 'C' (Great Malvern and Upton-on-Severn), 'D' (Evesham), 'E' (Droitwich), 'F' (Pershore), 'G' (Bromsgrove) and 'H' (Redditch). The Corps was re-designated as 2nd Volunteer Battalion Worcestershire Regiment in 1883. A new company was sanctioned in 1900, but the battalion's establishment was back to eight companies in 1905. A cadet corps was formed and affiliated at the Victoria Institute, Worcester in 1903. Transfer to the Territorial Force in 1908 was as 8th Battalion Worcestershire Regiment.

Cadet Battalions

2nd (Dudley Grammar School) Cadet Battalion Affiliated to 7th Battalion.

3rd (Kidderminster Grammar School) Cadet Battalion Affiliated to 7th Battalion.

Illustration credits: Anne SK Brown Military Collection, Brown University Library (324), (325) and (326), Bruce Bassett-Powell and Bob Bennet (322)

EAST LANCASHIRE REGIMENT

30th (Cambridgeshire) Regiment

Colonel Thomas Saunderson raised a regiment in 1694, but this was disbanded four years later. Having been on half-pay since, he re-raised the regiment in 1702 under the name of Thomas Saunderson's Regiment of Marines. Successive Colonels' names prior to 1751 were: Thomas Pownall, Sir Charles Willis, George Forrester, Thomas Stanwix, Andrew Bissett, Henry de Grangues, Charles Frampton and John Campbell. As the 30th, Cambridgeshire was added to the title in 1782, all connections with the university county being lost when it became 1st Battalion East Lancashire Regiment in 1881. The 30th wore yellow facings, the

Carl Franklin plate also showing the lace of c1768 which has a blue line around the edge. The regiment's Sphinx badge superscribed Egypt was authorised in July 1802.

59th (2nd Nottinghamshire) Regiment

Raised by Colonel Sir Charles Montague as the 61st and recruited 1755 in Leicestershire and Nottinghamshire, the regiment wore red coats with light crimson facings. White facings were introduced in 1776, the regiment from this soon acquiring the nickname of The Lilly Whites. Re-numbering as 59th was in 1757, 2nd Nottinghamshire being added in 1782. In 1881 the 59th provided the 2nd Battalion of the East Lancashire Regiment.

Regular Battalions

1st and 2nd Battalions In 1881 the former 30th (Cambridgeshire) Regiment provided the 1st Battalion, the 2nd coming from the 59th (2nd Nottinghamshire). In **(330)** we see the Sphinx superscribed Egypt badge if the former 30th Regiment, the red rose of Lancaster being a device worn by the 5th Royal Lancashire Militia. Both devices were used in the regiment's cap badges, a Victorian crown version is illustrated in **(331)**, and an officer's forage cap in **(332)**.

The work of three important military artists, Harry Payne, Frank Feller and Richard Simkin, is featured in **(333)**, **(334)** and **(335)**. All three images show clearly the regiment's white facings, illustration (335) being No 67 from the series of supplements produce by Richard Simkin for publication with the *Army and Navy Gazette*, this particular image appearing on 1 July 1893. Illustration **(336)** is from Gale & Polden's 'History and Traditions' postcard series and features a sergeant in conversation with a private. Both wear rose collar badges, the private also having both the

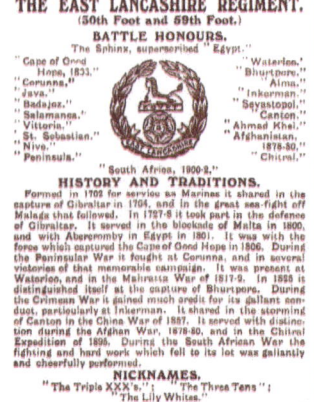

Queen's and King's Medals awarded for service in the Second Boar War. The 1st Battalion had sailed for South Africa on the *Bavarian* in January 1900.

Militia Battalion

3rd Battalion   Formed from the 5th Royal Lancashire Militia at Burnley.

Territorial Battalions

4th Battalion   Formed in 1908 from the former 1st Volunteer Battalion. Headquarters were in Blackburn and the eight companies located: 'A' to 'E' (Blackburn), 'F', 'G' (Darwen) and 'H' (Clitheroe). Although both the Sphinx device was permitted to be included on the badges of the Territorial battalions and their Volunteer predecessors, the word Egypt was not, the tablet as in **(337)** being left blank. Volunteers had served alongside the Regulars during the Boar War, gaining for their battalion the battle honour 'South Africa 1900-02' which was carried forward in 1908.

5th Battalion   Formed from the 2nd Volunteer Battalion with headquarters at Burnley and companies: 'A' (Burnley), 'B' (Burnley and Padiham), 'C', 'D' (Burnley), 'E' (Padiham), 'F' (Accrington), 'G' (Haslingden and Ramsbottom) and 'H' (Bacup). From the three-tier shoulder title, the men in this photograph **(338)** can be placed as members of one or other of the regiment's two Territorial battalions. The number is not clear, however, but black collars and cuffs lead us to the 5th, the 4th having white.

Volunteer Battalions

1st Volunteer Battalion   The 2nd Lancashire Rifle Volunteer Corps had its headquarters at Blackburn and ten companies located: 'A' to 'F' (Blackburn), 'G' and 'H' (Over Darwen), 'J' and 'K' (Clitheroe). Re-designation as 1st Volunteer Battalion East Lancashire Regiment was in June 1889 and transfer to the Territorial Force as the regiment's 4th Battalion was in 1908. The Stonyhurst College Cadet Corps which had been formed and affiliated in January 1901 at the same time joined the OTC.

2nd Volunteer Battalion   Burnley was the headquarters of the 3rd Lancashire Rifle Volunteer Corps, its twelve companies being located: 'A' to 'D' (Burnley), 'E' (Padiham), 'F' to 'H' (Accrington), 'J' (Haslingden), 'K' (Ramsbottom), 'L' (Stacksteads) and 'M' (Lytham). Re-designation as 2nd Volunteer Battalion East Lancashire Regiment was notified by Army Order 263 of June 1889. Transfer to the Territorial Force was as 5th Battalion. Illustration **(339)** shows an example of the battalion's cap badge.

Illustration credits: Anne SK Brown Military Collection, Brown University Library (333), Bruce Bassett-Powell (330) and (332)

EAST SURREY REGIMENT

31st (Huntingdonshire) Regiment

Colonel George Villier's Regiment of Marines appeared in the Army List from 1702 and, having been disbanded, was later restored and placed back on the establishment under its colonel's name. Subsequent colonels prior to 1751 were: Alexander Luttrell, Joshua Churchill, Sir Harry Goring, Lord John Kerr, Charles Cathcart, William Hargrave, William Handasyde, Lord Henry Beauclerk and Henry Holmes. Listed as the 31st (Huntingdonshire) from 1782, there would be no connection with the birthplace of Oliver Cromwell when in 1881 it became 1st Battalion of the East Surrey Regiment. WY Carman records that when serving as marines high crowned leather caps were worn with red coats lined yellow. Buff facings were noted when re-raised.

70th (Surrey) Regiment

Raised 1756 as 2nd Battalion 31st Regiment, being regimented two years later as 70th. Surry (sic) was added to the title in 1782. John Parslow, formally of the 1st Foot Guards, was the first colonel. Having returned from duty in the West Indies in 1812, the King graciously approved the changing of the subtitle from Surry to Glasgow Lowland. But a return to Surrey (this time with the 'e') was made in 1825. The 70th, in 1881, would be reunited with the 31st when the two provided the 1st and 2nd Battalions of the East Surrey Regiment. Much of the regiment was provided by men from Glasgow which, together with the facing colour, led to the nickname Glasgow Greys. Black, however, made an appearance by 1763.

Regular Battalions

1st and 2nd Battalions The 1st Battalion was formed by the 31st (Huntingdonshire) Regiment, the 2nd coming from the 70th (Surrey). The arms of Guildford were adopted as a badge of the regiment in 1881, a star from the old 3rd Royal Surrey Militia appearing at the same time. Here in Bruce Bassett-Powell's detailed illustration we see how the devices were used on the officers' helmet plate, collar badges, buttons and waist-belt plates **(340)**. Also illustrated are

examples of the cap badge **(341)**, officers' glengarry badge **(342)** and other ranks brass helmet plate **(343)**. The Guildford arms collar badge can be seen in **(344)**, the crossed flags being worn by the sergeant above his chevrons indicating that he is an instructor in signalling. He wears the glengarry cap, its two-piece badge comprising the centre from the helmet plate with a separate crown above.

The regiment's white facings can be seen in **(345)** and **(346)**, the former being original artwork by Harry Payne for a Gale & Polden postcard. The second image, No 68 in a series of supplements produced for the *Army and Navy Gazette*, is by Richard Simkin.

Militia Battalions

3rd and 4th Battalions The 1st Royal Surrey Militia provided the 3rd Battalion the 3rd Royal Surrey the 4th. Both had their headquarters at Kingston.

Territorial Battalions

5th Battalion Formed from the former 2nd Volunteer Battalion. Headquarters were at 17 St George's Road, Wimbledon and the companies: 'A' (Streatham), 'B' (Leatherhead, Bookham and Walton-on-the-Hill), 'C' (Sutton), 'D' (Mitcham), 'E', 'F', 'G' (Wimbledon) and 'H' (Epsom). War having been declared, the 5th

Battalion as part of the Home Counties Division embarked at Southampton for India on 29 October 1914. Here in **(347)** we see the battalion orchestra wearing foreign service dress, the helmets having diamond patches with the title, 5 over E.SURREY. Note also how the bass drum proudly displays South Africa 1900-02', the battle honour awarded to the battalion's Volunteer predecessors.

6th Battalion Formed by the 3rd Volunteer Battalion. Headquarters were at Woodville, Surbiton Crescent, Kingston-upon-Thames, moving by 1912 to Orchard Road, Kingston-upon-Thames. The companies were located: 'A' (Esher, Cobham and Hersham), 'B', 'C' (Richmond), 'D', 'E', 'F' (Kingston-upon-Thames), 'G' (Chertsey and Weybridge) and 'H' (Egham). Affiliated to the battalion were the Richmond County School Cadet Corps, the Richmond Hill Cadets and Weybridge and District Scout Cadets. Recognition of the latter being withdrawn under Army Order 260 of 1912.

Easily identified by its special cap badge is the 6th Battalion **(348)**. In blackened brass, the badge

was a Maltese cross, the edge of the top arm being inscribed South Africa and the edge of the bottom arm, 1900-1902. The Guildford arms appear in the centre surrounded by a circle inscribed 'The East Surrey Regt. 6th Battalion.' Also in black are the T over 6 over E.SURREY shoulder titles and the buttons. Note also how each man wears the Imperial Service brooch.

Although only required to serve as home defence, officers and men of the peacetime Territorial Force could also offer to serve outside of the United Kingdom in time of national emergency. Under the conditions set out for the Imperial Service Section, a Territorial could undertake to serve abroad, but only with his own unit, or part of his own unit. He could not be drafted as an individual to any other regiment or corps, except at his own request. Upon 90% of a unit's strength having volunteered, the words 'Imperial Service' were placed on signboards, in the Army List and other official documentation. The 6th Battalion East Surrey Regiment was one of the few Territorial Force units that qualified. Members could be identified in uniform by a metal badge. Worn on the right breast, the badge (referred to as a 'brooch') comprised a tablet, bearing the words 'Imperial Service', surmounted by a crown.

Volunteer Battalions

1st (South London) Volunteer Rifle Corps The 1st Surrey Rifle Volunteer Corps had its headquarters at Camberwell and became a volunteer battalion of the East Surrey Regiment in 1881, but although ranked as 1st, there was no change in title. There was a cadet corps affiliated at Dulwich College. Transfer to the Territorial Force in 1908 was as 21st Battalion London Regiment, Dulwich College at the same time joining the OTC.

2nd Volunteer Battalion In 1881 the 3rd Surrey Rifle Volunteer Corps in Thornton Road, Clapham Park had seven companies: 'A', 'B' and 'C' (Brixton), 'D' (Carshalton), 'E' and 'F' (Wimbledon) and 'G' (Epsom). There was also a half-company at Brixton. Headquarters were moved to St George's Road, Wimbledon in 1884, two new companies being added in 1886. In December 1887 the 3rd Surrey was re-designated as 2nd Volunteer Battalion East Surrey Regiment. Another two companies joined in 1900 and by 1904, after several reorganisations, company locations stood at: 'A' and 'B' (Streatham), 'C' and 'D' (Sutton) 'E', 'F' and 'G' (Wimbledon) 'H' (Epsom) 'I' (Wimbledon) and 'K' (Epsom). A cadet corps at Epsom College was formed and affiliated in 1890. Transfer to the Territorial Force in 1908 was as 5th Battalion East Surrey Regiment, Epsom College at the same time joining the OTC.

3rd Volunteer Battalion Headquarters of the 5th Surrey Rifle Volunteer Corps were at Kingston-upon-Thames, its eight companies in 1881 being found at: 'A' (Esher), 'B' and 'C' (Richmond), 'D', 'E', 'F' and 'G' (Kingston-upon-Thames) and 'H' (Chertsey). Re-designation as 3rd Volunteer Battalion East Surrey Regiment was in December 1887. Two new companies, one at Egham, one at Richmond, were added in 1900. Also in that year Richmond County School Cadet Corps was formed and affiliated, as was Beaumont College at Old Windsor in 1906. Transfer to the Territorial Force in 1908 was as 6th Battalion East Surrey Regiment, Beaumont College at the same time joining the OTC.

349

The fine silver pouch-belt plate shown in **(349)** is easily identified by the inscription around the centre circle. Also shown, on the four arms of the Maltese cross, are four of the battalions company locations: Kington, Esher, Richmond and Chertsey.

4th Volunteer Battalion The 7th Surrey Rifle Volunteer Corps in 1881 had ten companies with headquarters at Upper Kennington Lane, Southwark. The corps was designated as 4th Volunteer Battalion East Surrey Regiment in December 1887, headquarters transferring to

Clapham Junction in 1902. A cyclist company was added there in 1900 and transfer to the Territorial Force was as the 23rd Battalion London Regiment.

Wearing green jackets with scarlet facings, members of the Cyclist section parade with their machines (350). Note the cycle wheel insignia, the bugler closest to the camera also having a double bugle arm badge and one efficiency star. Guildford arms collar badges and 4 over V over E.SURREY shoulder titles are also worn.

Cadet Battalion

1st Cadet Battalion Formed with headquarters at 71 Upper Kennington Lane, London in 1890 with four companies. Disbanded in 1896.

Illustration credits: Bruce Bassett-Powell and Bob Bennet (340)

DUKE OF CORNWALL'S LIGHT INFANTRY

32nd (Cornwall) Light Infantry

Raised in 1702, the regiment first served under their colonels' names as marines—Edward Fox (killed at Gibraltar), Jacob Borr, Charles Dubourgay, Thomas Paget, Simon Descury, John Huske, Henry Skelton, William Douglas and Francis Leighton. Cornwall was added to the numerical title in 1782, followed by Light Infantry in 1858, and 1st Battalion Duke of Cornwall's Light Infantry in 1881. When known as Fox's Marines, the uniforms were red faced and lined with green. Later, however, cuffs were noted as being white. Regarding badges, bugle-horns were adopted in 1858, the light infantry title having been given as a distinction for the gallantry shown during the defence of the residency at Lucknow during the Indian Mutiny. Adopted as a collar badge in 1876 was the coronet of the Duke of Cornwall together with the fifteen bezants from the county arms and the motto *One and All*.

46th (South Devonshire) Regiment

The regiment was raised under a Royal Warrant dated 13 January 1741 by Colonel John Price of the 1st Foot Guards. Colonel Price was removed to the 14th Regiment in 1743, his replacement being Thomas Murray. South Devonshire was added to the numerical title in 1782, the regiment providing the 2nd Battalion of the Duke of Cornwall's Light Infantry in 1881. The uniforms had yellow facings. Two red feathers, a badge distinction of the 46th, dates from the American War of 1777 when, after inflicting heavy casualties on the opposing side, the American battalion concerned vowed to take revenge the next day. In defiance, the 46th dyed their white feather red so as they could be easily recognised.

Regular Battalions

1st and 2nd Battalions The 2nd Battalion was from the 32nd (Cornwall) Light Infantry, the 2nd the former 46th (South Devonshire) Regiment. Here in the centre of the officers' helmet plate (351) is the bugle horn device taken into use by the 32nd Regiment when styled as light infantry in 1858. The two red feathers are from the 46th and serve as a reminder of how the regiment severely handled a force of Americans commanded by General Wayne at Brandywine during the American War of Independence. It was on 11 September 1777 that the enemy sent word that they were going to seek revenge, the British troops indignant of the fact replied that they were not bothered by the threat and as a help to the Americans dyed their hat feather red so as they could be more easily recognised. The silver turreted archway has been described as the gateway as shown on the great seal of the Duke of Cornwall, the design, records Major HG Parkyn, 'is of the ancient gateway of Launceston Castle.' The ducal coronet can be seen on the waist-

belt clap, button and collar badges, the latter having the fifteen roundels from the Cornwall arms. Illustration **(352)** shows an officer's forage cap.

Richard Simkin's illustration for No 69 in his 'Military Types' series shows a party of infantry advancing during an exercise **(353)**. The print appeared as a supplement to the *Army and Navy Gazette* on 2 September 1893 and shows the regiment's white facings. From Gale & Polden's 'History and Traditions' series of postcards, we a group of three from the regiment, artist J McNeill showing a sergeant seated and two privates **(354)**. Each man wears two medals, these being the Queen's and King's Medals awarded for service during the Second Boar War. It was the 2nd Battalion that on 5 November 1899 sailed for South Africa in the *Formosa*, arriving at the Cape on the 29th. The same medals are being worn in Harry Payne's watercolour of an officer. **(355)**.

In the two photographs illustrated we see the Colours of the 1st Battalion, together with a set of eight silver bugles **(356)**, and a regimental band somewhere in India with their local servants **(357)**.

When war was declared in August 1914, the 1st Battalion was stationed in Ireland, the 2nd being overseas in Hong Kong. Both would be in France

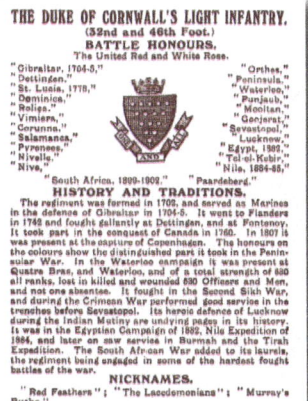

before the end of the year, the channel crossing not, it must be assumed, being via a Cornish pasty **(358)**.

Militia Battalion

3rd Battalion From the Royal Cornwall Rangers Duke of Cornwall's Own Militia with headquarters at Bodmin.

Territorial Battalions

4th Battalion Formed from the former 1st Volunteer Battalion with headquarters at Truro and companies located: 'A' (Penzance), 'B' (Camborne), 'C' (Falmouth), 'D' (Helston), 'E' (Truro), 'F' (Hayle), 'G' (Redruth) and 'H' (St Just and Pendeen). 'A' Company of the 1st Cadet Battalion of Cornwall at Falmouth was affiliated.

5th Battalion Formed from the former 2nd Volunteer Battalion at Bodmin. The eight companies were located: 'A'(Liskeard), 'B' (Saltash and Callington), 'C' (Launceston), 'D' (St Austell and St Stephen), 'E' (Bodmin and Lostwithiel), 'F' (Camelford, Wadebridge and Delabole), 'G' (St Columb and Newquay) and 'H' (Bude, Stratton, Kilkhampton and Morwenstow).

Volunteer Battalions

1st (The Duke of Cornwall's) Volunteer Battalion Headquarters of the 1st (The Duke of Cornwall's) Rifle Volunteer Corps was at Penzance and its eleven companies located: 'A' (Penzance), 'B' (Camborne), 'C' (Falmouth), 'D' (Helston), 'E' and 'F' (Truro), 'G' (Hayle), 'H' (Redruth), 'I' (Trelowarren), 'J' (St Just-in-Penwith) and 'K' (Penryn). Headquarters moved from Penzance to Falmouth in 1881. The corps was designated as 1st Volunteer Battalion Duke of Cornwall's Light Infantry in 1885 and headquarters moved again, this time to Truro, in 1902. Two new companies were sanctioned in 1900 and transfer to the Territorial Force in 1908 was as 4th Battalion. Illustration **(359)** shows the cap badge worn by the 1st Volunteer Battalion. In white metal, it is the same as that worn by the regular battalions, but with the additional scroll.

2nd (The Duke of Cornwall's) Volunteer Battalion Headquarters of the 2nd (The Duke of Cornwall's) Rifle Volunteer Corps were at Bodmin and its nine companies located: 'A' (Liskeard), 'B' (Callington), 'C' (Launceston), 'D' (St Austell), 'E' (Bodmin), 'F' (Wadebridge), 'G' (St Columb), 'H' (Camelford) and 'I' (Saltash). The corps was re-designated as 2nd Volunteer Battalion Duke of Cornwall's Light Infantry in 1885 and 'J' Company was added at Bude in 1900. Transfer to the Territorial Force in 1908 was as 5th Battalion.

Illustration credit: Bruce Bassett-Powell and Bob Bennet (351) and (352)

DUKE OF WELLINGTON'S (WEST RIDING REGIMENT)

33rd (Duke of Wellington's) Regiment

The 33rd began in 1702 as the George Hastings, 8th Earl of Huntingdon's Regiment, taking on its Yorkshire connection as 33rd (1st Yorkshire West Riding) Regiment in 1782. Subsequent colonels prior to 1751 were: Henry Leigh, Robert Duncanson (killed at Alcantara), George Wade, Henry Hawley, Robert Dalzell and John Johnson. Sir Arthur Wellesley, 1st Duke of Wellington, had been colonel of the regiment from January 1806 to January 1813 and it would be in 1853 that his name was added to the title, making the regiment the first to be named after a subject. The title assumed in 1881 was 1st Battalion Duke of Wellington's (West Riding Regiment). With the 1853 title came the Duke's crest and motto, *Virtutis fortuna comes* (Fortune accompanies honour) as a badge. The dress of the Earl of Huntingdon's Regiment consisted of red coats lined with yellow and worn with yellow breeches. Later, however, a change was made to red facings with white linings.

76th (Hindoostan) Regiment

Raised in 1787 by Thomas Musgrave whose commission was dated 12 October. Hindoostan was included in the title from 1807 and until 1812, the 76th providing the 2nd Battalion Duke of Wellington's (West Riding Regiment) in 1881. The facings were red. For services in India, the badge of an Elephant with Howdah was authorized 17 January 1807.

Regular Battalions

1st and 2nd Battalions The 1st battalion was the former 33rd (The Duke of Wellington's) Regiment, the 2nd being the 76th. Here in **(360)** we see the crest and motto of the Duke of Wellington, an old badge of the 33rd Regiment, and the elephant and howdah conferred on the 76th in 1807 to commemorate its long service in India, 1788-1806. A photograph of an officer's forage cap is shown in **(361)**.

Both the 33rd and 76th Regiments had worn red facings, but the regulations that came with the 1881 reorganisation of the line infantry required that they should be changed to white, this being the prescribed colour for all non-royal English regiments. Published on 7 October 1893, artist Richard Simkin correctly shows the white in his supplement No 70 produced for the *Army and Navy Gazette* **(362)**. The image featuring two officers and a bugler. But the old red would be back in 1905, Richard Simkin showing this in his fine 1910 study of an officer **(363)**.

One of Harry Payne's postcards for Gale & Polden showed an officer inspecting the rifle of a private **(364)**, J McNeill's artwork of a signaller

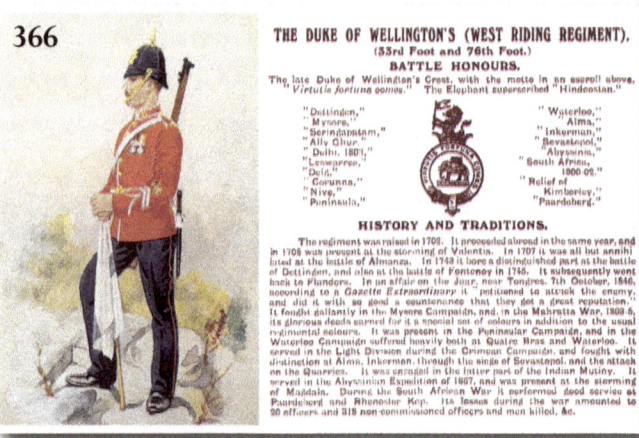

(365) also finding its way to the Aldershot publishing company, this time for its 'History and Traditions' series (366). The 1st Battalion had sailed on the *Orient* on 30 December 1899 for war service in South Africa, both Harry Payne and J McNeill showing their subjects wearing the Queen's and King's Medals awarded for that campaign.

Militia Battalions

3rd and 4th Battalions Formed from the 6th West Yorkshire Militia which comprised two battalions with headquarters at Halifax. The two were amalgamated as 3rd in 1890.

Territorial Battalions

4th Battalion Formed from the former 1st Volunteer Battalion with headquarters at Halifax and eight companies: 'A', 'B', 'C' (Halifax), 'D' (Brighouse), 'E' (Cleckheaton), 'F' (Halifax), 'G' (Elland) and 'H' (Sowerby Bridge).

5th Battalion From part of the 2nd Volunteer Battalion with headquarters at Huddersfield and eight companies located: 'A' (Huddersfield and Meltham), 'B' to 'E' (Huddersfield), 'F' (Holmfirth), 'G' (Kirkburton) and 'H' (Mirfield). Illustration (367) shows a bandsman of the 5th Battalion wearing three efficiency stars.

6th Battalion From the former 3rd Volunteer Battalion with headquarters at Skipton-in-Craven and companies at: 'A' (Skipton-in-Craven and Barnoldswick), 'B' (Skipton-in-Craven), 'C' (Guiseley), 'D', 'E' (Keighley), 'F' (Settle and Ingleton), 'G' (Haworth) and 'H' (Bingley). The Settle Cadet Battalion was affiliated.

7th Battalion Formed from part of the 2nd Volunteer Battalion with headquarters at Milnsbridge. The companies were located: 'A', 'B' (Milnsbridge), 'C' (Slaithwaite), 'D' (Marsden), 'E' (Upper Mill), 'F' (Mossley), 'G' (Lees) and 'H' (Mossley).

Volunteer Battalions

1st Volunteer Battalion With headquarters in Halifax, the 4th Yorkshire (West Riding) Rifle Volunteer Corps was re-designated as 1st Volunteer Battalion Duke of Wellington's Regiment in 1883 and by 1908 had four companies at Halifax and one each at Brighthouse and Check Heaton. Transfer to the Territorial Force in 1908 was as 4th Battalion Duke of Wellington's Regiment.

2nd Volunteer Battalion The 6th Corps Yorkshire (West Riding) Rifle Volunteer Corps at Huddersfield had ten companies: 'A', 'B', 'C' and 'D' (Huddersfield), 'E' (Holmfirth), 'F', 'G', 'H' and 'J' (Saddleworth) and 'K' (Mirfield). The corps was re-designated as 2nd Volunteer Battalion Duke of Wellington's Regiment in February 1883, headquarters at this time being at The Armoury in Ramsden Street. A new company was raised at Huddersfield in 1900 and transfer to the Territorial Force was as part of both the 5th and 7th Battalions Duke of Wellington's Regiment.

3rd Volunteer Battalion With headquarters at Skipton-in-Craven, the 9th Yorkshire (West Riding) Rifle Volunteer Corps had eight companies: 'A' (Skipton-in-Craven), 'B' (Settle), 'C' (Burley), 'D', 'E' and 'F' (Keighley), 'G' (Haworth) and 'H' (Bingley). Re-designation as 3rd Volunteer Battalion Duke of Wellington's Regiment was in February 1883. New companies were added in 1884 and 1900 and transfer to the Territorial Force was as 6th Battalion Duke of Wellington's Regiment.

Illustration credits: ASK Brown Military Collection, Brown University Library (363), Bruce Bassett-Powell (360)

BORDER REGIMENT

34th (Cumberland) Regiment

Raised 1702 in the southern counties and known as Lord Robert Lucas's Regiment of Foot, the 34th took on its Cumberland title eighty years later in 1782 and in 1881 provided the 1st Battalion of the Border Regiment. Robert Lord Lucas was the Lieutenant of the Tower of London and often used his regiment for guard duty there. Colonels who succeeded Robert Lucas prior to 1751 were: Hans Hamilton, Thomas Chudleigh, Robert Hayes, Stephen Cornwallis, Lord James Cavendish, James Cholmondeley and Henry Seymour Conway.

The first uniforms on record were red coats lined with grey, worn with waistcoats and breeches of the same colour. Later, facings appeared as light yellow and the waistcoats and breeches red. W Y Carman explains the origins of the regiment's half-red and half-white ball tuft distinction. White ball-tufts were introduced for battalion company shakos in 1835, but in memory of the 34th's capture of the French 34th Regiment at Arroyo dos Molinos during the Peninsular War it was allowed to have one made up of the two colours. Some ten years later, however, all battalion companies were issued with two colour ornaments on their shakos, but the 34th would retain its distinction by keeping the half-and-half pattern as opposed to the rest that had two thirds white and one third red. The red and white custom did, however, go back a little further to when feathers were worn in the headdress.

When helmets replaced shakos in 1879, a piece of red and white cloth was used as a backing to the number 34 in the centre of the plate. Although a Maltese Cross had featured on the regiment's badges for some years, it was not until July 1881 that this device was authorised.

55th (Westmoreland) Regiment

Raised at Stirling as the 57th Regiment in 1755 under a warrant dated 31 December wearing dark green facings and white linings to red coats. The colonel was Charles Barry, the regiment being re-numbered as

55th in 1757. Westmoreland was added to the title in 1782 and the regiment provided the 2nd Battalion Border Regiment in 1881. For its services in the China War the regiment received authorization to adopt the badge of a Dragon superscribed China in January 1843.

Regular Battalions

1st and 2nd Battalions The 1st Battalion was formed by the 34th (Cumberland) Regiment, the 2nd by the 55th (Westmoreland) Regiment. Much of the regiment's long history is represented in the centre of the helmet plate and on the collar badges **(368)**. The wreath is an old badge of the 34th, tradition recording that this was in memory of the battle of Fontenoy. The dragon superscribed China also remembers active service, on this occasion that of the 55th during the China War. For an explanation of the red and white backing we turn to Major HG Parkyn who records in his book, *(Military) Shoulder-Belt Plates and Buttons,* how for many years the 34th had worn red and white feathers (later tufts) in their headdress in memory of its gallantry

at Arroyo dos Molinos during the Peninsular War. A battle honour, Molinos dos Molinos appears on a silver scroll at the bottom of the helmet plate. On the waist-belt clasp, the Star of the Order of the Garter was originally the badge of the Royal Westmoreland Militia. Illustration **(369)** shows the officers' forage cap, the Regimental Colour and cap badge appearing on a Player's cigarette card in 1903 **(370)**.

White facings were ordered for the regiment in 1881 and here were see them in supplement No 71 (published on 4 November 1893) of Richard Simkin's 'Military Types' series produced for the *Army and Navy Gazette* **(371)**. The white, however, gave way to the former yellow of the 34th in 1913. The new colour can be seen in Harry Payne's water-colour of a corporal wearing both the Queen's and King's Medals for South Africa **(372)**. In **(373)** a photograph of another corporal taken in 1914 also shows yellow collars and cuffs. Seated with his brother by

his side, he wears a distance judging star on his lower right arm and on his lower left the star over crossed rifles badge indicating that the wearer has been judged as best shot in his company.

Militia Battalions

3rd and 4th Battalions The 3rd Battalion was formed by the Royal Cumberland Militia, the 4th by the Royal Westmoreland Light Infantry Militia. Both had their headquarters at Carlisle, the 4th being disbanded in 1908.

Territorial Battalions

4th (Cumberland and Westmorland) Battalion Formed from the former 1st and 2nd Volunteer Battalions. Headquarters were at Penrith, moving to Kendal in 1909, then Strand Road, Carlisle in 1911. The eight companies were located: 'A', 'B' (Carlisle), 'C' (Keswick and Brampton), 'D' (Penrith), 'E' (Kirkby Lonsdale, Sedbergh, Endmoor and Milnthorpe, Kirkby Stephen and Appleby), 'F' (Kendal), 'G' (Kendal, Burneside and Staveley) and 'H' (Windermere, Ambleside and Elterwater). The Kirkby Lonsdale Cadet Company was affiliated. Illustration **(374)** shows the special badge worn by the 4th Battalion.

When war was declared in August 1914 the Territorials, most of them already at annual camp, were recalled and sent to war stations. The 4th Border Regiment first moved to Barrow, later taking up billets in Sittingbourne during September. In the photograph shown **(375)** we see a group having just arrived at their new lodgings. Note how 4B has been chalked onto the wall of the house, the owners and their family all keen to share in the photograph. Also of interest is the mixture of scarlet jackets and khaki service dress, hats with and without badges.

5th (Cumberland) Battalion Formed from the former 3rd Volunteer Battalion with headquarters at Workington. The companies were located: 'A' (Whitehaven), 'B' and 'C' (Workington), 'D' (Cockermouth), 'E' (Egremont, St Bees and Cleator), 'F' (Wigton), 'G' (Frizington) and 'H' (Aspatria, Dearham and Bullgill).

Volunteer Battalions

1st (Cumberland) Volunteer Battalion With headquarters at Keswick, the 1st Cumberland Rifle Volunteer Corps had thirteen companies: 'A', 'B' and 'C' (Carlisle), 'D' (Whitehaven), 'E' (Keswick), 'F' (Brampton), 'G' and 'H' (Penrith), 'I' (Alston), 'K' (Workington), 'L' (Cockermouth), 'M' (Egremont) and 'N' (Wigton). Re-designation as 1st (Cumberland) Volunteer Battalion was notified by General Order 181 of December 1887. Headquarters were moved to Carlisle in 1896 and in 1900 the companies at Whitehaven,

Workington, Cockermouth, Egremont and Wigton were detached to form the 3rd (Cumberland) Volunteer Battalion. Four companies of the 4th Battalion Border Regiment were provided in 1908.

2nd (Westmoreland) Volunteer Battalion The 1st Westmoreland Rifle Volunteer Corps at Kendal had nine companies: 'A' (Kirkby Lonsdale), 'B' (Appleby), 'C' to 'E' (Kendal), 'F' (Stavely), 'G' (Windermere), 'H' (Ambleside) and 'J' (Grasmere). Re-designation as 2nd (Westmorland) Volunteer Battalion Border Regiment was notified in General Order 181 of December 1887. The Sedbergh School Cadet Corps was formed and affiliated in 1901 and the Kirkby Lonsdale Cadet Company in April 1902. Four companies of 4th Battalion Border Regiment were provided in 1908, Sedbergh School at the same time joining the OTC.

3rd (Cumberland) Volunteer Battalion Formed with headquarters at Workington in 1900 by the withdrawal of the Whitehaven, Workington, Cockermouth, Egremont and Wigton Companies of the 1st (Cumberland) Volunteer Battalion Border Regiment. New personnel were also added at Workington, Frizington and Aspatria bringing the new battalion's establishment to eight companies. St Bees south of Whitehaven, the ancient grammar school, formed a cadet corps in 1903. The 5th Battalion Border Regiment was provided in 1908, St Bees School becoming a contingent of the Junior Division OTC at the same time.

Illustration credit: Bruce Bassett-Powell and Bob Bennet (368) and (369)

ROYAL SUSSEX REGIMENT

35th (Royal Sussex) Regiment

The regiment's first colonel, when raised 1701 in Ireland, was Arthur Chichester, the 3rd Earl of Donegal who was later killed at Alcantara. He was replaced in April 1706 by Richard Gorges, and then in 1717 by Charles Otway who held the position for forty-seven years. In 1782, Dorsetshire was added to the regimental number, this changing to Sussex in 1805 and Royal Sussex in 1832. With this distinction came a change to blue facing from the orange worn since formation. The 35th provided the 1st Battalion Royal Sussex Regiment in 1881. A feature of the regiment's badges was the Roussillon plume, worn since 1759 but not officially authorised until June 1880. It is said that this distinction was in memory of Quebec when the men of the regiment took the white plumes from the dead of the French Royal Roussillon Grenadiers. Thought to commemorate the capture of Malta in 1899, a Maltese Cross appears on several of the regiment's badges and appointments.

107th (Bengal Infantry) Regiment

Raised 1854 in India as the Honourable East India Company's 3rd Bengal European Light Infantry Regiment, becoming the 107th in 1862 and providing the 2nd Battalion Royal Sussex Regiment in 1881. After serving in Bengal and Madras, the regiment came to England in 1875. It wore white facings.

Regular Battalions

1st and 2nd Battalions The 1st Battalion was formed from the 35th (Royal Sussex) Regiment, the 2nd coming from the 107th (Bengal Infantry) Regiment. Three examples of the regiment's badges can be seen in illustration **(376)**, the Roussillon plume, a Maltese Cross and the Star of the Order of the Garter. The photograph in the second illustration **(377)** showing the forage cap worn by officers and senior NCOs was taken at the studio of J Russell & Sons which could be found at 65 East Street, Chichester. The next photograph **(378)** was taken in India and represents a fine study of a drum major.

In his watercolour representing the Royal Sussex Regiment in Gale & Polden's 'History and Traditions' postcard series, artist J McNeill show a sergeant writing in a notebook, his medals indicating service in both India and South Africa **(379)**. The regiment wore dark blue facings, clearly seen in this colour plate from *Her Majesty's Army* by Walter Richards **(380)**.

Militia Battalions

3rd and 4th Battalions Formed from the Royal Sussex Infantry Militia with headquarters at Chichester. The two were amalgamated as 3rd Battalion in 1890. In **(381)** a scarce image of the 3rd Battalion band in 1910.

Territorial Battalions

4th Battalion Formed from the former 2nd Volunteer Battalion with headquarters at 34 Tevil's Road, Worthing, moving to Horsham in 1909. The eight companies were located: 'A' Company (Haywards Heath and Cuckfield), 'B' (Hurstpierpoint, Burgess Hill, Henfield and Steyning), 'C' (East Grinstead, Crawley and Forest Row), 'D' (Petworth, Midhurst, Graffham and North Chapel), 'E' (Horsham and Warnham), 'F' (Arundel, Ashington, Littlehampton and Storrington), 'G' (Chichester, Bognor and Eastergate) and 'H' (Worthing). The Brighton Preparatory Schools Cadet Corps and Cottesmore School Cadets were affiliated. In **(382)** a pioneer section cart. Note the crossed hatchets arm badges.

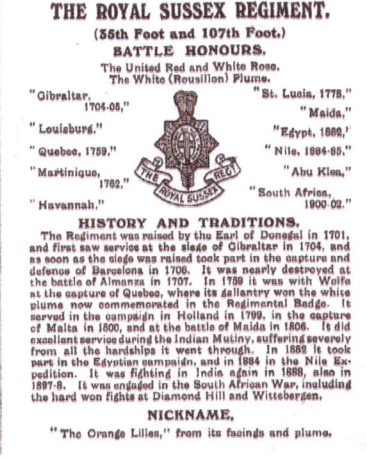

5th (Cinque Ports) Battalion Formed by the former 1st Cinque Ports Volunteer Rifle Corps with headquarters in Middle Street, Hastings. The eight companies were located: 'A' (Hastings, Eastbourne and Hailsham), 'B' (Battle, Dallington, Sedlescombe, Staplecross, Robertsbridge and Bexhill), 'C' (Wadhurst, Burwash, Flimwell, Hurst Green, Ticehurst and Frant), 'D' (Lewes, Glynde and Stanmer), 'E' (Rye, Icklesham, Winchelsea, Peasmarsh and Northiam), 'F' (Uckfield, East Hoathly, Hadlow Down, Nutley,

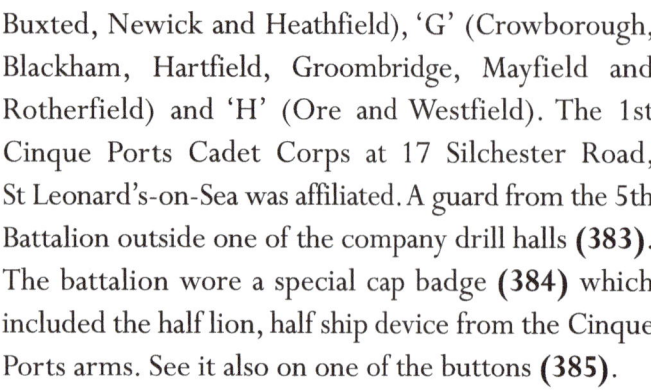

Buxted, Newick and Heathfield), 'G' (Crowborough, Blackham, Hartfield, Groombridge, Mayfield and Rotherfield) and 'H' (Ore and Westfield). The 1st Cinque Ports Cadet Corps at 17 Silchester Road, St Leonard's-on-Sea was affiliated. A guard from the 5th Battalion outside one of the company drill halls **(383)**. The battalion wore a special cap badge **(384)** which included the half lion, half ship device from the Cinque Ports arms. See it also on one of the buttons **(385)**.

6th (Cyclist) Battalion: Formed in 1912 with headquarters at 9 Hampton Place, Brighton, moving to 18 Montpelier Place, Brighton in 1914. The companies were located: 'A', 'B' (Brighton), 'C' (Brighton and Portslade), 'D' (Brighton) and 'E' to 'H' (Lewes).

Volunteer Battalions

1st Volunteer Battalion Formed at Brighton on 23 November 1859, the 1st Sussex Rifle Volunteer Corps became 1st Volunteer Battalion Royal Sussex Regiment in 1887. A ninth company was added in 1900, the Brighton College Cadet Corps being affiliated in the same year. Christ's Hospital Cadet Corps joined in 1904, Cottesmore School (re-designated Brighton and Preparatory Schools in 1907) in 1905. Transfer to the Territorial Force was to see the 1st Volunteer Battalion convert to artillery, but this was unpopular and the officers, having refused to comply, were then placed onto the unattached list. Brighton College and Christ's Hospital joined the OTC. The 1st VB eventually, in 1912, became 6th (Cyclist) Battalion Royal

Sussex Regiment.

Illustration **(386)** shows a 1st Volunteer Battalion, post 1902, 'King's' crown officers' helmet plate. Volunteers from almost every regiment served with 'Volunteer Service Companies' alongside their regular counterparts during the war in South Africa. Here in **(387)** we see members from Brighton just after their return in June 1901, and in **(388)** a detailed watercolour of the battalion on exercise by Orlando Norie.

2nd Volunteer Battalion The 2nd Sussex Rifle Volunteer Corps with headquarters in Chichester had eleven companies: 'A' and 'B' (Cuckfield), 'C' (East Grinstead), 'D' (Petworth), 'E' (Horsham), 'F' (Arundel), 'G' (Chichester), 'H' (Worthing), 'I' (Westbourne), 'K' (Hurstpierpoint) and 'L' (Henfield). The corps was re-designated as 2nd Volunteer Battalion Royal Sussex Regiment in 1887 and increased to twelve companies in 1900. The St John's College, Hurstpierpoint Cadet Corps was affiliated in 1887, Lancing College at Shoreham in 1900, Ardingly College at Hayward's Heath in 1902. Thee 4th Battalion Royal Sussex Regiment was formed in 1908, all three schools at the same time joining the OTC.

1st Cinque Ports Volunteer Rifle Corps The 1st Cinque Ports Rifle Volunteer Corps at Hastings had companies located: 'A' (Hastings), 'B' (Battle), 'C' (Ticehurst) and 'D' (Lewes). It became a Volunteer battalion of the Royal Sussex Regiment in 1881, but no change in title was ever conferred. 'E' Company was formed at Rye in 1885, 'F' at Hastings in 1887, 'G' Crowborough and 'H' at Ore in 1890, 'I' Hastings and 'K' Ore in 1900. Eastbourne College provided a cadet corps in 1896. Transfer to the Territorial Force in 1908 was as 5th (Cinque Ports) Battalion Royal Sussex Regiment, the Eastbourne College Cadet Corps at the same time becoming a contingent of the Junior Division OTC.

Illustration credit: Anne SK Brown Military Collection, Brown University Library (388), Bruce Bassett-Powell and Bob Bennet (376)

HAMPSHIRE REGIMENT

37th (North Hampshire) Regiment

Raised 1702 in Ireland, the regiment's succession of colonels until 1751 were: Thomas Meredith, William Windress, John Fane (7th Earl of Westmorland), Edward Richard Montagu (Viscount Hinchinbroke), Robert Murray, Henry Ponsonby, Sir Robert Munro and Lewis Dejean. Henry Ponsonby was killed at Fontenoy, Sir Robert Munro at Falkirk in 1746. North Hampshire was added to the numerical title in 1782, the 37th providing the 1st Battalion Hampshire Regiment in 1881. By 1742 the facings of the regiment were yellow. Thomas Carlyle, in his history of Frederick the Great, wrote 'A really splendid victory, this of Minden, August 1st. These unsurpassable Six, in industrious valour, unsurpassable.' The six regiments he was referring to include the 37th which, on Minden Day (1st August) celebrated the victory by wearing roses in their hats and decorating the Colours and drums with the same. The custom recalls how advancing troops during the battle passed among rose briers, snatching up the blossoms and placing them in their headdress and equipment.

67th (South Hampshire) Regiment

Raised 1756 as 2nd Battalion of the 20th Regiment and regimented two years later as 67th. The new regiment retained the yellow facings of the 20th, keeping these until providing the 2nd Battalion of the Hampshire Regiment in 1881. The regiment's Royal Tiger badge was authorized on 20 December 1826 in recognition of its services in India 1805-26.

Regular Battalions

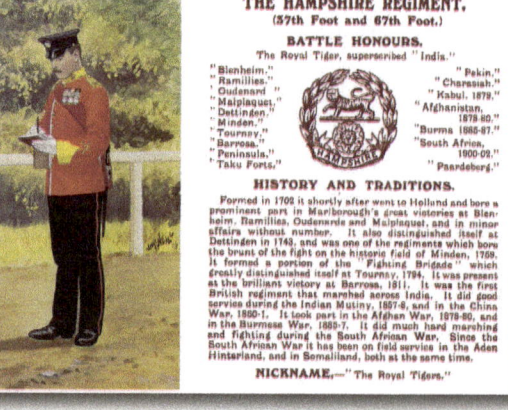

1st and 2nd Battalions 1st Battalion formed by the 37th (North Hampshire) Regiment, the 2nd from 67th (South Hampshire) Regiment. Here in Gale & Polden's 'History and Traditions' postcard **(389)** we see the regiment's cap badge, the tiger being an old badge of the 67th who were awarded it for service in India between 1805 and 1826, and the rose (the Hampshire Rose) which was formerly worn by the Hampshire Militia. From a painting by J McNeill, the image shows a sergeant, notebook in hand, talking to a private who wears a brass scout badge. The 37th's former yellow facings are shown, but from 1881 to 1903 the Hampshire Regiment was required to wear white, as seen in Richard Simkin's 1894 painting for his 'Military Types' series **(390)**. The yellow is seen again in Harry Payne's original artwork for another of Gale & Polden's postcard projects **(391)**. The medals worn by the mounted officer were awarded for service during the Boer War, the 2nd Battalion arriving in South Africa in January 1900. Going by the vast array of medals and cups seen in this photograph **(392)**, it

would seem that the 2nd Battalion's football team were quite successful. Conveniently, the football identifies the battalion and year, the 2nd Hampshire being in South Africa in 1910.

Militia Battalion

3rd Battalion Formed by the Hampshire Militia with headquarters at Winchester.

Territorial Battalions

4th Battalion Formed by the former 1st Volunteer Battalion at Winchester with companies located: 'A', 'B' (Winchester), 'C' (Romsey, Botley, Chandler's Ford, Bishop's Waltham, Hursley, Mottisfont, Twyford, East Tytherley and Newtown), 'D' (Andover, Tidworth, Highclere, Burghclere, Kingsclere, Woodhay, Whitchurch and Cholderton), 'E' (Aldershot, Farnborough, Fleet, Cove and Redfields), 'F' (Yateley, Crowthorne, Blackwater and Eversley), 'G' (Basingstoke, Hartley Wintney, Silchester, Odiham and

Strathfieldsaye) and 'H' (Alton, Alresford and Selborne). The Peter Symonds School Cadet Corps at Winchester and the Basingstoke and Eastrop Cadet Company were affiliated, the latter disappearing from the Army List in 1913.

5th Battalion Formed from the former 2nd Volunteer Battalion with headquarters at Carlton Place, Southampton. The companies were located: 'A' to 'E' (Southampton, Sarisbury, Woolston, Bitterne, Shirley and Westend), 'F' (Eastleigh and Fair Oak), 'G' (Southampton) and 'H' (Southampton and Bursledon).

6th (Duke of Connaught's Own) Battalion Formed from the former 3rd Volunteer Battalion with headquarters at Connaught Hall in Portsmouth. The companies were located: *Companies:* 'A' to 'D' (Portsmouth), 'E' (Gosport and Lee-on-Solent), 'F' (Havant, Waterlooville, South Hayling and Rowlands Castle), 'G' (Petersfield, Greatham, Liphook, Headley and Clanfield) and 'H' (Fareham, Titchfield, Swanwick, Wickham and Portchester). Illustration **(393)** shows the special cap badge worn by the 6th Battalion.

7th Battalion Formed from the former 4th Volunteer Battalion with headquarters at 177 Holdenhurst Road, Bournemouth. The companies were located: 'A' (Lymington, East Boldre, Milford-on-Sea, Brockenhurst and South Baddesley), 'B' (Christchurch, Highcliffe and Milton), 'C' (Ringwood, Burley, Fordingbridge and Damerham), 'D' (Totton, Hythe, Fawley and Marchwood) and 'E' to 'H' (Bournemouth). The Lymington Cadet Corps was affiliated. In illustration **(394)** the sergeant wears the battalion's unique badge on the collar (see 4th Volunteer Battalion below).

8th (Isle of Wight Rifles, 'Princess Beatrice's') Battalion Formed by the former 5th Volunteer Battalion with headquarters at Newport. The companies were located: 'A' (Ryde, Havenstreet, Binstead and Fishbourne), 'B' (St Helens, Bembridge, Seaview and Brading), 'C' (Newport, Calbourne and Yarmouth), 'D' (Newport, Wootton and Lock's Green), 'E' (Sandown, Shanklin and Newchurch), 'F' (Ventnor and Wroxall), 'G' (Newport, Niton, Whitwell, Godshill, Chillerton and Brighstone) and 'H' (Cowes and Northwood). The Ventnor Cadet Company and Cowes Cadet Company were both affiliated. Whereas the other Territorial battalions wore the scarlet with yellow facings of the regiment, the 8th were dress as rifles, the photograph in **(395)** showing the battalion on parade in their green with black facings uniforms. In service dress the cap badge illustrated **(396)** was worn, the central device being a representation of Carisbrooke Castle.

9th (Cyclist) Battalion Formed in 1911 with headquarters at 32 Queen's Terrace, Southampton, in 1914 later moving to Hamilton House in Commercial Road, Southampton. There were eight companies: 'A' (Southampton and

Swanwick), 'B' (Bournemouth and Dorchester), 'C' (Romsey), 'D' (Portsmouth), 'E' (Rowland's Castle, Horndean and Petersfield), 'F' (West Meon), 'G' (Basingstoke and Herriard) and 'H' (Highclere and Whitchurch).

Volunteer Battalions

1st Volunteer Battalion The 1st Hampshire Rifle Volunteer Corps at Winchester had ten companies: 'A' and 'B' (Winchester), 'C' (Botley), 'D' (Romsey), 'E' (Andover), 'F' (Hartley Wintney), 'G' (Alresford), 'H' (Alton), 'I' (Winchester) and 'K' (Basingstoke). Changes made in 1884 when 'L' Company was added at St Mary's College, Winchester, then in 1889 'M' Company was raised from the Aldershot section of 'H'. In 1892 another company was formed at Stockbridge. Which, according to CT Atkinson's *Regimental History of the Hampshire Regiment* (Vol. 1), became an ASC (Volunteers) company in 1903. The total establishment by 1900 stood at eighteen companies. There had also been a cadet corps affiliated at Winchester College since 1870. The 1st Hampshire was re-designated as 1st Volunteer Battalion Hampshire Regiment under General Order 91 of 1885, forming in 1908 the regiment's 4th Battalion. The Winchester College company, together with the cadet corps, at the same time became a contingent of the OTC. A glengarry badge of the battalion is illustrated **(397)**.

2nd Volunteer Battalion The 2nd Hampshire Rifle Volunteer Corps at Southampton had nine companies: 'A' to 'D' (Southampton), 'E' (Lymington), 'F' (Christchurch), 'G' (Lyndhurst) and 'H' and 'I' (Bournemouth). By 1883 the establishment of the 2nd had reached twelve companies, but in 1885 this was reduced to eight when part of the corps was detached to form the new 4th Hampshire RVC. According to the regimental history of the Royal Hampshire Regiment, the companies removed were those from the Bournemouth, Christchurch, Lymington and Ringwood. This would suggest that one of the Bournemouth companies ('H' or 'I') had been lost and its place taken by another at Ringwood. Also, in 1885 the corps took the title of 2nd Volunteer Battalion Hampshire Regiment. Another new company was raised in 1900 and transfer to the Territorial Force eight years later was as 5th Battalion Hampshire Regiment.

3rd (Duke of Connaught's Own) Volunteer Battalion The 3rd Corps Hampshire Rifle Volunteer Corps at Portsmouth had eleven companies: 'A' to 'E' (Portsmouth), 'F' and 'G' (Gosport), 'H' (Havant), 'I' (Petersfield), 'K' (Fareham) and 'L' (Porchester). A new company was added in 1884 and in 1897 a cadet corps was formed and affiliated by Portsmouth Grammar School. In 1900 an additional six companies were raised, followed in 1905 by another cadet corps at Churcher's College near Petersfield. The 3rd Corps was re-designated as 3rd Volunteer Battalion Hampshire Regiment by General Order 91 of September 1885. In 1893 HRH the Duke of Connaught was made Hon Colonel and from that year the title of the battalion became 3rd (The Duke of Connaught's Own) Volunteer Battalion. Transfer to the Territorial Force was as 6th Battalion Hampshire Regiment, the Portsmouth Grammar School and Churcher's College cadets at the same time joining the OTC.

4th Volunteer Battalion We have seen how in April 1885 the Bournemouth, Christchurch, Lymington and Ringwood companies of the 2nd Hampshire Rifle Volunteer Corps were detached so as to form a new 4th Corps of six companies. Headquarters were placed at Bournemouth and shortly after formation the title of the corps was changed to 4th Volunteer Battalion Hampshire Regiment. Bournemouth raised a new company in 1891, followed by another at Fordingbridge in 1895. Three more companies were added: Bournemouth again, and one of Mounted Infantry in 1900 which became known as the New Forest Scouts. Bournemouth School Cadet Corps was formed and affiliated in 1903 and a company at Lymington in 1905. Transfer to the Territorial Force was as 7th Battalion Hampshire Regiment, Bournemouth School cadets at the same time became a contingent of the OTC.

The central device of the badge shown in **(398)** is unique to the 4th Volunteer Battalion, and later 7th Hampshire Regiment. In the shape of a stirrup, this is the device once used in the New Forest to measure dogs. You can see the original chained to the wall in the old Verderers' Hall in the King's House at Lyndhurst.

5th (Isle of Wight, 'Princess Beatrice's) Volunteer Battalion
The 1st Isle of Wight Rifle Volunteer Corps at Newport had eight companies: 'A' and 'B' (Ryde), 'C' and 'D' (Newport), 'E' (Nunwell), 'F' and 'G' (Ventnor) and 'H' (Cowes). The corps was re-designated as 5th (Isle of Wight 'Princess Beatrice's') Volunteer Battalion Hampshire Regiment under General Order 91 of September 1885, Princess Beatrice being the wife of HRH Prince Henry of Battenberg, the battalion's first Hon Colonel. In 1900 a cyclist company was added at Newport and transfer to the Territorial Force was as 8th Battalion Hampshire Regiment.

Cadet Battalions

1st Cadet Battalion Headquarters at 41a Union Street, Aldershot. The battalion was affiliated to the 6th Battalion and originally called 1st Cadet Battalion of Hampshire (for 'G' and 'H' Companies see Farnham Cadet Corps) and re-designated in 1913.

2nd Cadet Battalion Headquarters were at the Connaught Drill Hall in Portsmouth. Affiliated to 6th Battalion.

Illustration credit: Anne SK Brown Military Collection, Brown University Library (391)

SOUTH STAFFORDSHIRE REGIMENT

38th (1st Staffordshire) Regiment

Raised in 1705, the regiment's successive colonels until 1751 were: Luke Lillingston, James Jones, Francis Alexander, Richard Lucas, Edward Jones, Robert Murray, Charles Spencer, Robert Dalzell, Richard Philipps and Alexander Duroure. After numbering in 1751, 1st Shropshire was added to the title in 1782, the regiment providing the 1st Battalion of the South Staffordshire Regiment in 1881. Just one year after its formation, Lillington's Regiment was sent to the West Indies where, some say, the War Office forgot all about it. It remained there for sixty years. Three generations of soldiers served in the heat of Antigua, many of them there to this day, having died from disease. With no supply of new uniforms over the period, it fell to the men to make repairs to what they had. A brown Holland material was most frequently used and to commemorate this, the regiment was authorised to feature this colour in its uniforms and as a backing to its badges. It is generally thought that grey garments were worn in the early years. Bright red coats with yellow facings were, however, recorded for the regiment by 1742, the Stafford Knot and crowned cypher GR being often seen in badges and appointments.

80th (Staffordshire Volunteers) Regiment

Formed September 1793 at Chatham by Henry William Paget who was at the time a captain in the

Staffordshire Militia. His commission, dated 12 September 1793, was the first ever to be held by the future Marquis of Anglesey. The men were mostly volunteers from the Staffordshire Militia, then embodied and doing duty at Portsmouth. The adopted yellow facings were also from that regiment. The 80th in 1881 would provide the 2nd Battalion South Staffordshire Regiment. The Stafford Knot was an early badge of the regiment, the Sphinx superscribed Egypt being authorized in July 1802.

Regular Battalions

1st and 2nd Battalions The 1st battalion was formed by the 38th (1st Staffordshire) Regiment, the 2nd from the 80th (Staffordshire Volunteers) Regiment. In Bruce asset-Powell's detailed image **(399)** we see three of the regiment's badges: the Sphinx superscribed Egypt, which commemorates the services of the old 80th Regiment in 1800, the Stafford Knot, and old badge of both battalions, and a representation of the Round Tower at Windsor Castle, the latter from the former 1st (King's Own) Staffordshire Militia. An officer's forage cap is shown in **(400)**, the cap badge in **(401)**. The regiment's white facings are shown in Richard Simkin's supplement No 74 of his 'Military Types' series for the *Army and Navy Gazette* **(402)** and in Harry Payne's original artwork for a Gale & Polden postcard **(403)**.

Militia Battalions

3rd and 4th Battalions Formed from the 1st (King's Own) 1st Staffordshire Militia at Lichfield.

Territorial Battalions

5th Battalion In 1908 most of the former 1st Volunteer Battalion transferred to the 1st North Midland Field Company Royal Engineers. The Handsworth companies, however, merged with those of the 2nd Volunteer Battalion and together provided the regiment's 5th Battalion. Headquarters were at Walsall and the companies located: 'A', 'B', 'C' (Walsall), 'D' (Bloxwich), 'E' (Brierley Hill), 'F' (Hednesford), 'G' (Handsworth) and 'H' (Wednesbury).

6th Battalion Formed from the former 3rd Volunteer Battalion with headquarters at Wolverhampton and companies located: 'A', 'B' (Wolverhampton), 'C' (Wednesfield), 'D' (Willenhall), 'E' (Tipton), 'F' (Darlaston), 'G' (Bilston) and 'H' (Tettenhall). The Brierley Hill Cadet Corps at The Temperance Hall, Brierley Hill was affiliated.

Volunteer Battalions

1st Volunteer Battalion The 1st Staffordshire Rifle Volunteer Corps at Handsworth had eight companies: 'A' and 'B' (Handsworth), 'C' (Brierley Hill), 'D' (Kingswinford), 'E' (West Bromwich), 'F' (Seisdon), 'G' (Patshull) and 'H' (Smethwick). Under General Order 63 of May 1883 the 1st Corps was re-designated as 1st Volunteer Battalion South Staffordshire Regiment, the headquarters of 'D' Company later transferring to Wordsley. 'I' Company was formed at Smethwick and 'K' at West Bromwich in 1900, followed by 'L' (Cyclist) at Handsworth in 1901. 'G' was later disbanded and at the same time a battalion reorganisation resulted in the following company locations: Handsworth (3), Brierley Hill (2), West Bromwich (2), Sutton Coldfield and Smethwick (2). Transfer to the Territorial Force in 1908 saw the bulk of the battalion converted to engineers and formed into the 1st North Midland Field Company RE. Some of the Handsworth personnel, however, remained as infantry and became part of the 5th Battalion South Staffordshire Regiment. The Handsworth Grammar School Cadets, which had been affiliated since 1907, at the same time joined the OTC.

2nd Volunteer Battalion Walsall was the headquarters of the 3rd Staffordshire Rifle Volunteer Corps which had six companies: 'A' and 'B' (Walsall), 'C' (Bloxwich), 'D' (Brownhills), 'E' (Cannock) and 'F' (Wednesbury). The corps was re-designated as 2nd Volunteer Battalion South Staffordshire Regiment under General Order 63 of May 1883. A new company was later added at Walsall, but this was soon disbanded. In 1884 another company was formed at Walsall, together with one at Wednesbury, 'E' Company at the same time moving to Brownhills. 'D' Company at Brownhills was disbanded before 1901 but reformed later at Walsall. 'I' was added at Walsall in 1901. Also in 1901, Queen Mary's School at Walsall provided a cadet corps. Transfer to the Territorial Force in 1908 was as part of 5th Battalion South Staffordshire Regiment. Queen Mary's School at the same time joined the OTC.

3rd Volunteer Battalion Headquarters of the 4th Staffordshire Rifle Volunteer Corps were at Wolverhampton, its twelve companies being located: 'A', 'B' and 'C' (Wolverhampton), 'D' (Willenhall), 'E' (Tipton), 'F' (Sedgley), 'G' and 'H' (Bilston), 'I', 'K' and 'L' (Wolverhampton) and 'M' (Tettenhall). Re-designation as 3rd Volunteer Battalion South Staffordshire Regiment was notified By General Order 63 of May 1883. 'N' (Cyclist) Company was added at Wolverhampton in 1900, 'H' Company moved to Darlaston in the same year. The 6th Battalion South Staffordshire Regiment was formed in 1908.

Illustration credits: Anne SK Brown Military Collection, Brown University Library (403), Bruce Bassett-Powell and Bob Bennet (399) and (400)

DORSETSHIRE REGIMENT

39th (Dorsetshire) Regiment

Richard Coote, who was later killed in a duel with Lord Mohun, was the regiment's first colonel after it was raised in Ireland in 1702. He was replaced by Nicholas Sankey in March 1703, the successive colonels until 1751 being: Thomas Ferrers, William Newton, Sir John Cope, Thomas Wentworth, John Campbell, Richard Onslow, Robert Dalway, Samuel Walter Whished and Edward Richbell. Colonel Sankey, perhaps, would not have enjoyed his name being used as part of a nickname. In a hurry to get his men into battle at Almanza on 23 April 1707, he mounted them on mules and quickly the regiment became known, among others, as Sankey's Horse. East Middlesex was added to the numerical title in 1782, this being changed to Dorsetshire in 1807. The regiment provided the 1st Battalion Dorsetshire Regiment in 1881.

By 1742, pale green was being used for the uniform facings and waistcoats. After that the colour would appear described as willow green, popinjay or light green. From the facing colour came the nickname of the Green Linnets. The Castle, Key and motto of Gibraltar (*Montis insignia Calpe,* Badge of the Rock of Gibraltar) were authorized as a badge in commemoration of its services during the great siege of 1779-83. Also used on insignia was the motto *Primus in Indis* (First in India) which recognises that the 39th was the first British regiment of the Line to serve in India.

54th (West Norfolk) Regiment

Raised as the 56th in 1755 at Shrewsbury by Colonel John Campbell, 5th Duke of Argyll, the regiment wore red coats with popinjay green facings. It was re-numbered as 54th two years later, received the additional West Norfolk title in 1782 and provided the 2nd Battalion Dorsetshire Regiment in 1881. The sphinx superscribed Marabout as a badge was authorised in July 1802 which commemorated the services of the regiment the previous year.

Regular Battalions

1st and 2nd Battalions The 1st Battalion was formed from the 39th (Dorsetshire) Regiment, the 2nd by the 54th (West Norfolk) Regiment. Much of the regiment's history is represented in its badges **(404)**. Here is the Castle, Key and motto *Montis insignia Calpe* commemorating the services of the 39th during the siege of Gibraltar, 1779-1783 and the Sphinx superscribed Marabout which recalls the 54th Regiment's time in Egypt, 1801. Both the 39th and 54th Regiments wore green facings, that colour being used as a background to the word Marabout. Just visible above the helmet plate castle is the motto *Primus in Indis* which alludes to the claim of the 39th that they were the first in India. Illustration **(405)** shows the cap badge.

The former green facings were disallowed in 1881, the regiment now having to wear white. We can see this colour in No 75 of Richard Simkin's 'Military Types'

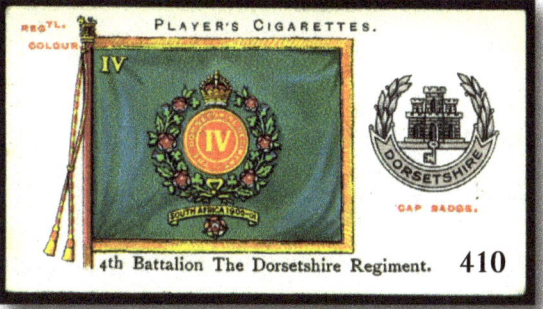

series for the *Army and Navy Gazette* which was published on 3 March 1894 **(406)** and in Orlando Norie's oil painting of the regiment on manoeuvres in 1890 **(407)**. White facings are also clear in this portrait of Samuel Vickery who with the 1st Battalion won the Victoria Cross during an attack on the Dargai Heights, North West Frontier, 20 October 1897 **(408)**. The green, however, was restored in 1904, Harry Payne showing this in his original artwork for one of Gale & Polden's uniform postcard series **(409)**.

Militia Battalion

3rd Battalion From the Dorsetshire Militia with headquarters at Dorchester.

Territorial Battalion

4th Battalion Formed from the former 1st Volunteer Battalion with headquarters at Dorchester. The companies were located: 'A' (Bridport, Beaminster, Chideock and Netherbury), 'B' (Wareham, Corfe Castle, Bere Regis and Wool), 'C' (Dorchester and Broadwey), 'D' (Poole and Parkstone), 'E' (Gillingham and Shaftesbury), 'F' (Wimborne, Witchampton, Broadstone, Horton Heath and Woodlands), 'G' (Sherborne and Milborne Port) and 'H' (Blandford, Sturminster Newton and Marnhull). The John Player cigarette card shown in illustration **(410)** features the 4th Battalion Regimental Colour with its 'South Africa 1900-01'. The former 1st Volunteer Battalion had provided a service company to fight alongside the regulars during the Second Boar War.

Volunteer Battalion

1st Volunteer Battalion Headquarters of the 1st Dorsetshire Rifle Volunteer Corps were at Dorchester, its eleven companies being located: 'A' (Bridport), 'B' (Wareham), 'C' (Dorchester), 'D' (Poole), 'E' (Weymouth), 'F' (Wimborne), 'G' (Sherborne), 'H' (Blandford), 'I' (Shaftesbury), 'K' (Stalbridge) and 'L' (Gillingham). Re-designation as 1st Volunteer Battalion Dorsetshire Regiment was notified by General Order 181 of December 1887. The Sherborne School Cadet Corps was affiliated in 1888 and the County School Cadet Corps at Dorchester in 1893. The latter, however, was removed from the Army List in January 1897. Transfer to the Territorial Force was as 4th Battalion Dorsetshire Regiment, Sherborne School at the same time joining the OTC.

Illustration credits: Anne SK Brown Military Collection, Brown University Library (407) and (409), Bruce Bassett-Powell and Bob Bennet (404)

PRINCE OF WALES'S VOLUNTEERS (SOUTH LANCASHIRE REGIMENT)

40th (2nd Somersetshire) Regiment

The 40th Regiment had its origins in a number of independent companies which had for many years served in the West Indies and were, in 1717, located in Canada. They were regimented at Annapolis Royal that year under the command of Colonel Richard Philipps who, at the time, was governor of Nova Scotia. The regiment wore light buff facings and white lace with an orange stripe. Richard Philipps' successor was Edward Cornwallis. The 2nd Somersetshire title was added in 1782 and in 1881 the 40th provided the 1st Battalion Prince of Wales's Volunteers (South Lancashire Regiment). From America, the Flank companies left for Egypt and in 1801 provided the regiment with the right to wear the Sphinx superscribed Egypt as a badge. The distinction was authorized on 6 July of the following year.

82nd (Prince of Wales's Volunteers) Regiment

Raised under a letter of service dated 27 September 1793 by Major-General Charles Leigh of the 3rd Foot Guards. Charles Leigh had for some time served on the Staff of the Prince of Wales and it is thought that the regiment's title was in view of this. The 82nd provided the 2nd Battalion Prince of Wales's Volunteers (South Lancashire Regiment) in 1881. From its formation, the regiment wore buff facings and the Prince of Wales's coronet, plumes and *Ich Dien* (I Serve) motto as its badge. Major HG Parkyn in his book *(Military) Shoulder-Belt Plates and Buttons* notes that the badge was not authorized until 20 December 1831.

Regular Battalions

1st and 2nd Battalions The 1st Battalion came from the 40th (2nd Somersetshire) Regiment, the 2nd from the 82nd (Prince of Wales's Volunteers) Regiment. Here in the cap badge (**411**) we see the Sphinx superscribed Egypt from the former 40th Regiment and the Prince of Wales's plumes, coronet and motto from the 82nd. The devices can be seen in a portrait photograph of a bandmaster (**412**) and in a Gale & Polden postcard featuring

regimental badges **(413)**. In 1881 the regiment was not permitted to continue with the buff facings worn by both the 40th or 82nd Regiments and instead adopted the white seen in Richard Simkin's 'Military Types' No 76 issued as a supplement with the *Army and Navy Gazette* on 7 April 1894 **(414)**. Illustration **(415)** is the original artwork for another of one of Gale & Polden's postcards.

Militia Battalion

3rd Battalion From the 4th Royal Lancashire Militia with headquarters at Warrington.

Territorial Battalions

4th Battalion Formed by the former 1st Volunteer Battalion with headquarters at Warrington. The eight companies were located: 'A' to 'D' (Warrington), 'E' (Newton-le-Willows), 'F' (Warrington), 'G' (Newton-le-Willows) and 'H' (Warrington).

5th Battalion Formed from the former 2nd Volunteer Battalion with headquarters at St Helens and companies located: 'A' (St Helens), 'B' (Prescot), 'C' (St Helens), 'D' (St Helens and Haydock), 'E' (St Helens),

'F' (Prescot), 'G' (St Helens) and 'H' (Widnes). Illustration **(416)** shows two members of the 5th Battalion in their full dress green with scarlet facings uniforms.

Volunteer Battalions

1st Volunteer Battalion The 9th Lancashire Rifle Volunteer Corps at Warrington had seven companies located: 'A' to 'F' (Warrington) and 'G' (Newton-le-Willows). Re-designation as 1st Volunteer Battalion South Lancashire Regiment was in 1886. During 1900-1903 additional personnel were sanctioned, bringing the establishment of the battalion up to eleven companies. The 4th Battalion South Lancashire Regiment was formed in 1908.

2nd Volunteer Battalion The 21st Lancashire Rifle Volunteer Corps at St Helens in 1881 had five companies at St Helens and one at Prescot. It was later increased to eight and in 1886 re-designated as 2nd Volunteer Battalion South Lancashire Regiment. The 5th Battalion was formed in 1908.

WELSH REGIMENT

41st (The Welsh) Regiment

A Royal Warrant dated 11 March 1719 authorised the formation of a regiment of army invalids to be known under its colonel's name, Edmund Fielding. He was succeeded in 1743 by Colonel Tomkyn Wardour who was buried in Westminster Abbey on 22 February 1752. The regiment was raised entirely from out-pensioners on the rolls of Chelsea Hospital, with headquarters being set up at Portsmouth. Having been designated as the 41st Regiment of Invalids in 1751, there then followed a series of title changes beginning with the exclusion of the word Invalids in 1787. Almost seventy years after its formation, it was felt that the 41st should now take its place in the Line and subsequently both officers and men were replaced by drafts from other regiments. One notable officer was Arthur Wellesley, the future Duke of Wellington. Welsh appeared in the title in 1831, the regiment in 1881 providing the 1st Battalion of the Welsh Regiment. The regiment's uniform was much as that worn by the Chelsea Pensioners today, the long, loose-fitting coats having blue cuffs and linings and worn with blue waistcoats and breeches. There was no lace. When the 41st ceased to be made up of pensioners in 1787, red facings were introduced, but the colour was changed to white in 1822.

Displayed on the Colours in 1747 was the Rose and Thistle within the Garter and with a crown above. With the introduction of the word Welsh to the title in 1831, the Prince of Wales's Coronet, Plumes and motto *Ich Dien* (I serve) were also authorized.

69th (South Lincolnshire) Regiment

Raised 1756 as 2nd Battalion of the 24th Regiment, being regimented as 69th two years later. The green facings of the 24th were retained, the December 1880 Army List giving Lincoln green. South Lincolnshire was added to the title in 1782, the 69th providing the 2nd Battalion Welsh Regiment in 1881. With the regiment's number appearing the same either way it was viewed, the 69th acquired the nickname of The Ups and Downs.

Regular Battalions

1st and 2nd Battalions Formed respectively by the 41st (The Welsh) and 69th (South Lincolnshire) Regiments. Illustration **(417)** shows examples of the officers' helmet plate, waist-belt clasp, button and collar badges, the Red Dragon of Wales being an old badge of the Glamorgan Militia and introduced to the Welsh Regiment in 1881. In this photograph taken by WM Crockett of Plymouth **(418)** we see Drum-Major McKelvey of the 1st Battalion with the regimental goat. The goat again in No 77 of Richard Simkin's 'Military Types' series of supplements for the *Army and Navy Gazette*, published on 5 May 1894 **(419)**. The 2nd Battalion were quick to arrive in France, having landed at Havre on 13 August 1914 as part of the 1st Division. In the early months of the war the Aldershot firm of Gale & Polden produced a number of

postcard sets featuring both ceremonial and active service regimental studies. Illustration **(420)**, showing a French officer pointing out the damage caused by recent shelling to a member of the Welsh Regiment, is the original artwork by artist Edgar Holloway that was used.

Militia Battalion

3rd Battalion Formed by the Royal Glamorganshire Light Infantry Militia with headquarters in Cardiff.

Territorial Battalions

4th Battalion Formed by the former 1st (Pembrokeshire) Volunteer Battalion with headquarters at Haverfordwest, moving to Llanelli in 1909, then in 1913 to Carmarthen. There were eight companies: 'A' (Haverfordwest and Milford Haven), 'B' (Pembroke and Narberth), 'C' (Cardigan), 'D' (Llandeilo and Llandovery), 'E' (Carmarthen), 'F' (Llanelli and Tumble), 'G' (Llanelli) and 'H' (Ammanford).

5th Battalion Formed by the former 3rd Volunteer Battalion at Pontypridd. The companies were located: 'A', 'B' (Pontypridd), 'C', 'D' (Mountain Ash), 'E' (Aberdare), 'F' (Treharris), 'G' (Merthyr Tydfil and Dowlais) and 'H' (Merthyr Tydfil).

6th (Glamorgan) Battalion Formed by the former 3rd Glamorganshire Rifle Volunteer Corps at Swansea. The companies were located: 'A' (Maesteg), 'B', 'C', 'D' (Swansea), 'E' (Hafod and Morriston), 'F' (Neath), 'G' (Gorseinon and Clydach) and 'H' (Gorseinon).

7th (Cyclist) Battalion Although a number from the former 2nd Volunteer Battalion joined, the 7th (Cyclist) Battalion was in 1908 considered a new unit. Headquarters were originally at 28 Park Road, Cardiff, a move being made to 11 Newport Road, Cardiff in 1911. The companies were located: 'A', 'B' (Cardiff), 'C' (Barry), 'D' (Bridgend), 'E', 'F' (Swansea), 'G' (Neath) and 'H' (Aberavon). A sergeant of the battalion wearing a green uniform with scarlet facings and T over 7 over WELSH metal shoulder titles is seen in illustration **(421)**, and from the Regimental Museum of the Royal Welsh at Brecon, a photograph of a pouch-belt plate which features the Welsh Dragon superimposed upon a cycle wheel **(422)**. Outside City Hall in Cardiff, the National Museum next door not yet completed, members of the 7th Battalion parade just after war was declared in August 1914 **(423)**.

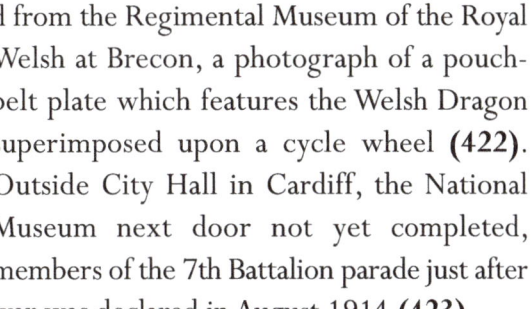

Volunteer Battalions

1st (Pembrokeshire) Volunteer Battalion The 1st Pembrokeshire Rifle Volunteer Corps at Haverfordwest had ten companies: 'A' (Milford Haven), 'B' to 'D' (Haverfordwest), 'E' (Pembroke), 'F' (Cardigan), 'G' (Llandeilo), 'H' and 'I' (Carmarthen) and 'K' (Llanelli). Re-designation as 1st (Pembrokeshire)

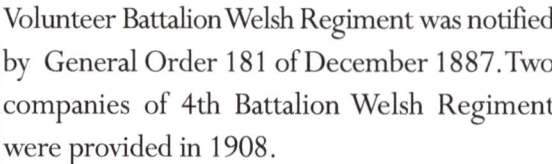

Volunteer Battalion Welsh Regiment was notified by General Order 181 of December 1887. Two companies of 4th Battalion Welsh Regiment were provided in 1908.

2nd Volunteer Battalion The 1st Glamorganshire Rifle Volunteer Corps at Margam had twelve companies: 'A' and 'B' (Margam), 'C' to 'E' (Swansea), 'F' and 'G' (Taibach), 'H' (Cwm Avon), 'I' (Bridgend), 'K' and 'L' (Neath) and 'M' (Cowbridge). Re-designation as 2nd (Glamorgan) Volunteer Battalion Welsh Regiment was notified by General Order 181 of December 1887. The sub-title was not, however, shown in the Army List after December 1888. Headquarters moved to Bridgend in 1896 and an even greater reorganisations in 1905 saw the three Swansea Companies ('C', 'D' and 'E') transferred to the 3rd Corps. At the same time, personnel from around the Cardiff area then serving with the 3rd Volunteer Battalion Welsh Regiment was absorbed. This was to bring 2nd Volunteer Battalion's establishment up to fourteen companies, headquarters at the same time changing to Cardiff. In 1908 much of the battalion was converted as 2nd Welsh Brigade RFA, some members joined the Glamorgan Battery RHA and others the 7th Battalion Welsh Regiment. A 1st Glamorgan Rifle Volunteer Corps officers' helmet is illustrated **(424)**.

3rd Volunteer Battalion The 2nd Glamorganshire Rifle Volunteer Corps had twenty-two companies: 'A' and 'B' (Dowlais), 'C' to 'E' (Mountain Ash), 'F' and 'G' (Cardiff), 'H', 'I', 'K' and 'L' (Merthyr Tydfil), 'M' and 'N' (Taff's Well), 'O' and 'P' (Aberdare), 'Q' to 'U' (Cardiff), 'V' (Pontypridd) and 'W' (Hirwain). Headquarters were in Cardiff. Under General Order 181 of December 1887 the 2nd Corps was re-designated as 3rd (Glamorgan) Volunteer Battalion Welsh Regiment, the sub-title, however, being removed from the Army List in March 1891. An increase in establishment to twenty-four companies took place in 1900, but this

was reduced to fifteen upon transfer of personnel from around the Cardiff area to the 2nd Volunteer Battalion Welsh Regiment in 1905. Headquarters at the same time moved to Pontypridd. A cadet corps was formed and affiliated to the battalion at Cardiff in 1889, but this was not shown in the Army List after August 1892. The 5th Battalion Welsh Regiment was formed in 1908. Posing for a portrait photograph in **(425)** is Sergeant ER McGregor who wears a scarlet jacket with dark blue facings, dragon collar badges and the white metal shoulder title, 3 over V over WELSH.

3rd Glamorganshire Rifle Volunteer Corps Formed at Swansea on 12 October 1859 and soon comprised four companies under the command of Major Lewis Llewelyn Dillwyn. Later increased to six and became a volunteer battalion (without change in title) of the Welsh Regiment in 1881. Increased from six to nine companies in 1900 and then twelve as the Swansea personnel of 2nd Volunteer Battalion Welsh Regiment were transferred in 1905. The 6th Battalion Welsh Regiment was formed in 1908.

Illustration credits: Anne SK Brown Military Collection, Brown University Library (420), Bruce Bassett-Powell and Bob Bennet (417)

BLACK WATCH (ROYAL HIGHLANDERS)

42nd Royal Highland (The Black Watch) Regiment

The Black Watch: the name is said to have come from the regiment's dark tartan and the fact that it was formed for the protection (Watch) of Edinburgh, originated in 1739 from a number of independent Highland companies that had been raised for service in Scotland between 1725 and 1729. John Lindsay, Earl of Crawford, became colonel, replaced by Lord Hugh Forbes in 1741 and Lord John Murray, 1745. Besides being referred to by its colonels' names, the regiment was also known as the Highland Regiment. Title changes from 1751 were as 42nd Highland Regiment and 42nd Royal Highland Regiment in 1758. Black Watch was added in 1861, the regiment providing the 1st Battalion of the Black Watch (Royal Highlanders) in 1881.

The regiment's short red coats had buff facing until blue was introduced along with the granting of the Royal title in 1758. The Royal Cypher within the Garter was first shown as a badge in the Army List for 1868, the Sphinx superscribed Egypt appearing after the 42nd's service during the 1801 campaign. The Thistle and Crown was in use for some time, appearing on the Colours in 1747, the Royal Cypher within the Collar of St Andrew being shown prior to 1751.

A feature of the 42nd's dress was its red plumes, the origins of which have been subject to much conjecture. One strong contention is that the distinction was authorised as a reward for war service, Archibald Forbes giving the following reason in his 1896 regimental history. The author bases his account on statements made by two old soldiers, Rowland Cameron and Private Andrew Dowie. On 4 January 1795, the 42nd were occupying positions at the village of Geldermalsen on the River Waal in Holland. During an attack by the French, two British guns were left behind and were about to be captured by the enemy's cavalry. At this point it is alleged that the British cavalry regiment, the 11th Dragoons, detailed to recover the guns, did not, and instead retreated at a furious rate. Private Dowie, who witnessed the whole affair, asserts that the order was then given by General Sir David Dundas, 'Forty-Second, for God's sake and for the honour of your country, retake those guns.' The Highlanders complied, the general then calling out 'Forty-Second, the 11th Dragoons shall never wear the red plume on their helmets any more, and I hope the 42nd will carry it so long as they are the Black Watch.' As fascinating as this account is, there is evidence to dispute its authenticity. For the 'against', see *Military Customs* by Major T J Edwards (Gale & Polden, Aldershot, 1954).

73rd (Perthshire) Regiment

Raised 1758 at Perth as 2nd Battalion of the 42nd Regiment and in 1786 was regimented as the 73rd (Highland) with General Sir George Osborn as its first colonel. Highland was dropped from the title in 1809, but the Scottish connection was again established when in 1862 Perthshire was added. The regiment provided the 2nd Battalion Black Watch (Royal Highlanders) in 1881. When regimented, the 73rd did not assume the blue facings of the 42nd, but instead chose dark green. Highland dress was worn until 1809, it being restored, in part, when Perthshire became part of the title in 1862. The arms of Perth were worn as a collar badge from 1874.

Regular Battalions

1st and 2nd Battalions The 1st Battalion was the former 42nd Royal Highland (The Black Watch) Regiment, the 2nd being the old 73rd (Perthshire) Regiment. Artist Harry Payne's fine study of a sentry at ease is shown in **(426)**, Richard Simkin's private, officer and piper **(427)** being supplement No 78 in his 'Military Types' series for the *Army and Navy Gazette*. Edgar Holloway contributed to a number of the Gale & Polden sets of postcards featuring both ceremonial and active service scenes, each containing six cards. Here in **(428)** we have a colonel and bugler, **(429)** showing an officer and rear view of a private and sergeant. Both illustrations are in fact the original artwork provided by the artist. From Mitchell & Co, a fine study of a piper **(430)**. Photographers Mitchell & Co had studios at East High Street in Forfar and Marywell Street, Kirriemuir.

Militia Battalion

3rd Battalion Formed by the Royal Perthshire Militia with headquarters at Perth.

Territorial Battalions

4th (City of Dundee) Battalion Formed by the former 1st (City of Dundee) Volunteer Battalion with headquarters and all eight companies at Dundee. To illustrate the Dundee Territorial Force Association in Volume 1 of *His Majesty's Territorial Army*, Walter Richards chose a fine study of a Black Watch sentry **(431)**. By R Caton Woodville, the painting clearly shows the regiment's red plume and dark blue facings and a rear view of a sergeant in drill order.

5th (Angus & Dundee) Battalion Formed by the amalgamation of the

former 2nd (Angus) and 3rd (Dundee Highland) Volunteer Battalions with headquarters at Arbroath. The companies were located: 'A' (Kirriemuir, Glamis and Newtyle), 'B' (Forfar), 'C' (Montrose and Craigo), 'D' (Brechin and Edzell), 'E' (Arbroath and Friockheim), 'F' (Arbroath, Carnoustie and Monifleth) and, 'G', 'H' (Dundee).

6th (Perthshire) Battalion Formed by the former 4th (Perthshire) Volunteer Battalion at Tay Street, Perth. The companies were located: 'A', 'B' (Perth), 'C' (Dunblane, Bridge of Allan, Doune and Callander), 'D' (Crieff and Comrie), 'E' (Blairgowrie, Coupar Angus and Alyth), 'F' (Auchterarder, Blackford and Dunning), 'G' (Birnam, Pitlochry, Bankfoot, Ballinluig, Stanley, Luncarty, Strathbraun and Blair Atholl) and 'H' (Aberfeldy, Kenmore, Fortingall, Grandtully and Killin). Members of the battalion are seen at camp in **(432)**, the men identified by their T over 6 over RH brass shoulder title.

7th (Fife) Battalion Formed from the former 6th (Fifeshire) Volunteer Battalion at St Andrews. The companies were located: 'A' (Dunfermline), 'B' (Lochgelly), 'C' (Kirkcaldy), 'D' (Cowdenbeath), 'E' (Cupar, Newburgh, Auchtermuchty and Abernethy), 'F' (Leven, Colinsburgh and Largoward), 'G' (St Andrews, Guardbridge, Anstruther and Crail) and, 'H' (Leslie, Markinch and Thornton).

8th Battalion It was originally intend for the formed 5th (Perthshire) Volunteer Battalion to provide personnel for an 8th Battalion Black Watch. Before the end of 1908, however, plans for this were cancelled and instead the men were formed into the independent Highland Cyclist Battalion.

Volunteer Battalions

1st (City of Dundee) Volunteer Battalion The 1st Forfarshire Rifle Volunteer Corps was formed as the result of a public meeting held in Dundee on 20 May 1859, its service being accepted in the following November with Sir John Ogilvy, Bart in command. Five companies were authorized, followed by two more in February 1860 and another in April. Re-designation as 1st (Dundee) Volunteer Battalion Black Watch was notified in General Order 181 of December 1887, the sub-title changing, however, to (City of Dundee) in February 1889. Formed and attached in 1879 was a company of cadets, but this was later disbanded and last seen in the Army List for September 1888. Two new companies (one a Cyclist) were added in 1900 and another cadet corps, that raised at Morgan Academy, was affiliated in the same year. Battalion headquarters and drill hall were in the Albany Quarters, Bell Street, Dundee and its rifle range just over seven miles off at Monifieth Links. Transfer to the Territorial Force in 1908 was as 4th Battalion Black Watch was.

2nd (Angus) Volunteer Battalion The 2nd Forfarshire Rifle Volunteer Corps had fourteen companies: 'A' and 'B' (Forfar), 'C' to 'F' (Arbroath), 'G' and 'H' (Montrose), 'I' and 'K' (Brechin), 'L' (Newtyle), 'M' (Glamis), 'N' (Kirriemuir) and 'O' (Friockheim). Headquarters were at Friockheim by Arbroath. Forfarshire or Angus was at first included in the title of the corps, but this was changed to just Angus in 1883. Next came the re-designation in 1887 as 2nd (Angus) Volunteer Battalion Black Watch, that same year seeing headquarters moved to Arbroath. In 1894 the company structure of the battalion underwent a number of changes beginning with the disbandment of 'F' and the amalgamation of 'L' and 'M' as 'K'. Further reorganisations saw 'G' designated as 'F', 'H' as 'G', 'I' as 'H', the original 'K' as 'I', 'N' as 'L' and 'O' as 'M'. A cadet corps formed at the Chapel Works in Montrose was affiliated in 1907. Transfer to the Territorial Force was as Six companies of 5th Battalion Black Watch.

3rd (Dundee Highland) Volunteer Battalion The 3rd (Dundee Highland) Rifle Volunteer Corps was re-designated as 3rd (Dundee Highland) Volunteer Battalion Black Watch under General Order 181 of December 1887 and increased to eight companies in 1900. Two companies of the 5th Battalion Black Watch were provided in 1908. Headquarters of the battalion and its drill hall were at Albany Quarters, Bell Street, Dundee, its musketry being carried out at the Barry Links government range.

4th (Perthshire) Volunteer Battalion The 1st Perthshire Rifle Volunteer Corps had seven companies: 'A' and 'B' (Perth), 'C' (Dunblane), 'D' (Crieff), 'E' (Doune), 'F' (Auchterarder) and 'G' (Perth). Headquarters were in Tay Street, Perth and affiliated since 1875 was a cadet corps at Glenalmond Collage. A new company ('H') was added at Bridge of Allan in March 1885 and by General Order 181 of December 1887 the 1st Corps was re-designated as 4th (Perthshire) Volunteer Battalion Black Watch. Three new companies were added at Perth in 1900. 'I' Company was disbanded in 1902, as were 'K' and 'L' in 1905. Transfer to the Territorial Force in 1908 was as 6th Battalion Black Watch, the Glenalmond College at the same time joining the OTC. Illustration **(433)** is from *Records of the Scottish Volunteer Force 1859-1908* by Lieutenant-General Sir James Moncrieff Grierson and shows a private of the battalion for the period 1901-1908.

5th (Perthshire Highland) Volunteer Battalion The 2nd Perthshire Rifle Volunteer Corps had eight companies: 'A' (Aberfeldy), 'B' (Killin), 'C' (Blairgowrie), 'D' (Couper Angus), 'E' (Alyth), 'F' (St Martin's), 'G' (Birnam) and 'H' (Pitlochry). 'B' Company also had detachments at Crainlarich, Lochearnhead and Kenmore. Re-designation as 5th (Perthshire Highland) Volunteer Battalion Black Watch was notified in General Order 181 of December 1887. The headquarters of 'F' Company were moved to New Scone in 1899; two new companies, 'I' (Blairgowrie) and 'K' (Birnam), being added in the same year. 'I', however, was disbanded in 1904, followed by 'K' in 1905. Transfer to the Territorial Force in 1908 was to be as 8th Battalion Black Watch, but this was cancelled and instead the 5th Volunteer Battalion personnel went to form the independent Highland Cyclist Battalion.

6th (Fifeshire) Volunteer Battalion The 1st Fifeshire Rifle Volunteer had twelve companies: 'A' and 'B' (Dunfermline), 'C' and 'D' (Cupar), 'E' (East Anstruther), 'F' (Colinsburgh), 'G' (St Andrews), 'H' (Leslie), 'I' (Falkland), 'K' (Kirkcaldy), 'L' (Lochgelly) and 'M' (Newburgh). Re-designation as 6th (Fifeshire) Volunteer Battalion Black Watch was notified by General Order 181 of December 1887. In March 1900 both 'C' and 'D' Companies moved to Kirkcaldy, 'K'

at the same time going to Cupar. A Cyclist Company ('O') was added at Dunfermline in January 1901, and in 1906 'F' was moved to Leven. The 7th Battalion Black Watch was formed in 1908. Illustration **(434)** is from *Records of the Scottish Volunteer Force 1859-1908* by Lieutenant-General Sir James Moncrieff Grierson and shows a sergeant of the battalion for the period 1880-1908.

Illustration credit: Anne SK Brown Military Collection, Brown University Library (426)

OXFORDSHIRE AND BUCKINGHAMSHIRE LIGHT INFANTRY

The Oxfordshire Light Infantry was the title assumed in 1881, Buckinghamshire being added in 1908.

43rd (Monmouthshire Light Infantry)

Colonel Thomas Fowke's Regiment was raised in 1741 and was known by that name until the appointments of William Graham in August 1741 and James Kennedy, 1746. Thomas Fowke had been dismissed for failing to reinforce Minorca when requested to do so. Monmouthshire was added to the numerical title in 1782, this changing to Monmouthshire Light Infantry with effect from 17 July 1803. The regiment provided the 1st Battalion Oxfordshire Light Infantry in 1881.   Colonel Fowke had served with the 7th Dragoons who wore white facings and it is said that that colour was chosen for the 43rd for that reason. The bugle-horn was introduced after 1803.

52nd (Oxfordshire Light Infantry) Regiment

Raised as the 54th Regiment by Colonel Hedworth Lampton under a letter of service dated 25 December 1755. Recruiting seems to have taken place in no specific areas, but assembly was organised at Coventry. The uniforms were red with buff facings, the men's lace being white with one red stripe and one orange. The regiment was re-numbered as 52nd on 8 February 1757. Oxfordshire was added to the title in 1782, Light Infantry in 1803. The 52nd provided the 2nd Battalion Oxfordshire Light Infantry in 1881. Bugle-horn badges were worn after 1803.

Regular Battalions

1st and 2nd Battalions The 1st Battalion was formed by the 43rd (Monmouthshire Light Infantry), the 2nd from the 52nd (Oxfordshire Light Infantry). Both illustrations **(435)** and **(436)** are examples of the original artwork produced for the Aldershot firm of Gale & Polden and their several series of uniform postcards. The first is by Harry Payne who shows a sergeant and private, their white facings and bugle over OXF & BUCKS brass shoulder titles clearly seen. The sergeant wears both the Queen's and

King's Medals for South Africa as does the two men in J McNeill's watercolour. It was the 1st Battalion of the regiment that sailed on the *Gaika* for South Africa on 22 December 1899. Richard Simkin's supplement No 79, produced for the *Army and Navy Gazette* and published on 7 July 1894, **(437)** shows an officer standing at the rear of four men firing. Note his collar decoration, a button at the end of a piece of gold Russia braid 2½ inches long. See also illustration **(438)**. With the Colours cased, the 2nd Battalion are seen here arriving at Aldershot in 1911 **(439)**. Note how full-dress helmets are being worn with service dress.

Militia Battalion

3rd Battalion The original 3rd Battalion was formed in 1881 by the Royal Buckinghamshire Militia (King's Own) with headquarters at High Wycombe. Disbanded in 1908.

4th, later 3rd Battalion The Oxfordshire Militia became 4th Battalion of the regiment in 1881 with headquarters at Oxford, being re-numbered as 3rd in 1908.

Territorial Battalions

4th Battalion Formed by the former 2nd Volunteer Battalion at Oxford and with companies located: 'A' (Oxford), 'B' (Oxford and Thame), 'C' (Banbury and Brackley), 'D' (Henley-on-Thames and Culham), 'E' (Chipping Norton, Kingham, Charlbury, Shipton-under-Wychwood and Stow-on-the-Wold), 'F' (Witney, Woodstock, Burford and Eynsham), 'G' (Banbury and Bicester) and 'H' (Oxford and Woodburn).

The Burford Grammar School Cadet Corps at 14 Holywell Street, Oxford and the Cowley Cadet Corps were affiliated. Illustration **(440)** shows a 4th Battalion Colour party.

Buckinghamshire Battalion Formed by the 1st Buckinghamshire Volunteer Rifle Corps which had served as a volunteer battalion of the regiment since 1881. Headquarters were at Marlow, moving to Aylesbury before the end of 1908, and the companies located: 'A' (Marlow), 'B' (High Wycombe and Winslow), 'C' (Buckingham, Tingewick and Chesham), 'D' (Aylesbury), 'E' (Slough and Datchet), 'F', 'G'

(Wolverton) and 'H' (High Wycombe). General Swann, in his book, *The Citizen Soldiers of Buckinghamshire,* records how Headquarters in 1908 were moved to Temple Square, Aylesbury, a small shed of corrugated iron being erected in the yard for drill purposes. Most of the battalion stores had to be kept at Wycombe, owing to lack of accommodation. The London & North Western Railway Company continued to find accommodation for the Wolverton Companies ('F' and 'G'), until a new drill hall was opened towards the end of 1914. The Aylesbury Grammar School Cadet Corps was affiliated. The battalion wore dark grey uniforms with scarlet facings, as seen in illustration **(441)**. In service dress the cap badge shown at **(442)** was worn.

Volunteer Battalions

1st (Oxford University) Volunteer Battalion On 8 August 1859 three companies of rifle volunteers were formed within Oxford University. A fourth followed on 16 December. In the Army List for February 1860 all four companies are shown as having been amalgamated under the title of 1st University of Oxford Rifle Volunteer Corps. Fifth and sixth Companies were added in March 1860 with, in command, the Hon Robert CH Spencer, late of the Royal Artillery. In 1887, under General Order 181 of December, the corps was re-designated as 1st (Oxford University) Volunteer Battalion Oxfordshire Light Infantry. Magdalen College School Cadet Corps was formed and affiliated in May 1873, but this disbanded late in 1884. Another unit known as the Oxford Military College Cadet Corps was formed in July 1885, but again, this was to be removed from the Army List in January 1898. In 1908 the corps became the Oxford University Contingent Senior Division OTC. Seen in **(443)** is an other ranks helmet plate displaying in its centre the university arms.

2nd Volunteer Battalion The 1st Administrative Battalion of Oxfordshire Rifle Volunteers was formed with headquarters at Oxford in May 1860 and consolidated as the 2nd Oxfordshire Rifle Volunteer Corps of six companies on 8 July 1875—a seventh being added at Chipping Norton in 1876. The title of 2nd Volunteer Battalion Oxfordshire Light Infantry was assumed under General Order 181 of December 1887. Two new companies were formed in 1900 and transfer to the Territorial Force in 1908 was as 4th Battalion Oxfordshire Light Infantry. Helmet plates had the ox passing through a ford from the City of Oxford arms as a central device **(444)**.

1st Buckinghamshire Volunteer Rifle Corps The 1st Administrative Battalion of Buckinghamshire Rifle Volunteers was formed with headquarters at Aylesbury in July 1862. Great Marlow became headquarters in 1872 and in 1875 the battalion was consolidated to form the new 1st Buckinghamshire Rifle Volunteer Corps which first appeared in the Army List for April. There were five companies: Great Marlow, Buckingham, Aylesbury, Slough and Eton College. New companies were later formed at High Wycombe, Buckingham and Wolverton—No 6 Company at Wolverton being in the main recruited from men employed at the London and North

Western Railway Carriage Works and the volunteers at High Wycombe were from the staff of a local chair manufacturer. In 1876 a cadet corps was also provided by St Paul's College at Stony Stratford which, however, disappeared from the Army List in May 1883. The Eton College personnel were detached to form a new 2nd Corps in 1878. The 1st Corps became a volunteer battalion (without change of title) of the Oxfordshire Light Infantry in 1881, the companies in 1897 being redistributed: two at High Wycombe (still mainly chair-makers), one-and-a-half at Wolverton (LNWR carriage works), half at Buckingham and one each at Marlow, Aylesbury, Slough and Stony Stratford. A ninth company was added in 1900. Transfer to the Territorial Force was as The Buckinghamshire Battalion Oxfordshire Light Infantry.

4th (Eton College) Volunteer Battalion Formed as 8th Buckinghamshire Rifle Volunteer Corps at Eton College in May 1867 with a cadet corps attached. Commanding Officers' commissions for both units: Captain Samuel Thomas George Evans (8th Corps) and Hon Captain Rev Edmond Warre (cadets), being dated 22 January 1868. Became part of the new 1st Corps in 1875. In June 1878, however, it was decided to remove the Eton College elements and form the companies into an independent corps designated 2nd Buckinghamshire (Eton College) Rifle Volunteer Corps which was re-designated as 4th (Eton College) Volunteer Battalion Oxfordshire Light Infantry in 1887. The battalion, however, reverted to its former title, 2nd (Eton College), in 1902. Establishment was increased from four to five companies in 1900 and transfer to the Territorial Force in 1908 saw the Eton College Volunteers as a contingent of the Junior Division OTC.

Illustration credits: Anne SK Brown Military Collection, Brown University Library (435) and (436)

ESSEX REGIMENT

44th (East Essex) Regiment

Raised by Colonel James Long of the 1st Foot Guards in 1741, the regiment would bear his name until succeeded by Colonel John Lee (11 March 1743) and Sir Peter Halkett, February 1751. Sir Peter, along with his youngest son, was killed in America during a disastrous attempt to take For du Quesne in 1755. East Essex was added to the numerical title in 1782, the 44th providing the 1st Battalion Essex Regiment in 1881. Yellow facings were worn, the regiment's Sphinx superscribed Egypt badge being authorized in 1802 for its services the previous year.

56th (West Essex) Regiment

The regiment's facings were deep crimson when it was raised in 1755 by Lord Charles Manners as the 58th. Re-numbering took place two years later, the facings about 1764 changing to purple. The colour is said to have been associated with that favoured by the Marchioness de Pompadour, the mistress of Louis XV and this led to the nickname The Pompadours. West Essex was added to the title in 1782, the regiment providing the 2nd Battalion Essex Regiment in 1881. The arms of Essex, three seaxes, formed part of pre-1881 badges.

Regular Battalions

1st and 2nd Battalions The 1st Battalion was provided by the 44th (East Essex) Regiment, the 2nd by the 56th (West Essex) Regiment. Richard

Simkin's supplement No 80 for the *Army and Navy Gazette* is shown in illustration **(445)**. Published on 4 August 1894, the artist clearly shows the regiment's white facings. Harry Payne chose a corporal of the regiment for one of his Gale & Polden postcards **(446)** who is shown wearing both the Queen's and King's Medals for South Africa. It was the 1st Battalion that sailed for the Cape in November 1899. Note also the Essex arms collar badges which had be seen in a photograph taken at the Grand Studio, 268 Sda Reale, Valletta, Malta **(447)**. The sergeant also wears a star over crossed rifles badge indicating that he had been judged as the best shot in his company, and an Indian General Service Medal. More shooting awards in **(448)** and **(449)**.

Militia Battalions

3rd and 4th Battalions The 3rd Battalion was provided by the Essex Rifle Militia at Colchester, the 4th by the West Essex Militia which had its headquarters at Warley. The latter was disbanded in 1908.

Territorial Battalions

4th Battalion Formed by the former 1st Volunteer Battalion with headquarters at Brentwood. The companies were located: 'A' (Romford and Harold Wood), 'B' (Manor Park), 'C' (Ilford), 'D' (Barking), 'E' (Loughton, Abridge and Woodford), 'F' (Brentwood, Southminster, Wickford, Billericay, Althorne, Bradwell-on-Sea, Burnham-on-Crouch, Mountnessing and Tillingham), 'G' (Ongar, Epping and Harlow) and 'H' (Hornchurch, Dagenham, Rainham and, transferred from 'A' Company in 1913, Harold Wood). The following cadet corps were affiliated: Cranbrook College Cadets in Ilford, the Manor Park Cadet Company at 63 Carlyce Road, Ongar Grammar School Cadets, Warley Garrison Cadets and East Ham Secondary School Cadets.

5th Battalion Formed by the former 2nd Volunteer Battalion with headquarters at 35 Salisbury Avenue, Colchester, moving to Association Buildings, Market Road, Chelmsford in 1912. The companies at this time were located: 'A' (Chelmsford, Broomfield, Writtle and Great Waltham), 'B' (Chelmsford,

Boreham, Hatfield and Danbury), 'C' (Colchester), 'D' (Manningtree, Dedham and Bradfield), 'E' (Halstead, Hedingham, Yeldham, Pebmarsh, Earls Colne and Maplestead), 'F' (Braintree, Bocking, Dunmow, Thaxted, Great Bardfield, Felstead and Coggeshall), 'G' (Maldon, Wickham Bishops, Witham, Terling, Tiptree and Tollesbury) and 'H' (Clacton-on-Sea, Wivenhoe and Walton-on-the-Naze). The King Edward VI School Cadet Corps at Chelmsford and the Colchester Royal Grammar School Cadets were affiliated.

6th Battalion Formed by the former 3rd Volunteer Battalion with headquarters at West Ham and companies: 'A' to 'G' (West Ham), 'H' (Prittlewell and Grays). The Church of the Ascension Cadet Corps, which according to Army Order 65 of 1911 became 'E' Company of the 1st Cadet Battalion Essex Regiment, the Palmer's School Cadet Corps at Grays, the Given Wilson Institute Cadets in London Road, Plaistow and the Southend Technical School Cadet Corps were all affiliated. The latter in 1913 was re-designated as Southend High School.

7th Battalion Formed from the 4th Volunteer Battalion with headquarters at Park Road, Leyton, moving to Walthamstow Lodge, Church Hill, Walthamstow in 1913. The companies were: 'A', 'B', 'C' (Hackney, moving to Walthamstow in 1913), 'D', 'E' (Leyton, moving to Walthamstow in 1913), 'F' (Silvertown, moving to Walthamstow in 1913), 'G' (Walthamstow) and 'H' (Walthamstow and Chingford). The Forest Cadet Corps at Walthamstow was affiliated,

but recognition was withdrawn by the Essex Territorial Force Association in 1912. Another unit was the Walthamstow Cadets which could be found at 26 Chester Road, Walthamstow. T over 7 over ESSEX shoulder titles are being worn in **(450)** and just identifiable are the battalion's Essex Regiment cap badges with the additional 'South Africa 1900-02' scroll below.

8th (Cyclist) Battalion A new battalion with headquarters at Colchester and companies: 'A' (Leyton), 'B' (West Ham), 'C' (Colchester, Braintree, Dunmow and Maldon), 'D' (Saffron Waldon and Stansted Mountfitchet), 'E' (East Ham), 'F' (Ilford), 'G' (Brentwood) and 'H' (Coggeshall). The battalion was originally raised in 1908 as part of the Essex and Suffolk Cyclist Battalion which was divided in 1911. A member of the battalion is seen in **(451)**.

Volunteer Battalions

1st Volunteer Battalion The 1st Essex Rifle Volunteer Corps at Ilford had eight companies: 'A' and 'B' (Romford), 'C' (Ilford), 'D' (Barking), 'E' (Walthamstow), 'F' (Brentwood), 'G' (Chipping Ongar) and 'H' (Hornchurch). Re-designation as 1st Volunteer Battalion Essex Regiment was notified by General Order 14 of February 1883. Headquarters moved to Brentwood in 1890 and two new companies were added in 1896, followed by four more in 1900. Several cadet units have been associated with the battalion: one at Ongar Grammar School in 1865, then a company raised at Forest School, Walthamstow in May 1883. Chigwell School raised a company in 1900 and three years later a unit at Loughton and Buckhurst Hill appeared. The 4th Battalion Essex Regiment was formed in 1908, the Forest and Chigwell Schools becoming contingents of the OTC at the same time. The cloth shoulder title, ESSEX over 1 over V worn by the cadet see in **(452)** identifies him as a member of one of the 1st Volunteer Battalion's several cadet corps.

2nd Volunteer Battalion The 2nd Essex Rifle Volunteer Corps at Braintree had eight companies: 'A' and 'B' (Chelmsford), 'C' and 'D' (Colchester), 'E' (Witham), 'F' (Braintree), 'G' (Maldon) and 'H' (Walton-on-the-Naze). Re-designation as 2nd Volunteer Battalion Essex Regiment was notified in General Order 14 of February 1883 and in 1895 headquarters moved to Colchester. Two new companies were added in 1900. The Felstead School Cadet Corps was affiliated in 1883 and in 1904 the King Edward VI School Cadet Corps was formed at Chelmsford. The 5th Battalion Essex Regiment was formed in 1908.

3rd Volunteer Battalion Formed at Plaistow in 1860 with four companies, much of the 3rd Essex Rifle Volunteer Corps was recruited from the Royal Victoria Dock, its commanding officer being docks manager, Mr Charles Cooper. Re-designation as 3rd Volunteer Battalion Essex Regiment was in 1883, headquarters moving to West Ham two years later. The battalion reached an establishment of thirteen companies in 1900 and a cadet corps was formed and affiliated in 1907. Transfer to the Territorial Force was as 6th Battalion Essex Regiment.

4th Volunteer Battalion Formed at Silvertown in 1860, the 4th Essex Rifle Volunteer Corps was re-designated as 4th Volunteer Battalion Essex Regiment in 1883. Headquarters moved to Leyton in 1900 and in that same year the battalion's establishment was increased to eleven companies. The 7th Battalion Essex Regiment was formed in 1908.

Cadet Battalion

1st Cadet Battalion Headquarters were in Wellington Street, Canning Town, the battalion having been formed by the amalgamation of the West Ham, St Gabriel's Canning Town, St Matthew's (Custom House) and Church of the Ascension cadet units.

SHERWOOD FORESTERS (NOTTINGHAMSHIRE AND DERBYSHIRE REGIMENT)

The title assumed in 1881 was The Sherwood Foresters (Derbyshire) Regiment, the change to that above being in 1902.

45th (Nottinghamshire Sherwood Foresters) Regiment

When raised at Buckingham and Aylesbury in 1741, the regiment was known by its colonel's name, Colonel Daniel Houghton, who was succeeded by Hugh Warburton in June 1745. Colonel Warburton was later to serve as Member of Parliament for Nottingham. With their deep green facings (afterwards referred to as Lincoln green), the regiment added Nottingham to its numerical title in 1782, and then Sherwood Foresters in 1866. The 1st Battalion Sherwood Foresters (Derbyshire) Regiment was provided in 1881. An interesting custom relating to an item of uniform was upheld by the 45th. Distinguishing himself at the Battle of Badajoz on 6 April 1812, Lieutenant Macpherson, despite being wounded, scaled the walls of the enemy's defences under heavy fire. Reaching a tower where a French flag was flying, he then removed it and, in its place, hoisted his own scarlet jacket. In memory of this, a red coat was flown on every Badajoz Day.

95th (Derbyshire) Regiment

The 95th was raised in January 1824, its colonelcy going to Sir Colin Halkett who later, in 1849, became Governor of the Royal Hospital. Derbyshire was added to the title in 1825, the 95th providing the 2nd Battalion Sherwood Foresters (Derbyshire) Regiment in 1881. Yellow facing were worn, and a Maltese Cross featured on badges. The latter, although there is no evidence to support it, is said to have derived from the fact that many of the officers formerly served with the old 95th, then the Rifle Brigade.

Regular Battalions

1st and 2nd Battalions The 1st Battalion was provided by the 45th (Nottinghamshire Sherwood Foresters) Regiment, the 2nd by the 95th (Derbyshire) Regiment. Bruce Bassett-Powell's detailed image of officers' badges **(453)** shows items that were in use prior to the change of title in 1902. The white hart lodged within park gates was an old badge of the Derbyshire Militia. Illustration **(454)** is by Richard Simkin and shows a colour sergeant talking to an officer as his squad stands to attention and a bugler sounds a call in the distance. The image was published on 1 September 1894 as a supplement to the *Army and Navy Gazette*. The image includes the regiment's white facings introduced in 1881, but the original artwork by Ernest Ibbetson for a Gale & Polden postcard set **(455)** has the green that was reintroduced in 1913. Illustration **(456)** is one of the postcards from the set and features the commanding officer talking to the regimental sergeant major as a young bugler tends his horse.

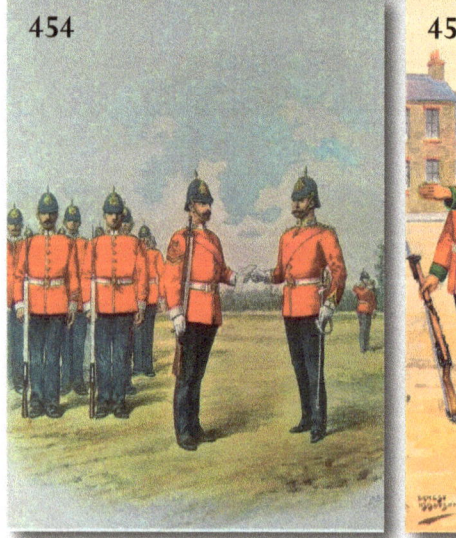

Militia Battalions

3rd Battalion Formed by the 2nd Derbyshire Militia (The Chatsworth Rifles) with headquarters at Chesterfield. Amalgamated with the 5th Battalion in 1891 and headquarters transferred to Derby.

4th Battalion From the Royal Nottingham or Sherwood Foresters Militia with headquarters at Newark.

5th Battalion From the 1st Derbyshire Militia with headquarters at Derby. Amalgamated with the 3rd Battalion in 1891.

Territorial Battalions

5th Battalion Formed by the former 1st Volunteer Battalion with headquarters at Derby. The companies were located: 'A' (Derby), 'B' (Melbourne, moving to

Derby c1913), 'C' (Derby), 'D' (Derby, moving to Long Eaton c1913 and, transferred from 'B' Company about the same time, Melbourne), 'E' (Ripley, Codnor Park, Horsley Woodhouse, Kilburn, Alfreton and Butterley), 'F' (Belper, Crich, Horsley and, transferred from 'E' Company c1913, Woodhouse and Kilburn), 'G' (Ilkeston, Long Eaton, Heanor and Langley Mill) and 'H' (Swadlincote and Repton). The Derby Post Office Cadet Corps was affiliated, but recognition was withdrawn on 6 December 1913. The colour sergeant shown in **(457)** wears an Imperial Service broach on his sash which indicates that he had agreed to serve overseas if required. His arm badge is a National Rifle Association shooting award carrying a date of 1909.

6th Battalion Formed from the former 2nd Volunteer Battalion with headquarters at 10 Corporation Street, Chesterfield. The companies were: 'A' (Chesterfield), 'B' (Chapel-en-le-Frith, Edale, Hathersage, Peak Dale and Chinley), 'C' (Buxton and Ashbourne), 'D' (Bakewell and Stoney Middleton), 'E' (Wirksworth, Cromford and Matlock), 'F' (Staveley, Clowne, Eckington and Brimington), 'G' (Clay Cross, New Tupton and South Wingfield) and 'H' (Whaley Bridge, New Mills, Disley and Hayfield). The White Cross Cadet Corps was affiliated, but recognition was withdrawn with effect from 4 September 1911. The metal shoulder title worn by the battalion is shown in **(458)**.

7th (Robin Hood) Battalion Formed by the former 1st Nottinghamshire (Robin Hood) Volunteer Rifle Corps. Headquarters and all eight companies were at 168 Derby Road, Nottingham.

8th Battalion Formed from the former 4th (Nottinghamshire) Volunteer Battalion with headquarters at Newark. The companies were located: 'A' (Retford and Ollerton), 'B' (Newark), 'C' (Sutton-in-Ashfield), 'D' (Mansfield), 'E' (Carlton, Burton Joyce and Bingham), 'F' (Arnold, Basford, Eastwood, Daybrook and Hucknall), 'G' (Worksop and Shireoaks) and 'H' (Southwell, Calverton and Farnsfield). The Welbeck Cadet Battalion at the Cadet Drill Hall in Mansfield was affiliated.

Volunteer Battalions

1st Volunteer Battalion The 1st Derbyshire Rifle Volunteer Corps had twelve companies: 'A' to 'D' (Derby), 'E' (Butterley), 'F' (Condor Park), 'G' (Belper), 'H', 'I' and 'K' (Derby) and 'L' and 'M' (Long Eaton). A cadet corps at Derby School was formed and affiliated, also another at Trent College in 1886. But this was disbanded towards the end of 1889. Repton School provided a company in December 1900, followed by a unit raised by the Derby General Post Office called the Postal Telegraph Messengers Cadet Corps in 1905. The 1st Derbyshire was re-designated as 1st Volunteer Battalion Sherwood Foresters under General Order 39 of April 1887 and transferred to the Territorial Force in 1908 as 5th Battalion Sherwood Foresters. Both Derby and Repton Schools at the same time joined the OTC.

2nd Volunteer Battalion The 2nd Derbyshire Rifle Volunteer Corps at Bakewell had ten companies: 'A' (Chesterfield), 'B' (Chapel-en-le-Frith), 'C' (Ashbourne), 'D' (Bakewell), 'E' (Wirksworth), 'F' (Matlock), 'G' (Clay Cross), 'H' (Whaley Bridge), 'I' (Hartington) and 'K' (Staveley). Headquarters were at Bakewell. Re-designation as 2nd Volunteer Battalion was notified by General Order 39 of April 1887. Headquarters moved from Bakewell to Chesterfield in 1898 and in 1900 three new companies (two at Chesterfield, one Buxton) were formed. Transfer to the Territorial Force in 1908 was as 6th Battalion Sherwood Foresters.

1st Nottinghamshire (Robin Hood) Volunteer Rifle Corps In the Army List for October 1859, five separate companies of unnumbered rifle volunteers are shown as having been formed at Nottingham. In that for December the five now appear as having been amalgamated under the title of The Robin Hood Rifle Volunteer Corps, the officers' commissions being dated 15 November 1859. By March 1860 the corps had been designated as the 1st Nottinghamshire (Robin Hood) RVC and comprised nine companies, a former Rifle Brigade officer, Robert Crawford, being appointed as lieutenant-colonel commandant. The corps became a volunteer battalion (without change in title) of the Sherwood Foresters in 1881. By 1881 the Robin Hoods comprised ten companies, an eleventh was added in 1895, a twelfth, a year later, and in 1900/01 a further six brought the establishment up to eighteen companies. These were then divided equally into two battalions. A cadet corps was also formed at this time by Nottingham High School. Transfer to the Territorial Force in 1908 was as 7th Battalion Sherwood Foresters, the Nottingham High School Cadet Corps at the same time becoming part of the OTC. The photograph shown at **(459)** was taken in the 24 Moorgate Street, New Radford studio of EA Carnell and shows a volunteer of the 1st Nottinghamshire RVC wearing a green uniform with black facings.

459

4th (Nottinghamshire) Volunteer Battalion The 2nd Nottinghamshire Rifle Volunteer Corps at East Retford had eight companies: 'A' (East Retford), 'B' and 'C' (Newark), 'D' (Mansfield), 'E' (Thorney Wood Chase), 'F' (Collingham), 'G' (Worksop) and 'H' (Southwell). In 1887, under General Order 39 of April, the 2nd Corps was re-designated as 4th (Nottinghamshire) Volunteer Battalion Sherwood Foresters, headquarters transferring to Newark in 1890. Two cadet corps were associated with the battalion: Worksop College in 1900 and the Queen Elizabeth School at Mansfield in 1906. Transfer to the Territorial Force in 1908 was as 8th Battalion Sherwood Foresters, both Worksop College and Queen Elizabeth School at the same time joining the OTC.

1st Cadet Battalion: *Headquarters:* 48-50 St James's Street, Nottingham. Affiliated to 7th Battalion.

Illustration credits: Anne SK Brown Military Collection, Brown University Library (455), Bruce Bassett-Powell and Bob Bennet (453)

LOYAL NORTH LANCASHIRE REGIMENT

47th (Lancashire) Regiment

Raised 1741 in Scotland, the 47th was known by two of its colonels' names prior to 1751, Sir John Mordaunt and Peregrine Lascelles who was appointed 13 March 1743. Lancashire was added to the numerical title in 1782, the 47th providing the 1st Battalion Loyal North Lancashire Regiment in 1881. White facings were worn. The Royal Crest, which was also that of the Duchy of Lancaster, is displayed on a button found at Ticonderoga which dates this device prior to 1781 when the regiment returned home from America. The Red Rose of Lancaster was also a feature of a shoulder-belt plate dated pre-1855.

81st (Loyal Lincoln Volunteers) Regiment

Raised 1793 in Lincolnshire by Major-General Albemarle Bertie, 9th Earl of Lindsey whose commission was dated 19 September 1793. During its first year of existence the 81st also held the title of Loyal Lincoln Volunteers, but this was absent for the period 1794 to 1833 when it was once again seen in the Army List. All three words were in respect of the fact that the regiment had been raised almost entirely from men of the Lincoln Militia. The regiment, which wore buff facings, provided the 2nd Battalion Loyal North Lancashire Regiment in 1881.

Regular Battalions

1st and 2nd Battalions The 1st Battalion was formed by the 47th (Lancashire) Regiment, the 2nd by the 81st (Loyal Lincoln Volunteers) Regiment. The painting showing a detail from the regiment being inspected by an officer in **(460)** is by Richard Simkin and was produced as part of the series of supplements published with the *Army and Navy Gazette*. Illustration **(461)**, this time by Harry Payne, is the original artwork supplied to Gale & Polden for one of their uniform postcard series. The royal crest, red rose of Lancaster and City of Lincoln arms badge are seen in **(462)**. Members of 'B' Company, 2nd Battalion are seen in a photograph taken in 1897 **(463)**, the group including one man wearing the crossed axes badge of a pioneer, another, in the back row, with a patch of scarlet cloth on his left shoulder to protect the uniform from the rifle when at the shoulder arms position.

Militia Battalions

3rd and 4th Battalions Formed by the 3rd Royal Lancashire Militia (The Duke of Lancaster's Own) with headquarters at Preston. The battalions were amalgamated as 3rd Battalion in 1896.

Territorial Battalions

4th Battalion Formed by the former 1st Volunteer Battalion with headquarters at St

Winifred Street, Preston, moving to 97 Avenham Lane, Preston in 1913. The companies were located: 'A' (Preston), 'B' (Longridge), 'C' (Preston and Bamber Bridge), 'D' (Preston and Leyland), 'E' (Lytham), 'F' (Horwich) and 'G', 'H' (Chorley). The Arnold House School Cadet Corps at South Shore, Blackpool was affiliated.

5th Battalion Formed from the former 2nd Volunteer Battalion at Bolton. The companies were located: 'A', 'B', 'C' (Bolton), 'D' (Farnworth), 'E' (Bolton), 'F' (Astley Bridge), 'G' (Hindley) and 'H' (Little Hulton).

Volunteer Battalions

1st Volunteer Battalion The 11th Lancashire Rifle Volunteer Corps had nine companies: 'A' to 'E' (Preston), 'F' (Leyland) and 'G', 'H' and 'J' (Chorley). Headquarters were in Preston. Re-designation as 1st Volunteer Battalion Loyal North Lancashire Regiment was notified by General Order 14 of February 1883. Two new companies were sanctioned in 1900 and transfer to the Territorial Force in 1908 was as 4th Battalion Loyal North Lancashire Regiment. An other ranks glengarry badge is shown in **(464)**.

2nd Volunteer Battalion The 14th Lancashire Rifle Volunteer Corps at Bolton was re-designated 2nd Volunteer Battalion Loyal North Lancashire Regiment in 1883. In the same year 'L' and 'M' (Farnworth) Companies of the 4th Corps were transferred to the battalion. Two new companies were sanctioned in 1900 and transfer to the Territorial Force in 1908 was as 5th Battalion Loyal North Lancashire Regiment.

Illustration Credits: Alan Seymore (463), Anne SK Brown Military Collection, Brown University Library (461), Bruce Bassett-Powell and Bob Bennet (462)

NORTHAMPTONSHIRE REGIMENT

48th (Northamptonshire) Regiment

Raised in 1741, the regiment would be known by the following names of its colonels prior to 1751: James Cholmondely, Lord Henry Beauclerk, Francis Ligonier, Henry Seymour Conway, George Byng (3rd Viscount Torrington) and William Home (8th Earl Home). Northamptonshire was added to the numerical title in 1782, the 48th providing the 1st Battalion Northamptonshire Regiment in 1881. Uniform facings and linings were buff. Major H G Parkyn, in his book *(Military) Shoulder-Belt Plates and Buttons,* illustrates an officers' oval gilt plate which has the two lions and castle tower from the arms of Northampton. He dates the item at c1792.

58th (Rutlandshire) Regiment

Raised as the 60th Regiment by Colonel John Anstruther under a letter of service dated 28 December 1755 and re-numbered as 58th in 1757. The uniforms were red with black facings, buff waistcoats and linings. From the facing colour the regiment acquired the nickname The Black Cuffs. Rutlandshire was added to the title in 1782, the 58th providing the 2nd Battalion Northamptonshire Regiment in 1881. The Gibraltar Castle, Key and motto *(Montis insignia Calpe,* The badge of the Rock of Gibraltar) were authorized as a badge on 2 May 1836, the 58th having served during the defence of the Rock between 1779-83. Another badge, the Sphinx superscribed Egypt, was permitted in July 1802.

Regular Battalions

1st and 2nd Battalions The 1st Battalion was formed by the 48th (Northamptonshire) Regiment, the 2nd by the 58th (Rutlandshire) Regiment. In Harry Payne's original artwork for one of Gale & Polden's postcards, an officer returns the salute of a sentry **(465)**. Illustration **(466)** by Richard Simkin shows a mounted officer, his bugle by his side awaiting orders, reviewing a march past. In **(467)**, **(468)** and **(469)**, three photographs of the 1st Battalion taken at Poona, India in 1908, the drums, Sergeant Major JJ Christie and the machine gun section.

Militia Battalions

3rd and 4th Battalions Formed from the Northamptonshire and Rutland Militia with headquarters at Northampton. The two were amalgamated as 3rd Battalion in 1899.

Territorial Battalion

4th Battalion Formed from the former 1st Volunteer Battalion with headquarters at 83 Sheep Street, Northampton, moving in 1913 to Territorial Headquarters, Clare Street. The eight companies were located: 'A' (Northampton), 'B' (Northampton, Daventry and Weedon), 'C' (Northampton, Althorp Park, Long Buckby and Harpole), 'D' (Northampton), 'E' (Wellingborough and Finedon), 'F' (Kettering), 'G' (Desborough and Rothwell) and 'H' (Higham Ferrers, Rushden and Irthlingborough). The King's School Peterborough Cadet Corps and Northampton School Cadet Corps were affiliated.

Volunteer Battalion

1st Volunteer Battalion With headquarters at Northampton, the 1st Northamptonshire Rifle

Volunteer Corps had thirteen companies: 'A' (Althorp), 'B' (Towcester), 'C' to 'G' (Northampton), 'H' and 'I' (Peterborough), 'K' and 'L' (Wellingborough), 'M' (Daventry) and 'N' (Kettering). Re-designation as 1st Volunteer Battalion Northamptonshire Regiment was notified in General Order 181 of December 1887. Three new companies were added in 1900. The Wellingborough Grammar School Cadet Corps was formed and affiliated in 1900, then Oundle School Cadet Corps in 1902. Transfer to the Territorial Force in 1908 was as 4th Battalion Northamptonshire Regiment. Two of the Peterborough companies, however, were converted to artillery, under the title of Northamptonshire Battery RFA, and as supply and transport troops, the East Midland Brigade Company ASC. Wellingborough and Oundle Schools became contingents of the Junior Division, OTC. Illustration **(470)** shows a member of the battalion in grey uniform with scarlet facings.

Photo Credit: Anne SK Brown Military Collection, Brown University Library (465)

PRINCESS CHARLOTTE OF WALES'S (ROYAL BERKSHIRE REGIMENT)

49th (Hertfordshire) (Princess Charlotte of Wales's) Regiment

The regiment was known by one name, Colonel Edward Trelawny's, from its formation in 1743 until 1751. Hertfordshire was added to the numerical title in 1782, the Princess of Wales giving her name in 1816. The 49th provided the 1st Battalion Princess Charlotte of Wales's (Berkshire Regiment) in 1881. Regimental facing were at first described as full green, but Lincoln green was the colour in use at 1881. For its services during the China War of 1840-42, the 49th were awarded their Dragon badge.

66th (Berkshire) Regiment

Raised 1756 as 2nd Battalion 19th Regiment and regimented as 66th two years later. Berkshire was added to the title in 1782, the 66th providing the 2nd Battalion Princess Charlotte of Wales's (Royal Berkshire Regiment) in 1881. The Royal title was added in 1885. Various shades of green facings have been worn from formation and up until 1881: yellowish green, gosling green, emerald green and grass green.

Regular Battalions

1st and 2nd Battalions 1st Battalion formed by the 49th (Hertfordshire) (Princess Charlotte of Wales's) Regiment, the 2nd from the 66th (Berkshire) Regiment. In Bruce Bassett-Powell's detailed illustration **(471)** we see the dragon badge of the 49th Regiment, the helmet plate displaying a former badge of the Royal Berkshire Militia, a stag under and oak tree. The cap badge is shown in illustration **(472)** and an example of the officers' forage cap in **(473)**. Richard Simkin's painting showing a mixed group of officers and other ranks was published as a supplement to the *Army and Navy Gazette's* on 1 December 1894 **(474)**, the Harry Payne original in **(475)** becoming one of the postcards published by Gale & Polden.

Militia Battalion

3rd Battalion From the Royal Berkshire Militia with headquarters at Reading. Illustration **(476)** shows the band of the 3rd Battalion at Pernham Camp in 1913.

Territorial Battalion

4th Battalion Formed from the former 1st Volunteer Battalion with headquarters at St Mary's Butts, Reading. The eight companies were located: 'A' (Reading and Englefield), 'B' (Reading), 'C' (Wantage and Wallingford), 'D' (Windsor), 'E' (Newbury, Bucklebury, Aldermaston and Hungerford), 'F' (Abingdon), 'G' (Maidenhead) and 'H' (Wokingham). There were also the following cadet units affiliated: 1st Cadet Company at Maidenhead County Boys School, the Reading Cadet Company at Elm Lodge Avenue and the Windsor Cadet Companies which were located at the County Boys' School in Windsor.

Volunteer Battalion

1st Volunteer Battalion With headquarters at Reading, the 1st Berkshire Rifle Volunteer Corps had thirteen companies: 'A', 'B' and 'C' (Reading), 'D' (Windsor), 'E' (Newbury), 'F' (Abingdon), 'G' (Maidenhead), 'H' (Sandhurst), 'I' (Faringdon), 'K' (Wantage), 'L' (Winkfield), 'M' (Wallingford) and 'N' (Windsor Great Park). The corps was re-designated as 1st Volunteer Battalion Berkshire Regiment in 1882—the title 'Royal' not being conferred upon that regiment until three years later in 1885. A Mounted Infantry Company was formed in 1886, the total number of

companies amounting to fifteen by April 1897. Several cadet corps were formed and affiliated to the battalion: Wellington College Cadet Corps (formed in 1882) Bradfield College, which appeared in 1884, and a unit raised in the East Berkshire parish of Cookham Dean in 1900—the latter gone from the Army List, however, by July 1902. Transfer to the Territorial Force in 1908 was as 4th Battalion Royal Berkshire Regiment, both Wellington and Bradfield Colleges at the same time becoming contingents of the Junior Division OTC. Illustration **(477)** shows a member of the mounted infantry company wearing a leather ammunition bandolier and a dark blue uniform.

Illustration credits: Anne SK Brown Military Collection, Brown University Library (474), Bruce Bassett-Powell and Bob Bennet (471) and (473)

QUEEN'S OWN (ROYAL WEST KENT REGIMENT)

50th (Queen's Own) Regiment

When James Abercrombie raised his regiment in 1755, it was numbered as 52nd. Re-numbering as 50th was in 1757, West Kent being added to the title in 1782. After service in Jamaica, 1819-1827, the 50th returned home where new Colours were presented by the Duchess of Clarence. The Duke of Clarence's was then added to the title, this changing to Queen's Own with a change of facings from black to dark blue in 1831. The 50th provided the 1st Battalion Queen's Own (Royal West Kent Regiment) in 1881. There are two recorded cases where the regiment's number was reflected in nicknames. While in Egypt in 1801, many of the men suffered from ophthalmia which led to the name Blind Half Hundred. But during the Peninsular War it would be their black cuffs that caused the regiment to be known in the army as The Dirty Half Hundred. Wiping sweat away, the facing colour had left its mark on the faces of the heat-suffering troops. The Royal Crest was an old badge of the 50th, the Sphinx superscribed Egypt being authorized in 1802 for services the year before. With the Duke of Clarence title in 1827, also came his Cypher and Coronet.

97th (Earl of Ulster's) Regiment

Raised 1824 as the 97th Regiment, adding Earl of Ulster's to the title two years later. The facings were sky-blue, the colour of the ribbon of the Order of St Patrick, which led to the nickname the Celestials. The 97th provided the 2nd Battalion Queen's Own (Royal West Kent Regiment) in 1881.

Regular Battalions

1st and 2nd Battalions The 1st Battalion was from the 50th (Queen's Own) Regiment, the 2nd from the 97th (Earl of Ulster's) Regiment. An officers' helmet plate, collar badges, button and waist-belt plate are shown in **(478)**, illustration **(479)** being a good example of an officer's forage cap and badge. An officer's post 1902 helmet is shown in **(480)**. For supplement No 86 in the series produced for the *Army and Navy Gazette,* artist Richard Simkin

chose a rear view of the 2nd Battalion (note the painted identification of the packs) on a route march led by two mounted officers along a country lane **(481)**. The image was published on 2 February 1895. For one of Gale & Polden's postcard sets, J McNeill illustrated a colour sergeant talking to a private **(482)**, both the men wearing medals indicating service during the Second Boar War. It was the 2nd Battalion that sailed for South Africa on the *Bavarian* on 16 March 1900. Harry Payne's original artwork for the same company chose a study of a sergeant who also wears the Queen's and King's Medals for South Africa **(483)**.

Militia Battalions

3rd and 4th Battalions Formed by the West Kent Militia with headquarters at Maidstone. The two were amalgamated as 3rd Battalion in 1884.

Territorial Battalions

4th Battalion Formed from part of the former 1st Volunteer Battalion with headquarters at Tonbridge. The companies were located: 'A' (Maidstone), 'B' (Maidstone and West Malling), 'C' (Tonbridge and Hadlow), 'D', 'E' (Tunbridge Wells), 'F' (Orpington), 'G' (Sevenoaks) and 'H' (Westerham and Edenbridge). The Westerham and Chipstead Cadet Corps was affiliated.

5th Battalion Formed from part of the former 1st Volunteer Battalion with headquarters in East Street, Bromley. The companies were located: 'A', 'B' (Bromley), 'C' (Dartford), 'D' (Beckenham), 'E' (Sidcup and Dartford), 'F', 'G' (Chatham and Cliffe-at-Hoo) and 'H' (Swanley). The 1st Chatham Cadet Company RMLI at the Royal Marines barracks in Chatham was affiliated.

Volunteer Battalions

1st Volunteer Battalion With headquarters at Tonbridge the 1st Kent Rifle Volunteer Corps had eight companies: 'A' and 'B' (Maidstone), 'C' (Tonbridge), 'D' (Tunbridge Wells), 'E' (Penshurst), 'F' (Leeds Castle), 'G' (Sevenoaks) and 'H' (Westerham). Under General Order 14 of February 1883 the 1st Corps was re-designated as 1st Volunteer Battalion Queen's Own (Royal West Kent Regiment). The establishment was increased to eleven companies in 1900. Several cadet corps were formed and affiliated to the battalion: Skinner's School at Tunbridge Wells in 1901, a company at Westerham in 1904 and Maidstone Grammar School in 1906. Transfer to the Territorial Force in 1908 was as both the 4th and 5th Battalions Queen's Own (Royal West Kent Regiment), the Skinner's and Maidstone Schools at the same time joining the OTC.

2nd Volunteer Battalion With headquarters at Blackheath the 3rd Kent (West Kent) Rifle Volunteer Corps had eleven companies: 'A' and 'B' (Lee), 'C' and 'D' (Dartford), 'E' (Greenwich), 'F' (Bromley), 'G' and 'H' (Blackheath), 'I' (Deptford), 'K' (Charlton) and 'L' (Deptford). General Order 14 of February 1883 directed re-designation as 2nd Volunteer Battalion Queen's Own (Royal West Kent Regiment). By 1900 the strength of the battalion stood at thirteen companies and in that year the Proprietary School in Blackheath, and Quernmore School at Bromley, were affiliated. Transfer to the Territorial Force in 1908 was as part of the 20th Battalion London Regiment, Quernmore School at the same time becoming part of the OTC.

3rd Volunteer Battalion The 4th Kent (Royal Arsenal) RVC with an establishment of ten companies was re-designated as 3rd Volunteer Battalion Queen's Own (Royal West Kent Regiment) in 1883 and became part of the 20th Battalion London Regiment upon transfer to the Territorial Force in 1908.

4th Volunteer Battalion Formed with headquarters at Chatham on 27 April 1900 with nine companies and disbanded in 1908. The Borden School Cadet Corps was attached in 1903 but removed from Army List in November 1906—the officers, however, now appear under New College Schools (affiliated to 1st VB Buffs) at Herne Bay.

Cadet Battalion

1st Cadet Battalion Headquarters at 241 Stanstead Road, Forest Hill. Affiliated to 5th Battalion.

Illustration credits: Anne SK Brown Military Collection, Brown University Library (482) and (6), Bruce Bassett-Powell and Bob Bennet (478) and (479)

KING'S OWN (YORKSHIRE LIGHT INFANTRY)

51st (2nd Yorkshire, West Riding, King's Own Light Infantry) Regiment

Raised in 1755, the regiment was, notes Chichester and Burges Short, 'Yorkshire from its birth', letters of service for its formation having been issued to Yorkshire magnates Lord Rockingham and Sir Henry Savile. The regiment was originally numbered as 53rd, its first colonel being Robert Napier, and then re-numbered as 51st in 1757. Yorkshire was added to the title in 1782 and Light Infantry in 1809 after returning from Corunna the previous year. Further honour came with the addition of King's Own in 1821. The 51st provided the 1st Battalion King's Own Yorkshire Light Infantry (South Yorkshire Regiment) in 1881. The regiment's facings were at first described as sea green, later as dull green. With the King's title in 1821 came blue. The White Rose of York was an old badge, the French bugle-horn rather than the usual type being chosen, according to some accounts, after Waterloo where the 51st defeated a French regiment of mounted chasseurs whose badge it was. On Minden Day (1st August) roses decorated the hats and drums in memory of the battle there in 1759.

105th (Madras Light Infantry) Regiment

Raised at Arnee, India in 1839 as the Honourable East India Company's 2nd Madras European Regiment. Re-designated as 105th (Madras Light Infantry) in 1861, the regiment provided the 2nd Battalion King's Own Light Infantry (South Yorkshire Regiment) in 1881. The regiment had been employed during the expedition into the interior of Arabia during October to December 1873 and came to England for the first time in the following year. The uniform facings were pale buff.

The original title in 1881 was the King's Own Light Infantry (South Yorkshire Regiment), but this was changed to the above in 1887.

Regular Battalions

1st and 2nd Battalions 1st Battalion from the 51st (2nd Yorkshire, West Riding, King's Own Light Infantry) Regiment, the 2nd from the 105th (Madras Light Infantry) Regiment. The regiment's French horn and rose badge can be seen on the front of the officers' forage cap illustrated in **(484)** and again as collar badges in a Harry Payne postcard produced by Gale & Polden **(485)**. Both are also visible in a cigarette card featuring Frederick William Holmes who with the 2nd Battalion won the Victoria Cross at Le Cateau on 26 August 1914 **(486)**. The Minden Day celebration has been mentioned above, illustration **(487)** being a photograph taken at Aldershot on 1 August 1909. Illustration **(488)** is that by Richard Simkin which was published on 2 March 1895 as supplement No 87 with the *Army and Navy Gazette*.

Militia Battalion

3rd Battalion Formed from the 1st West Yorkshire Militia with headquarters at Pontefract.

Territorial Battalions

4th Battalion Formed from part of the former 1st Volunteer Battalion with headquarters at Wakefield. The companies were located: 'A', 'B' (Wakefield), 'C' (Normanton), 'D' (Ossett), 'E', 'F' (Dewsbury), 'G' (Batley) and 'H'

(Morley). Within days of war being declared in August 1914 territorial battalions were divided so as to separate those within their ranks who were willing to serve overseas from those that weren't. In this way a 1st Battalion was formed, this being indicated in the title by e.g. 1/4th. The 2nd, which was made up of those remaining at home to act in a recruiting and training role, becoming 2/4th. The postcard illustrated **(489)** was produced by the Wakefield company of Sanderson & Clayton.

5th Battalion Formed from part of the former 1st Volunteer Battalion with headquarters at French Gate, Doncaster. The companies were: 'A' (Pontefract), 'B', 'C' (Doncaster), 'D' (Goole), 'E' (Featherstone), 'F' (Doncaster), 'G' (Conisbrough) and 'H' (Castleford).

Volunteer Battalion

1st Volunteer Battalion With headquarters at Wakefield, the 5th Yorkshire (West Riding) Rifle Volunteer Corps had ten companies: 'A', 'B', 'C' and 'D' (Wakefield), 'E' (Goole), 'F', 'G' and 'H' (Dewsbury) and 'J' and 'K'

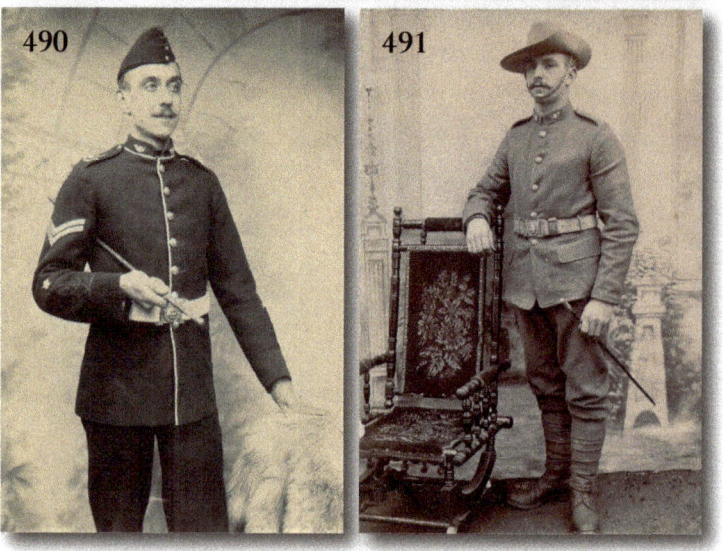

(Batley). Re-designated as 1st Volunteer Battalion King's Own Light Infantry (South Yorkshire Regiment) was in February 1883, the regiment itself being re-designated King's Own Yorkshire Light Infantry in 1887. Company locations by 1908 were: Wakefield (3), Normanton (1), Goole (1), Dewsbury (2), Ossett (1) and Batley (2) and transfer to the Territorial Force in 1908 saw the Wakefield, Dewsbury, Ossett and Batley companies as 4th Battalion King's Own (Yorkshire Light Infantry), while those from Normanton and Goole provided part of the 5th. Illustrations **(490)** and **(491)** are photographs of two members of the battalion, the latter being taken at the studio of CH Howes of Pontefract.

Illustration credit: Bruce Bassett-Powell and Bob Bennet (484)

KING'S (SHROPSHIRE LIGHT INFANTRY)

53rd (Shropshire) Regiment

The regiment was raised as 55th under a letter of service dated 21st December 1755. Its colonel was William Whitmore (he was in his second term as Member of Parliament for Bridgnorth) and the uniforms were red with red facings and yellow linings. Re-numbering as 53rd was in 1757, the Shropshire designation added in 1782. The 53rd provided the 1st Battalion King's Light Infantry (Shropshire Regiment) in 1881. The regiment's red facings led to the nickname The Brickdusts, Napoleon, as the regiment guarded the French leader at St Helena, referred to the 53rd as the Red Regiment. In 1768 the regiment was ordered to exchange their red facings for white.

85th (Bucks Volunteers) (King's Light Infantry) Regiment

Raised 1794 by Colonel (later Field-Marshal) Sir George Nugent chiefly in and around the estates of the Marquis of Buckingham. Light Infantry was added to the title in 1808 and the Duke of York's Own in 1815. The Duke having become king, the title in 1821 was amended to that above. The 85th provided the 2nd Battalion King's Light Infantry (Shropshire Regiment) in 1881. In the early 1820's, the 84th was given the privilege of not having to drink the King's health or to stand when the National Anthem was played. Officers of the regiment had come to the King's aid when he was in danger of being attacked by a mob while visiting Brighton. Yellow facings were at first worn, the royal connection of 1821 seeing a change to blue. Bugle-horn badges were introduced after 1808.

The original 1881 title was the King's Light Infantry (Shropshire Regiment), but this was changed to the above in 1882.

Regular Battalions

1st and 2nd Battalions The 1st Battalion was formed by the 53rd (Shropshire) Regiment, the 2nd by the 85th (Bucks Volunteers) (King's Light Infantry) Regiment. In some regiments the plate used on the old shako was retained after the helmet was introduced in 1878. Here in illustration **(492)** we see then worn by the band of the 1st Battalion. The second photograph **(493)** was taken at the same time and it shows two officers and six sergeants of 'B' Company, 1st Battalion. Glengarry caps are worn, one of the officers having a forage cap still with the old 53 numerals. Both photographs were taken at Chatham in 1881. Harry Payne's original artwork for a Gale & Polden postcard includes the star pattern helmet plate eventually adopted by the regiment, also the bugle horn collar badges that included the letters KSLI **(494)**. An officers' forage cap is shown in **(495)**, illustration **(496)** being Richard Simkin's supplement No 88 published on 6 April 1895 with the *Army and Navy Gazette*.

Militia Battalions

3rd Battalion Formed by the Shropshire Militia with headquarters at Shrewsbury.

4th Battalion Formed by the Herefordshire Militia with headquarters at Hereford. Disbanded in 1908.

Territorial Battalions

4th Battalion Formed from the former 1st and 2nd Volunteer Battalions with headquarters at Shrewsbury. The eight companies were located: 'A' (Shrewsbury), 'B' (Whitchurch and Wem), 'C' (Wellington, Market Drayton and Hodnet), 'D' (Ironbridge and Much Wenlock), 'E' (Shifnal, Oakengates and Newport), 'F' (Bridgnorth and Highley), 'G' (Ludlow, Craven Arms, Cleehill and Cleobury Mortimer) and 'H' (Oswestry and Ellesmere). The Bridgnorth Cadet Company at Eimslea, Bridgnorth was attached.

Herefordshire Battalion See 1st Herefordshire Volunteer Rifle Corps below.

Volunteer Battalions

1st Volunteer Battalion The 1st Shropshire Rifle Volunteer Corps had eight companies: 'A' and 'B' (Shrewsbury), 'C' (Condover), 'D' (Ironbridge), 'E' (Shifnal), 'F' (Bridgnorth), 'G' (Ludlow) and 'H' (Cleobury Mortimer). Headquarters were in Shrewsbury. Re-designation as 1st Volunteer Battalion King's (Shropshire Light Infantry) was notified in General Order 181 of December 1887. The Shrewsbury School Cadet Corps and the Bridgnorth Cadet Corps were formed and affiliated in 1900, the Shrewsbury Town Cadet Corps in 1906. Transfer to the Territorial Force in 1908 was as part of 4th Battalion King's (Shropshire Light Infantry), the Shrewsbury School Cadets at the same time joining the OTC.

2nd Volunteer Battalion The 2nd Shropshire Rifle Volunteer Corps had seven companies: 'A' (Market Drayton), 'B' (Whitchurch), 'C' (Wellington), 'D' (Hodnet), 'E' (Wem), 'F' (Oswestry) and 'G' (Newport). Headquarters were at Newport and an 'H' Company was added at Ellesmere in 1885. Re-designation as 2nd Volunteer Battalion was in 1887 under General Order 181 of December. The Ellesmere College Cadet Corps was formed and affiliated in 1900 and transfer to the Territorial Force was as part of 4th Battalion King's (Shropshire Light Infantry), Ellesmere College at the same time joining the OTC.

1st Herefordshire Volunteer Rifle Corps The 1st Herefordshire Rifle Volunteers was formed with headquarters at Hereford on 20 February 1861 and by 1881 comprised: 'A' Company at (Hereford), 'B' (Ross-on-Wye), 'C' (Ledbury), 'D' (Bromyard), 'E' (Ross-on-Wye), 'F' (Leominster), 'G' (Kington), 'H' (Hereford), 'I' (Presteigne) and 'K' (Rhayader). There was also a half-company at Hereford. The corps became a volunteer battalion (without change of title) of the King's Shropshire Light Infantry in 1881 and in the same year the two Ross companies ('B' and 'E') were merged as 'B'. A new 'E' Company was formed at Weobley in 1889. Also, in 1889 a Bearer Company was formed at Hereford to serve the Welsh Border Infantry Brigade. This company, as no authorization had been received to increase the establishment of the battalion, formed part of 'A' Company. In 1905 several further changes in organisation took place: 'L' Company was added at Hereford from members of the Cyclist Section created there in 1888, and 'M' was formed at Ruardean. An amalgamation between 'I' and 'G' Companies took place and the Bearer Company was constituted as a separate unit designated Welsh Border Brigade Company RAMC (Vols.). In 1902 the Hereford Cathedral School applied to the War Office to form a cadet corps which was affiliated to the 1st Herefordshire RVC on 28 March 1903. Transfer to the Territorial Force was as the Herefordshire Battalion King's (Shropshire Light Infantry); this was changed after a few months, however, to the Herefordshire Regiment. Hereford Cathedral School became a contingent of the OTC.

Illustration credits: Alan Seymore (492), (493), Anne SK Brown Military Collection, Brown University Library (494), Bruce Bassett-Powell and Bob Bennet (495)

DUKE OF CAMBRIDGE'S OWN (MIDDLESEX REGIMENT)

57th (West Middlesex) Regiment

Raised 1755 in Somersetshire and Gloucestershire as the 59th Regiment with John Arabin as colonel. His commission was dated 27 December 1755 and the red coats had yellow facings. Re-numbered as 57th in 1757, West Middlesex was added to the title in 1782. In 1881 the 57th provided the 1st Battalion Duke of Cambridge's Own (Middlesex Regiment). With the battle honour Albuhera had come a laurel wreath for use on badges and appointments. The Middlesex county arms of three seaxes also featured.

77th (East Middlesex) Regiment

Raised in 1787, the 77th received the additional title East Middlesex in 1807 and Duke of Cambridge's Own in 1876. Five years later it provided the 2nd Battalion Duke of Cambridge's Own (Middlesex Regiment). Yellow facings were worn. The Prince of Wales's plumes, Coronet and *Ich Dien* (I Serve) motto were granted in 1810, followed by the Duke of Cambridge's Cypher and Coronet being authorized as a badge in 1876.

Regular Battalions

1st, 2nd, 3rd and 4th Battalions The 1st Battalion was formed by the 57th (West Middlesex) Regiment, the 2nd by the 77th (East Regiment) Regiment. Both the 3rd and 4th were raised in 1900. Bruce Bassett-Powell's detailed image illustrates how the several badges of the 57th and 77th Regiments were incorporated into the helmet plate, collar badges, buttons and waist-belt plates **(497)**. Illustration **(498)** is a representation of the cap badge. An officers' forage cap can be seen in **(499)**, Richard Simkin including this headdress in his 'Military Types' series for the *Army and Navy Gazette* **(500)**. Illustrations **(501)** and **(502)** are from old Gale & Polden postcards, one by Harry Payne, the second from Ernest Ibbetson. In what could possibly be a photograph of three brothers, one man wears the brass arm badge of a scout **(503)**.

Militia Battalions

3rd, later 5th Battalion In 1881 the Royal Elthorne, or 5th Middlesex Militia provided the 3rd Battalion which in 1900 was re-numbered as 5th. Headquarters were at Hounslow.

4th, later 6th Battalion The Royal East Middlesex Militia had its headquarters at Hounslow, and this became the 4th Battalion in 1881. Re-designation as 6th was in 1900 upon the formation of the new regular battalion.

Territorial Battalions

7th Battalion Formed by the former 1st Volunteer Battalion with headquarters in Priory Road, Hornsey. The eight companies were located: 'A' (Hampstead), 'B' (Barnet), 'C' (Hornsey), 'D' (Highgate), 'E' (Tottenham), 'F' (Enfield Lock and Enfield Town), 'G' (Tottenham) and 'H' (Hornsey). The Christ's College Finchley Cadet Company, Friern Barnet School Cadet Company, Harringay Cadet Company and Tollington School Cadet Company were affiliated to the battalion. Both the 7th and 8th Battalions were 'Imperial Service' battalions which means that 90% of the battalion had volunteered to serve overseas if required. In this photograph **(504)** of the 7th Battalion drums and fifes at Falmer camp in 1912, most wear the white metal Imperial Service broach (see insert) on the right breast of their tunics.

8th Battalion Formed from the former 2nd Volunteer Battalion with headquarters at Whitton Park in Hounslow, moving in 1911 to 202a Hanworth Road, Hounslow. The companies were located: 'A' (Twickenham), 'B' (Brentford), 'C' (Hounslow), 'D' (Southall), 'E' (Uxbridge), 'F' (Ealing), 'G' (Hampton) and 'H' (Stains). The Ealing Cadet Company, Ealing County School Cadet Company and Mall School Cadet Company at 185 Hampton Road, Twickenham were affiliated.

9th Battalion Formed from the former 5th Middlesex Rifle Volunteer Corps with headquarters in Henry Street, St John's Wood moving in 1911 to Pound Lane, Willesden. The companies were located: 'A', 'B' (Willesden), 'C' (Willesden and Stanmore), 'D', 'E' (Willesden), 'F' (Harrow), 'G' (Wealdstone) and 'H' (Hendon). The Harrow Cadet Company, Kilburn Grammar School Cadet Company and

Sunbury House School Cadet Company were affiliated. The photograph at **(505)** was taken at a Harrow School Speech Day, members of the 9th Battalion forming a guard of honour.

10th Battalion The 10th Battalion was considered a new unit in 1908, although much of the strength was made up of former members of the 2nd Middlesex Rifle Volunteer Corps. Headquarters were at Stamford Brook Lodge, Ravenscourt Park and the companies located: 'A' (St John's College, Battersea), 'B' (St Mark's College, Chelsea) and 'C' to 'H' (Ravenscourt Park). The Acton Cadet Company and Bedford Park Cadet Company were affiliated, recognition of the latter, however, was withdrawn in 1913 (Army Order 187), but then given again in 1914 (Army Order 511).

Volunteer Battalions

1st Volunteer Battalion The 3rd Middlesex Rifle Volunteer Corps had nine companies: 'A', 'B' (Hampstead), 'C' (Barnet), 'D' (Hornsey), 'E', F' (Highgate), 'G' (Tottenham) and 'H' and 'I' (Enfield Lock). Headquarters were at Crouch End, Hornsey. A new company ('K') was added at Enfield Town in September 1881. Sanction to form a drill station attached to 'A' and 'B' (Hampstead) Companies at Hendon was obtained from the War Office in 1884, the first drill taking place at the Assembly Rooms, the Burroughs in the beginning of February 1885. In the same year, 'D' (Hornsey) Company began recruiting in Southgate, Wood Green and Finsbury Park. The new Southgate detachment carried out drills in the Village Hall. 'E' and 'F' (Highgate) Companies also recruited at North Finchley. The corps was

designated 1st Volunteer Battalion Middlesex Regiment in 1898. The Highgate School Cadet Corps was affiliated in 1883 but with no officers appointed, this was removed from the Army List by the end of 1884. The school appears again, however, in 1892. As a result of the war in South Africa permission was received to increase the battalion's establishment by three companies, the total establishment by the end of 1900 being now: Hampstead and Barnet, one company each; Hornsey four, Highgate two, Tottenham three and Enfield two. Transfer to the Territorial Force was as 7th Battalion Middlesex Regiment, Highgate School at the same time joining the Junior Division, OTC. In this colour plate from *Records of the Third Middlesex Rifle Volunteers* by ET Evans **(506)** we see a group of officers in, from left to right, undress, full dress and mess dress. The uniforms are described by the author as, 'Light grey, trimmed and edged with grey braid, small scarlet piping on forage cap and on mess-jacket, stripe on trousers, scarlet. Brown belts, silver ornaments. Brown gloves. Mess waistcoat, scarlet.'

2nd Volunteer Battalion With headquarters at Whitton Park, Hounslow the 8th Middlesex Rifle Volunteer Corps had eight companies: 'A', 'B', 'C', 'D' (Hounslow), 'E' (Uxbridge), 'F' (Ealing), 'G' (Sunbury) and 'H' (Stains). Re-designation as 2nd Volunteer Battalion Middlesex Regiment was in 1887. The Ealing Schools Cadet Corps was formed and affiliated in 1901 and an increase in establishment to ten companies was authorised in 1900, but this was reduced back to eight four years later. Transfer to the

Territorial Force was as 8th Battalion Middlesex Regiment.

11th Middlesex (Railway) Rifle Volunteer Corps The 11th Middlesex RVC was at first allotted to the King's Royal Rifle Corps as one of its volunteer battalions but transferred to the Middlesex Regiment in 1882. Eight years later, in 1890, there was another move, this time to the Royal Fusiliers.

17th Middlesex (North Middlesex) Rifle Volunteer Corps With headquarters in High Street, Camden the 17th maintained eight companies and in 1908 transferred to the Territorial Force as the 19th Battalion of the London Regiment.

Illustration credits: Anne SK Brown Military Collection, Brown University Library (501), Bruce Bassett-Powell and Bob Bennet (497), (499)

KING'S ROYAL RIFLE CORPS

60th (King's Royal Rifle Corps) Regiment

Under an order dated 24 December 1755, the regiment was raised in New York and Philadelphia as the 62nd (Royal American) Regiment by John, Earl of Loudoun. It was re-numbered as 60th two years later. Light Infantry was added to the title in 1815 and by June 1824 the regiment was organised: 1st Battalion Rifle Corps and 2nd Battalion Light Infantry. The Duke of York's was added in the following month and in August the title appeared as 60th (Duke of York's Own Rifle Corps), this changing to the 60th King's Royal Rifle Corps in 1830. Just the number would be discarded in 1881.

When first raised there were four battalions, all wearing red coats with blue facings, the men having no lace or braid. A 5th Battalion was added at the end of 1797 which wore green coats, this new conception brining about a change from red to green (with red facings) throughout the whole regiment by the end of 1815. The regiment's Maltese Cross badge, according to its published history, was adopted from Hompesch's Regiment from which the 5th Battalion was largely raised. The cross is said to have been copied from a Bavarian War Medal. The bugle-horn had also originated from the 5th Battalion. One of the regiment's nicknames, The Jaggers, also came from the 5th Battalion which was made up of German marksmen. The other, The Green Jackets, of course refers to the 60th's uniform.

Regular Battalions

1st, 2nd, 3rd, 4th All provided by the 60th (King's Royal Rifle Corps) Regiment. The regiment's dark green uniform and scarlet facings are seen here in a Gale & Polden postcard captioned by the artist 'Falling in on parade' **(507)** By Ernest Ibbetson, the card is one of a set of six which included: 'Guard Mounting' **(508)**, 'Charging from the trenches' **(509)** and ''The Colonel and Sergeant-Major **(510)**. Also to illustrate the regiment for postcard purposes was Harry Payne, illustration **(511)** being the original artwork supplied by the artist to Gale &

Polden. Generous in its number of colour plates was the Appendix volume published with Volumes 1 and 2 of the *Annals of The King's Royal Rifle Corps* in 1913. By PW Reynolds, the images include: **(512)** a sergeant-major and bugler in 1880, **(513)** two officers and a private in 1904 , and **(514)** a field officer of the 1st Battalion of 1885. Illustration **(515)** is from Richard Simkin's *Our Armies*.

Militia Battalions

5th Battalion Formed from the Huntingdonshire Rifle Militia with headquarters at Huntingdon.

6th Battalion Formed by the Royal Flint Rifles Militia with headquarters at Mold. The battalion was disbanded in 1889, the position of 6th being taken by the 7th Battalion in 1908.

7th Battalion Formed from the 2nd Middlesex or Edmonton Roya Rifle Regiment of Militia with headquarters at Barnet. Re-numbered as 6th Battalion in 1908.

8th Battalion Formed by the Carlow Rifle Militia with headquarters at Carlow. Disbanded in 1908.

9th Battalion Formed by the North Cork Rifles Militia with headquarters at Mallow. Disbanded in 1908.

Volunteer Battalions

The regiment's several volunteer battalions were provided by rifle volunteer corps from the Metropolitan area, all retained their volunteer titles. With the introduction of the Territorial Force in 1908, two battalions went to provide personnel for the 9th and 10th Battalions of the Middlesex Regiment, the remainder all transferring as battalions of the newly created London Regiment.

1st Middlesex (Victoria and St George's) Rifle Volunteer Corps Upon the general disbandment of volunteers in 1814 the Duke of Cumberland's Sharpshooter, which had been formed in 1803, was permitted to continue service—although not formally recognised as a military body, but as a rifle club. In 1835 permission was granted to style the club as the Royal Victoria Rifle Club and in 1853 sanction to form a volunteer corps was given. As the Victoria Volunteer Rifle Corps, whose first officers' commissions were dated 4 January 1853, the club subsequently, in 1859, became the 1st Middlesex RVC. The additional title Victoria was added by March 1860.

Headquarters were in Kilburn, but a move was made to Marlborough Place, off Hamilton Terrace, St John's Wood in 1867. Became a Volunteer battalion of the King's Royal Rifle Corps (without change in title) in 1881. Headquarters moved to 56 Davies Street, Westminster in 1892, and in the same year an amalgamation took place on 1 June with the 6th Middlesex (St George's) RVC. The new title adopted was 1st Middlesex (Victoria and St George's). Transfer to the Territorial Force in 1908 saw the 1st Middlesex amalgamated with the 19th Middlesex to form the 9th Battalion London Regiment. A cadet corps with headquarters in Marlborough Place was formed towards the end of 1866, but this was later disbanded and was last seen in the Army List for January 1898. Illustration **(516)** is by GD Giles and from *Her Majesty's Army* by Walter Richards.

516 THE 1st MIDDLESEX (VICTORIA RIFLES) VOLUNTEERS. (4TH VOLUNTEER BATTALION KING'S ROYAL RIFLE CORPS.)

2nd (South Middlesex) Rifle Volunteer Corps Formed with headquarters at Beaufort House, Waltham Green on 14 October 1859. Recruitment went well and within a few months the strength of the corps, one of the largest in the country, stood at sixteen companies. By the end of March 1860 some 1,261 members had subscribed twenty-one shillings each on being enrolled. In addition every man paid the cost of his uniform and equipment, besides an annual regimental subscription of twenty-one shillings. As founder of the 2nd Middlesex Viscount Ranelagh's crest of a dexter arm embowed in armour and grasping a dart was used on the later uniforms as a collar badge. His Lordship was to command the corps until his death in November 1885. Became a volunteer battalion (without change in title) of the King's Royal Rifle Corps in 1881 and in 1902, and with the tenancy at Beaufort House having come to an end, moved to new headquarters at Fulham House, 7 High Street, Fulham. This historic property had once been owned by Sir Ralph Warren, Lord Mayor of London in 1536 and 1543, and later the Cromwell family. A fine gateway was purported to have been built by Inigo Jones, and the Officers' Mess possessed a number of carvings by Grinling Gibbons.

The strength of the 2nd Middlesex eventually fell to twelve companies, the headquarters of these, in addition to Fulham, being found at Chelsea, Chiswick, Hammersmith, Kensington, Brompton, Knightsbridge and Acton. The headquarters of 'K' Company were at the War Office. A cadet corps was formed in 1865, but this was removed from the Army List in 1880. St Paul's School at West Kensington formed a cadet corps in 1890—BL Montgomery, the future field marshal, becoming a pupil of the Army Class in 1902. In 1908 some 300 officers and other ranks of the 2nd Middlesex provided a nucleus for the 10th Battalion Middlesex Regiment. However, the 10th was regarded as a new unit and no connection with any previous volunteer corps was permitted. Consequently, the battle honour 'South Africa 1900-02' gained by the volunteers from the 2nd Middlesex while serving as part of the City Imperial Volunteers was not carried forward. St Paul's School, in 1908, became part of the OTC.

4th (West London) Middlesex Rifle Volunteer Corps Headquarters were in Swallow Street, Piccadilly, the corps in 1881 providing a volunteer battalion (without change in title) of King's Royal Rifle Corps. Headquarters were moved to Adam and Eve Mews off Kensington High Street in 1885 having been situated in the West End of London since 1864. Having been designated 4th (Kensington) in 1905, the battalion joined the Territorial Force in 1908 as 13th Battalion London Regiment.

5th (West Middlesex) Rifle Volunteer Corps With headquarters at Lord's Cricket Ground, St John's Wood the 5th Middlesex RVC became a volunteer battalion (without change in title) of the Royal Fusiliers in 1881, transferring in 1883 to the King's Royal Rifle Corps. Headquarters later moved to 29 Park Road, Regents Park. The 9th Middlesex RVC at Harrow was absorbed in 1899, bringing with it the Harrow School Cadet Corps. The latter became the 27th Corps on 1 April 1902 and serving as such until disbandment in January 1906. The personnel then returned to the 5th Corps as a cadet company. The 9th Battalion Middlesex Regiment was formed in 1908, the cadet corps at the same time joining the OTC.

6th Middlesex (St George's) Rifle Volunteer Corps Formed in the Parish of St George's, Westminster with four companies recruited from the Bond Street, Grosvenor Square, Hanover Square and Belgravia areas. The corps became a volunteer battalion (without change in title) of the King's Royal Rifle Corps in 1881 and was amalgamated with 1st Middlesex RVC on 1 June 1892.

9th Middlesex Rifle Volunteer Corps Formed at Harrow as one company, much of the corps was recruited from the staff and senior boys of Harrow School which, in 1870, provided a cadet corps. The 9th became a volunteer battalion (without change of title) of the Royal Fusiliers in 1881, transferring to King's Royal Rifle Corps under General Order 99 of July 1883. An amalgamation took place with the 5th Corps (as 5th) in 1899.

10th Middlesex Rifle Volunteer Corps Formed in Bloomsbury of three companies on 13 December 1859 from members of the Working Men's College in Great Ormond Street, Holborn. The commanding officer was Thomas Hughes, the author of *Tom Brown's Schooldays*, which led to the corps often being referred to as 'Tom Brown's Corps'. The corps later comprised ten companies of which three were supplied by the college and others by the St John's Institute in Cleveland Street, the Price Belmont Works at Battersea, the Working Men's College in Paddington Green and the Westminster parishes of St Luke and St. Anne's. Headquarters later moved to 33 Fitzroy Square. The 10th became a volunteer battalion (without change in title) of the King's Royal Rifle Corps in 1881, General Order 99 of July 1883, however, directing a transfer to the Royal Fusiliers and re-designation as its 1st Volunteer Battalion.

11th Middlesex (Railway) Rifle Volunteer Corps The corps was formed with headquarters at Euston Square mainly from men employed by the London and North Western Railway Company and joined the King's Royal Rifle Corps (without change in title) as one of its volunteer battalions in 1881. It was transferred to the Middlesex Regiment in 1882 and then the Royal Fusiliers as its 3rd Volunteer Battalion in 1890.

12th Middlesex (Civil Service) Rifle Volunteer Corp From the very beginning of the Volunteer Movement it had been intended to merge all units raised by government departments into one corps.

Headquarters were placed at Somerset House and the several companies were organised: 'A' (Audit Office), 'B' (Post Office), 'C' (Post Office), 'D' (Inland Revenue), 'E' (Inland Revenue), 'F' (Whitehall), 'G' (Whitehall), 'H' (Admiralty) and 'K' (Bank of England). The 21st Corps became a volunteer battalion (without change in title) of the King's Royal Rifle Corps in 1881. In May 1898 the 12th became styled as The Prince of Wales's Own 12th Middlesex (Civil Service) RVC—HRH having been honorary colonel since its formation. An 'I' (Cyclist) Company was raised from employees of the London County Council in 1900 and a cadet corps was formed and affiliated in 1903. Transfer to the Territorial Force was as the 15th Battalion London Regiment.

13th Middlesex (Queen's) Rifle Volunteer Corps The corps comprised members from the parishes of St. John's, St. Margaret's, St Mary's Strand, St Paul's Covent Garden, St James, St Martin's in the Fields, St Anne's John Street, St Clement Danes and King's College. Also included in the corps was a number of men that had enrolled into a corps formed at Messrs J Broadwood & Sons Ltd of Horseferry Road, Westminster. With fifteen companies and headquarters in Westminster, the corps became a volunteer battalion (without change in title) of the King's Royal Rifle Corps in 1881. By 1900 the establishment had reached sixteen companies which were organised and named as follows: 'A', 'B', 'C', 'D' (Pimlico Division), 'E', 'F' (St John's Division), 'G' (St Margaret's Division), 'H' (St James's Division), 'I', 'K' (St Martin's Division), 'L' (Schoolbread's Company), 'M' (St Clement Dane's Division), 'O' (Royal Welsh), 'R' (Greater Westminster), 'S' (Mounted Infantry) and 'T' (Cyclists). A cadet corps was formed in 1900 and transfer to the Territorial Force was as 16th Battalion London Regiment. Illustration **(517)** show a member of 'T' (Cyclists) Company.

21st Middlesex (The Finsbury Rifle Volunteer Corps) Ten companies strong, the corps became a volunteer battalion (without change in title) of the Rifle Brigade in 1881, transferring to the King's Royal Rifle Corps in 1883. Two new companies were authorized in 1900. From headquarters in Penton Street, Pentonville, the 21st transferred to the Territorial Force in 1908 as the 11th Battalion London Regiment.

22nd Middlesex (Central London Rifle Rangers) Rifle Volunteer Corps This corps was formed from members of the legal profession at Gray's Inn, London and became a volunteer battalion (without change in title) of the Royal Fusiliers in 1881. Transfer to the King's Royal Rifle Corps was in 1882. The Mayall College Cadet Corps at Herne Hill was affiliated in 1891 but removed from the Army List in 1899. The 12th Battalion London Regiment was formed in 1908.

25th (Bank of England) Middlesex Rifle Volunteer Corps In July 1866 the clerks and senior staff of the Bank of England formed a company of Rifle Volunteers which became part of the 21st Middlesex (Civil Service) RVC. On 1 December 1875 a new company was formed, this time by the porters and messengers of the bank. The corps served with the 12th Middlesex RVC as a volunteer battalion of the King's Royal Rifle Corps until being disbanded in April 1907.

26th Middlesex Rifle Volunteer Corps (Cyclist) Notification of the acceptance of a corps of Cyclist in Middlesex was received on 11 February 1888. The new formation to rank after the 25th (Bank of England) Corps and to be made up of three troops lettered: 'A', 'B' and 'C—this would be the first battalion in the history of the British Army to be completely dedicated to a cyclist role. The cyclists functioned as scouts, signallers, pulled Colt machine guns into action attached to specially designed carriages and even, according to one source writing in the *Volunteer Gazette,* practised laying their machines down in the road so as to hinder oncoming enemy cavalry. The battalion's first headquarters was at Ashley Place where, seven years after formation of the corps, the first red bricks of John Francis Bentley's Westminster Cathedral would be set in place. By the end of 1888, however, a move had been made to Hare Court, this time in the City and within a few yards of the Temple Church and Fleet Street. Further moves would be made: first to 2 Queen's Road, West Chelsea (1890); 69 Lillie Road, West Brompton (1899) and Horseferry Road, Westminster (1904). Upon formation, the 26th Corps was allotted to the King's Royal Rifle Corps as one of its volunteer battalions. It transferred to the Rifle Brigade in 1889 and provided the 25th London Regiment in 1908.

27th Middlesex (Harrow School) Rifle Volunteer Corps On 1 April 1902 the cadet corps formed at Harrow School and hitherto attached to the 5th Middlesex RVC became a corps in its own right. Designated as 27th Middlesex, the new corps was allotted to the King's Royal Rifle Corps as one of its volunteer battalions. The 27th appeared as such for the last time in the Army List for April 1906, being disbanded officially with effect from the previous 31 January—the personnel returning to the 5th Corps as a cadet company.

1st (City of London Rifle Volunteer Brigade With headquarters at 17 Finsbury Place South and later 48 Finsbury Pavement, EC2, and after that, 130 Bunhill Row, EC1, the 1st London became a Volunteer battalion (without change of title) of the King's Royal Rifle Corps in 1881. After the Boer War the strength of the brigade fell off resulting in a reduction in establishment, first to ten, then to eight companies—in the last year of the Volunteer Force (1907) a strength of just 489 out of an establishment of 928 was returned. Transfer to the Territorial Force was as 5th Battalion London Regiment.

The first mention of a cadet corps having been formed within the brigade was in the Army List for May 1877. There was, however, a unit formed as early as 1860 which according to one source had a strength of 400 boys. Included in the c1860 cadet unit were boys from the Merchant Taylors, City of London, University College and King's College School, and in 1900 these school corps are shown in the Army List by name for the first time. By 1902 the schools, together with the 1877 unit, appear under the heading of 1st City of London Cadet Corps with a total establishment of five companies. Became part of the OTC in 1908.

2nd London Rifle Volunteer Corps Formed 16 May 1860 from employees of the newspaper and printing trade—much of the corps was made up of workers at the *Daily Mail* and the printing firms of Messrs Eyre and Spottiswoode and Messrs Harmsworth—George A Spottiswoode and William Spottiswoode being among the first officers to be commissioned. With headquarters at Little New Street, the 2nd London was known unofficially as The Printers' Battalion. Joined the King's Royal Rifle Corps (without change in title) as one of its Volunteer battalions in 1881. In 1887 the memorial stone to a new headquarters at 57a Farringdon Road was laid. The City of London School Cadet Corps became affiliated in 1905 and transfer to the Territorial Force in 1908 was as 6th Battalion London Regiment. The City of London School at the same time became part of the OTC.

3rd (City of) London Rifle Volunteer Corps Recruiting began late in 1860—a number coming forward from the ranks of the old Temple Bar and St Paul's Association Volunteers which had been formed in 1798—and the first officers' commissions were dated 8 March 1861. Twelve companies were soon established, the majority of the men being of the 'Artisan' class which led to the unofficial title of the Working Men's Brigade. Headquarters were at 26 Great Tower Street, moving later to 38 New Broad Street, then to 79 Farringdon Street, EC4 and finally to 24 Sun Street, Finsbury. Became a Volunteer Battalion of the King's Royal Rifle Corps (without change in title) in 1881, the additional title of (City of) being shown in the Army List by 1904. The 7th Battalion London Regiment was formed in 1908.

4th London Rifle Volunteer Corps Two companies were formed on 18 May 1900 from ex-members of the Grocers' Company Schools in Clapton, North East London. The corps, together with the

1st London RVC, provided a volunteer battalion of the King's Royal Rifle Corps until being disbanded in 1905, Major General Sir Frederick Maurice noting in his *History of the London Rifle Brigade* that 'the numbers having fell off, what remained of the 4th London was absorbed into 'E' company of 1st London'.

Cadet Battalion

1st Cadet Battalion Formed as 2nd Cadet Battalion Queen's (Royal West Surry Regiment) of four companies in November 1890. Headquarters were originally at the Lambeth Polytechnic, moving later to Kirkdale in Clapham, then to Brockwell Hall, Herne Hill. Increased to six companies in 1891 and in 1894 was re-designated as 1st Cadet Battalion KRRC. Headquarters at the same time moving to Finsbury Square EC London. The battalion published an interesting magazine called *The Monthly Record,* the cover for issue published in November 1902 being illustrated **(518)**. Illustration **(519)** features the Battalion's Maxim gun detachment, the photograph in **(520)** showing a party of cadets at camp.

DUKE OF EDINBURGH'S (WILTSHIRE REGIMENT)

62nd (Wiltshire) Regiment

Formed in the West of England in 1756 as 2nd Battalion 4th Regiment and regimented as 62nd on 21 April 1758, its facings being described as yellowish buff. Wiltshire was added to the title in 1782, the 62nd providing the 1st Battalion Duke of Edinburgh's (Wiltshire Regiment) in 1881. The regiment's Maltese Cross badge commemorates its service in Sicily in 1806.

99th (Duke of Edinburgh's) Regiment

Raised in 1824 as the 99th Regiment, the Lanarkshire sub-title being added in 1832. This was changed, however, in 1874 to The Duke of Edinburgh's. The 99th providing the 2nd Battalion Duke of Edinburgh's

(Wiltshire Regiment) in 1881. White facings were worn, the badges featuring the Duke of Edinburgh's Coronet and Cypher which were assumed with the title on 22 April 1874.

Regular Battalions

1st and 2nd Battalions 1st Battalion formed by the 62nd (Wiltshire) Regiment, the 2nd by the 99th (Duke of Edinburgh) Regiment. The regiment's Duke of Edinburgh's coronet and cypher from the 99th and Maltese Cross of the 62nd can be seen in Brice Bassett-Powell's detailed image of officers' insignia **(521)**. In Richard Simkin's No 91 in his 'Military Types' series for the *Army and Navy Gazette* an officer reads out some orders to a colour sergeant on a railway platform **(522)**. Published on 6 July 1895, the artist has shown the men wearing the white facings adopted in 1881. The later Harry Payne painting **(523)** includes collars and cuffs in the buff colour previously worn by the 62nd Regiment and restored in 1905. In **(524)** the corporal's medals indicate that he had served in the Second Boer War, the 2nd Battalion of the regiment having sailed for South Africa on 16 December 1899. His musketry efficiency is also noted by the two badges worn on the lower left arm: best shot in his company (top), best shot among corporals, lance corporals and privates in battalion (bottom).

Militia Battalion

3rd Battalion From the Royal Wiltshire Militia with headquarters at Devises.

Territorial Battalion

4th Battalion Formed from the former 2nd Volunteer Battalion and 1st Wiltshire Volunteer Rifle Corps with headquarters at Warminster, moving to Fore Street, Trowbridge in 1909. The eight companies were located: 'A' (Salisbury and Farley), 'B' (Wilton, Wishford and Barford St Martin), 'C' (Trowbridge and Steeple Ashton), 'D' (Chippenham and Calne), 'E' (Devizes, Lavington and Bromham), 'F' (Warminster, Westbury, Chitterne, Horningsham, Dilton March and Heytesbury), 'G' (Bradford-on-Avon, Melksham and Holt) and 'H' (Swindon and Marlborough). The Warminster Cadet Company was affiliated. The battalion left for India under the command of Lieutenant-Colonel the

Earl of Radnor in October 1914. The following two photographs of the signal section and the Colonel **(525)** and **(526)** were taken shortly after arrival.

Volunteer Battalions

1st Wiltshire Volunteer Rifle Corps With headquarters at Warminster the 1st Wiltshire Rifle Volunteer Corps had eight companies: 'A' and 'B' (Salisbury), 'C' and 'D' (Trowbridge), 'E' (Bradford-on-Avon), 'F' (Warminster), 'G' (Westbury) and 'H' (Wilton). The corps became a volunteer battalion (without change in title) of the Wiltshire Regiment in 1881. A new company ('I') was formed from around the Tisbury and Mere areas in 1892 and 'K' (Cyclist) was raised at Bradford-on-Avon in 1900. A cadet corps was formed at Salisbury and affiliated to the corps in 1890, but this had disappeared from the Army List by the end of 1897. Transfer to the Territorial Force in 1908 was as headquarters and five companies of the 4th Battalion Wiltshire Regiment. The badge of the corps **(527)** reflects that old Wiltshire legend of before 1787, the Moonrakers. In possession of several barrels of smuggled French brandy, and to defeat the customs men, some local people hid their contraband in the village pond. Caught while trying to retrieve one of the barrels at night, the excuse given was that they were in fact raking in a round of cheese. The cheese was the moon's reflection in the water. In **(528)** three members of the battalion are in khaki service dress with cloth embroidered shoulder tiles, WILTS over I over VRC.

2nd Volunteer Battalion With headquarters at Chippenham, the 2nd Wiltshire Rifle Volunteer Corps had twelve companies: 'A' (Malmesbury), 'B' (Chippenham), 'C' and 'D' (Devizes), 'E' (Market Lavington), 'F' and 'G' (Swindon), 'H' (Melksham), 'I' (Wootton Bassett), 'K' (Swindon), 'L' (Marlborough) and 'M' (Highworth). There was also a Sub-Division at Calne. The corps was reduced to eleven companies in 1882 and designated 2nd Volunteer Battalion Wiltshire Regiment under General Order 181 of December 1887. Transfer to the Territorial Force in 1908 was as three companies of 4th Battalion Wiltshire Regiment. The cadet corps at Marlborough College, which had been affiliated since 1864, at the same time became a contingent of the OTC.

Illustration credits: Alan Seymore (525), Bruce Bassett-Powell and Bob Bennet (521)

MANCHESTER REGIMENT

63rd (West Suffolk) Regiment

Raised as 2nd Battalion of the 8th Regiment in 1757 and regimented as 63rd in the following year with dark green facings. West Suffolk was added to the title in 1782, the 63rd providing the 1st Battalion Manchester Regiment in 1881.

96th (Queen's Own) Regiment

Although disbanded in 1818, it was confirmed that when a new 96th Regiment was raised in January 1824 it was to serve as the successor to the former regiment with that number. This was the 96th (Queen's Own) Regiment raised December 1798 by Lieutenant-General Sir Charles Stuart at Minorca from German-speaking members of Swiss regiments taken prisoner there and known as Stuart's or the Minorca Regiment. The 96th in 1881 become 2nd Battalion Manchester Regiment. The uniform facings were yellow and in June 1874 the Sphinx superscribed Egypt worn by the former 96th was authorized as a badge.

Regular Battalions

1st, 2nd, 3rd and 4th Battalions The 1st Battalion was formed by the 63rd (West Suffolk) Regiment, the 2nd by the 96th (Queen's Own) Regiment. The 3rd and 4th were added in 1900 and both disbanded in 1906. The several device of the regiment can be seen in Bruce Bassett-Powell's detailed image **(529)**. Illustrations **(530)** and **(531)** show the city arms cap badge and the post 1902 officers' helmet plate. Illustration **(532)** is Richard Simkin's 'Military Types' No 92, published on 3 August 1895 for the *Army and Navy Gazette*. Next we have three postcards from a set of six published by Gale & Polden featuring the artwork of Ernest Ibbetson: 'Changing Guard' **(533)**, the commanding officer, adjutant and sergeant major **(534)** and 'Arriving in France' **(535)**. Also produced for the postcard market was **(536)** by Harry Payne.

Militia Battalions

3rd and 4th, later 5th and 6th Battalions Formed as 3rd and 4th Battalion in 1881 from the former 6th Royal Lancashire Militia with headquarters at Ashton. Following the formation in 1900 of the 3rd and 4th Regular Battalions, the two were re-numbered as 5th and 6th.

Territorial Battalions

5th Battalion Formed by the former 1st Volunteer Battalion with headquarters at Bank Chambers, Wigan.

The companies were located: 'A' to 'E' (Wigan), 'F' (Patricroft), 'G' (Leigh) and 'H' (Atherton).

6th Battalion Formed from the former 2nd Volunteer Battalion with headquarters and all eight companies at 3 Stratford Road, Hulme.

7th Battalion Formed by the former 4th Volunteer Battalion with headquarters and all eight companies at Burlington Street, Manchester. Although the regiment as a whole changed its city arms cap badge for the fleur-de-lis in 1922, the 7th Battalion had itself adopted the device many years before **(537)**.

8th (Ardwick) Battalion Formed by the former 5th Volunteer Battalion with headquarters and all eight companies at Ardwick.

9th Battalion Formed by the former 3rd Volunteer Battalion with headquarters and all eight companies at Ashton-under-Lyne.

10th Battalion Formed by the former 6th Volunteer Battalion with headquarters and all eight companies at Oldham.

Volunteer Battalions

1st Volunteer Battalion The 4th Lancashire Rifle Volunteer Corps had thirteen companies: 'A' to 'E' (Wigan), 'F' (Swinton), 'G' (Eccles), 'H' (Leigh), 'J' (Atherton), 'K' (Worsley), 'L' and 'M' (Farnworth) and 'N' (Flixton). Headquarters were at Manchester. The Farnworth Companies ('L' and 'M') were transferred to the 14th Lancashire Rifle Volunteer Corps in 1883 and re-designation as 1st Volunteer Battalion Manchester Regiment took place in 1888. An additional company was sanctioned in 1900 and transfer to the Territorial Force in 1908 was as 5th Battalion Manchester Regiment. Illustration **(538)** shows the silver pouch-belt plate and pouch badge worn by officers.

2nd Volunteer Battalion Formed as the 6th (1st Manchester) Lancashire Rifle Volunteer Corps with twelve companies in Manchester on 25 August 1859, the Viscount Grey de Wilton being appointed as Lieutenant Colonel Commandant on 19 February 1860. A number of large Manchester firms such as Messrs JP and E Westhead, and Messrs J and N Phillips provided whole companies. The 6th Corps for many years occupied headquarters at Wolstenholme's Court, Market Street, Manchester and afterwards at 3 Stretford Road, Hulme. Re-designation as 2nd Volunteer Battalion Manchester Regiment was notified in Army Order 409 of 1888. A new company was sanctioned in 1890, followed by two more in 1900, and transfer to the Territorial Force in 1908 was as 6th Battalion Manchester Regiment, 'N' Company, however, which had been formed at Manchester University, became part of the Senior Division OTC.

538

3rd Volunteer Battalion With headquarters at Ashton-under-Lyne, the 7th Lancashire Rifle Volunteer Corps had twelve companies: 'A' to 'F' (Ashton-under-Lyne) and 'G' to 'M' (Oldham). The letter 'I' was not used. In 1882 the establishment was reduced when the Oldham companies were withdrawn to form a new Lancashire rifle volunteer corps numbered as 22nd, the remainder being designated as 3rd Volunteer Battalion Manchester Regiment in 1888. Three additional companies were sanctioned in 1900 and the 9th Battalion Manchester Regiment was formed in 1908.

4th Volunteer Battalion The 16th Lancashire Rifle Volunteer Corps was designated as 4th Volunteer Battalion Manchester Regiment in 1888, the headquarters at this time being in Burlington Street, Manchester and the strength twelve companies. Transfer to the Territorial Force was as 7th Battalion Manchester Regiment. He was one of the battalion's best shots and his left arm covered in prize shooting award badges **(539)**.

539

5th (Ardwick) Volunteer Battalion With fourteen companies, the 20th Lancashire Rifle Volunteer Corps was re-designated as 5th (Ardwick) Volunteer Battalion, Manchester Regiment in 1888. A cadet corps was formed and affiliated in the same year. An additional company was sanctioned in 1900 and transfer to the Territorial Force in 1908 was as 8th Battalion Manchester Regiment.

6th Volunteer Battalion The 22nd Lancashire Rifle Volunteer Corps was formed at Oldham on 29 July 1882 by the withdrawal of the Oldham companies from the 7th Lancashire RVC, the establishment by the end of the year rising to eight companies. Re-designation as 6th Volunteer Battalion Manchester Regiment was in 1888. Two additional companies were sanctioned in 1900 and transfer to the Territorial Force was as 10th Battalion Manchester Regiment.

17th Lancashire Rifle Volunteer Corps The 17th at Salford had become a volunteer battalion of the Manchester Regiment in 1881, but transferred to the Lancashire Fusiliers as 3rd Volunteer Battalion in March 1886.

Cadet Battalions

1st Cadet Battalion Formed in February 1889 with headquarters were at Tongue Street Manchester.

1st Territorial Cadet Battalion Headquarters Poplar Street, Ardwick and affiliated to the Manchester Infantry Brigade.

2nd Cadet Battalion Headquarters were at Coldhurst, Oldham, the battalion originally being called the 1st Coldhurst (Oldham) Cadet Corps. Re-designation was notified by Army Order 11 of 1912 and affiliation was with the 10th Manchester Regiment.

Illustration credits: Anne SK Brown Military Collection, Brown University Library (536), Bruce Bassett-Powell (529)

PRINCE OF WALES'S (NORTH STAFFORDSHIRE REGIMENT)

64th (2nd Staffordshire) Regiment

Raised in 1756 as 2nd Battalion of the 11th Regiment with green facings and regimented two years later as 64th with black. The county designation 2nd Staffordshire was added to the title in 1782, the 64th providing the 1st Battalion Prince of Wales's (North Staffordshire Regiment) in 1881. The Stafford Knot badge and black facings are the origins of the regiment's nickname, The Black Knots.

98th (Prince of Wales's) Regiment

Raised as the 98th Regiment in 1824, its first Colours being presented by the Duchess of Richmond at Chichester Cathedral on 6 October that year. The colonel, Henry Conron was commissioned on 25 March. The Prince of Wales's was added to the title in 1876, the 98th providing the 2nd Battalion Prince of Wales's (North Staffordshire Regiment) in 1881. White facings were worn, the regiment's Dragon of China badge being authorized in January 1843. The Coronet, Plumes and *Ich Dien* (I Serve) motto of the Prince of Wales were also badges.

Regular Battalions

1st and 2nd Battalions The 1st Battalion was formed by the 64th (2nd Staffordshire) Regiment, the 2nd by the 98th (Prince of Wales's) Regiment. From Richard Simkin, an unusual setting of three soldiers from the regiment which was produced by the artist for his 'Military Types' series for the *Army and Navy Gazette* and published on 7 September 1895 (**540**). The second illustration (**541**) is also by Richard Simkin an features a filed officer in 1914.

Militia Battalions

3rd and 4th Battalions The 3rd Battalion was formed by the 2nd (King's Own) Staffordshire Militia at Stafford, the 4th by the 3rd (King's Own) Staffordshire Militia at Newcastle-under-Lyne. Thanks to the Anne SK Brown Military Collection held at Brown University Library we have two delightful watercolours by the Dutch painter Jan Hoynck van Papendrecht (1858-1933). In **(542)** the artist shows men of the 4th Battalion resting as two of their officers observe operations. A scene set at Bulford Camp is next which this time features four soldiers outside a tent wearing greatcoats guarding the regimental safe **(543)**. The greatcoats, notes the artist on his artwork, were due '…on account of a heavy rain storm.'

Territorial Battalions

5th Battalion Formed by the former 1st Volunteer Battalion with headquarters at Hanley and companies located: 'A' (Longton), 'B' (Hanley), 'C' (Burslem), 'D' (Tunstall), 'E' (Stoke-on-Trent and Hanley), 'F' (Stone), 'G' (Newcastle-under-Lyme) and 'H' (Stoke-on-Trent).

6th Battalion Formed by the former 2nd Volunteer Battalion with headquarters at Burton-on-Trent and companies located: 'A' (Burton-on-Trent), 'B' (Burton-on-Trent and Tutbury), 'C' (Tamworth), 'D' (Rugeley), 'E' (Lichfield), 'F' (Stafford), 'G' (Uttoxeter) and 'H' (Burton-on-Trent).

Volunteer Battalions

1st Volunteer Battalion With headquarters at Stoke-upon-Trent, the 2nd Staffordshire Rifle Volunteer Corps had eleven companies: 'A' Longton (late 2nd Corps), 'B' Hanley (late 3rd Corps), 'C' Burslem (late 6th Corps), 'D' Tunstall (late 9th Corps), 'E' Stoke-upon-Trent (late 10th Corps), 'F' Kidsgrove (late 13th Corps), 'G' and 'H' Newcastle-under-Lyne (late 16th Corps), 'J' Leek (late 28th Corps), 'K' Hanley (late 36th Corps), 'L' Stone (late 40th Corps). Re-designation as 1st Volunteer Battalion North Staffordshire Regiment was notified in General Order 14 of February 1883. There was a cadet corps at Stoke-upon-Trent, but this was removed from the Army List in 1884. The battalion's establishment reached fourteen companies by 1900 but was later reduced to thirteen. The 5th Battalion North Staffordshire Regiment was formed in 1908.

2nd Volunteer Battalion With headquarters at Lichfield, the 5th Corps Staffordshire Rifle Volunteer Corps had eight companies: 'A' and 'B' (Burton-upon-Trent), 'C' (Tamworth), 'D' (Rugeley), 'E' (Lichfield), 'F' and 'G' (Stafford), and 'H' (Burton-upon-Trent). Re-designation as 2nd Volunteer Battalion North Staffordshire Regiment was notified in General Order 14 of February 1883, headquarters transferring to Burton-upon-Trent in 1884. A new company was added at Uttoxeter in 1900 and the Denstone College Cadet Corps affiliated in the same year. The 6th Battalion North Staffordshire Regiment was formed in 1908, Denstone College at the same time joining the OTC.

YORK AND LANCASTER REGIMENT

65th (2nd Yorkshire North Riding) Regiment

Raised 1756 as 2nd Battalion 12th Regiment and designated as 65th two years later. Yellow facings were first worn, these changing to white when regimented in 1758. The Yorkshire association appeared in the title in 1782, the 65th providing the 1st Battalion of the York and Lancaster Regiment in 1881.

84th (York and Lancaster) Regiment

Raised under a War Office letter dated 2 November 1793 by General George Bernard, his instruction being to form the regiment without levy money and for it to be completed in three months. The 84th was inspected at York on 23 February 1794. York and Lancaster was added to the title in 1809, the 84th providing the 2nd Battalion York and Lancaster Regiment in 1881. The regiment's facings were listed as various shades of yellow. Although the York and Lancaster title was assumed in 1809, it was not until 18 November 1823 that the Union Rose was authorized as a badge. A coronet also featured on badges and appointments, Major HG Parkyn suggesting that this was first used on the shoulder-belt plates around 1811. From its badge and title, the regiment acquired the nickname The Twin Roses. Illustration **(544)** is a detailed image of several officers'

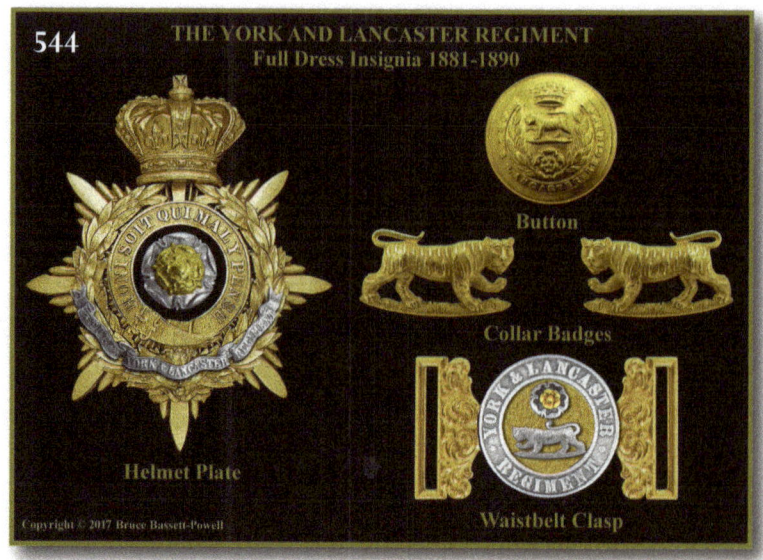

items by Bruce Bassett-Powell, **(545)** being a sketch of the cap badge. Artist Ernest Ibbetson produced a number of paintings for a series of regimental postcards published by Gale & Polden, three of which are illustrated here in **(547)**, **(548)** and **(549)**.

Regular Battalions

1st and 2nd Battalions The 1st Battalion was formed by the 65th (2nd Yorkshire North Riding) Regiment, the 2nd by the 84th (York and Lancaster) Regiment.

Militia Battalion

3rd Battalion Formed from the 3rd West Yorkshire Light Infantry Militia with headquarters at Pontefract.

Territorial Battalions

4th (Hallamshire) Battalion Formed from the former 1st Volunteer Battalion with headquarters and all eight companies at Sheffield.

5th Battalion Formed from part of the former 2nd Volunteer Battalion with headquarters at Rotherham and companies located: 'A', 'B' (Rotherham), 'C' (Barnsley), 'D' (Wath-upon-Dearne, Wombwell and Mexborough), 'E' (Barnsley), 'F' (Rotherham), 'G' (Treeton) and 'H' (Birdwell). The battalion's brass shoulder titles, T over 5 over Y&L are clearly seen in this photograph taken from high position **(550)**.

Volunteer Battalions

1st (Hallamshire) Volunteer Battalion According to Bartholomew's *Survey Gazetteer of the British Isles,* Hallamshire is an 'ancient lordship of the West Riding of Yorkshire'. It is mentioned in the *Doomsday Book* and is represented by the parishes of Sheffield and Ecclesfield. It was in Sheffield on 30 September 1859 that three separate companies were formed and designated as 2nd, 3rd and 4th Yorkshire West Riding RVC, the three being amalgamated by the end of the year under the new title of 2nd Yorkshire West Riding (Hallamshire) RVC and the command of Major Wilson Overend—his commission dated 22 December 1859. At the same time as the merger took place an additional company was raised, yet another being added when No 5 was formed from employees of the Atlas Works. The establishment of the 2nd Corps would reach seven companies by the end of 1861. Re-designation as 1st (Hallamshire) Volunteer Battalion York and Lancaster Regiment was notified by General Order 14 of February 1883, the 4th Battalion York and Lancaster Regiment being formed in 1908.

2nd Volunteer Battalion With headquarters at Doncaster, the 8th Yorkshire (West Riding) Rifle Volunteer Corps had nine companies: 'A' (Pontefract), 'B' (Rotherham), 'C' and 'D' (Doncaster), 'E' (Rotherham), 'F' (Barnsley), 'G' (Wath-upon-Dearne), 'H' (Barnsley) and 'J' (Rotherham). The corps was re-designated as 2nd Volunteer Battalion York and Lancaster

Regiment in February 1883. A new company was added in 1884 and a cadet corps was affiliated at Rotherham in 1894. This, however, had disappeared from the Army List during 1899. Two new companies were added in 1900, and company locations by 1908 were: Pontefract, Rotherham (3), Doncaster (5), Barnsley (2) and Wath-upon-Dearne. Transfer to the Territorial Force in 1908 saw the Rotherham, Barnsley and Wath-upon-Dearne personnel to the 5th Battalion York and Lancaster Regiment, while those from Doncaster and Pontefract formed part of the 5th Battalion King's Own Yorkshire Light Infantry. In illustration **(551)** a lance corporal of the battalion wears a star on his lower right arm indicating that he has been passed as efficient on five successive years.

Illustration credit: Bruce Bassett-Powell and Bob Bennet (544)

DURHAM LIGHT INFANTRY

68th (Durham Light Infantry) Regiment

Raised 1756 as 2nd Battalion 23rd Regiment and regimented as 68th in 1758. Durham was added to the title in 1782 and Durham Light Infantry in 1808. The 68th provided the 1st Battalion Durham Light Infantry in 1881. The regiment wore green facings, its bugle-horn badge accompanying the light infantry title in 1808.

106th (Bombay Light Infantry) Regiment

The regiment was raised in 1826 as the Honourable East India Company's 2nd Bombay European Light Infantry. The 106th title was assumed in 1861, the regiment providing the 2nd Battalion Durham Light Infantry in 1881. White facings and a French bugle-horn badge were worn.

Regular Battalions

1st and 2nd Battalions The 1st Battalion was formed by the 68th (Durham Light Infantry) Regiment, the 2nd by the 106th (Bombay Light Infantry) Regiment. Bruce Bassett-Powell illustrates several items worn by the regiment's officers **(552)**, image **(553)** being Richard Simkin's artwork for No 95 in his 'Military Types' series for the *Army and Navy Gazette*. Published on 2 November 1895, the regiment is shown with the white facings adopted in 1881. The old dark green of the 68th Regiment was later allowed and can be seen in the original artwork for one of Harry

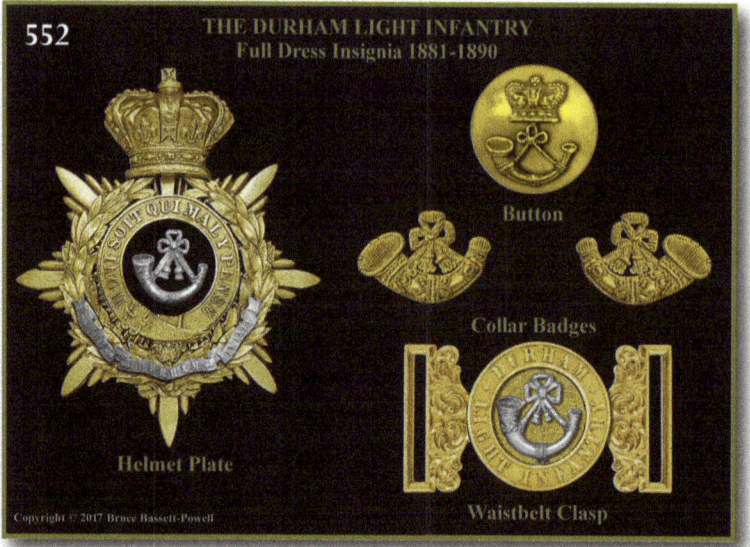

Payne's postcards for Gale & Polden **(554)**. Paintings for the same company were also produced by Ernest Ibbetson, two of which are shown in **(555)** and **(556)**.

Militia Battalions

3rd and 4th Battalions The original 3rd Battalion was formed in 1881 by the 2nd or North Durham Militia at Durham, the 4th at the same time being provided by the 1st Durham Fusiliers Militia which had its headquarters at Barnard Castle. In 1908 the numbers were reversed. In the 3rd Battalion photograph at **(557)** three officers are seen with one from the Northumberland Fusiliers and another from the Rifle Brigade.

Territorial Battalions

5th Battalion Formed from the former 1st Volunteer Battalion with headquarters at Stockton-on-Tees and companies located at 'A', 'B', 'C' (Stockton-on-Tees), 'D', 'E' (Darlington), 'F' (Castle Eden, Coxhoe and Trimdon), 'G' (Castle Eden and West Hartlepool) and 'H' (Darlington).

6th Battalion Formed by the former 2nd Volunteer Battalion with headquarters at Bishop Auckland and companies at: 'A' (Bishop Auckland and Coundon), 'B' (Bishop Auckland and West Auckland), 'C' (Spennymoor), 'D' (Crook and Willington), 'E' (Stanhope, St John's Chapel, Rookhope and Wolsingham), 'F' (Barnard Castle, Winston, Staindrop and Gainford) and 'G', 'H' (Consett).

7th Battalion Formed from the former 3rd Volunteer Battalion with headquarters at Livingstone Road, Sunderland and companies at: 'A' to 'F' (Sunderland) and 'G', 'H' (South Shields). In **(558)** the 7th Battalion are seen with its Colours.

8th Battalion Formed from the former 4th Volunteer Battalion with headquarters at Gilesgate, Durham and companies at: 'A' (Gilesgate, Sherburn Hill, Brandon and Sacriston), 'B' (Gilesgate), 'C' (Chester-le-Street), 'D' (Birtley), 'E' (Beamish and Burnhope), 'F' (Stanley), 'G' (Houghton-le-Spring, Pittington and Washington) and 'H' (Hamsteels, Langley Park and Sleetburn).

9th Battalion Formed from the former 5th Volunteer Battalion with headquarters at Burt Terrace, Gateshead and companies at: 'A' to 'D' (Gateshead), 'E' (Felling), 'F' (Chopwell) and 'G', 'H' (Blaydon and West Ryton).

Volunteer Battalions

1st Volunteer Battalion With headquarters at Stockton-on-Tees, the 1st Durham Rifle Volunteer Corps had eight companies: 'A' to 'C' (Stockton-on-Tees), 'D' and 'E' (Darlington), 'F' (Castle Eden) and 'G' and 'H' Middlesbrough. General Order 181 of December 1887 directed a change in designation to 1st Volunteer Battalion Durham Light Infantry. Four new companies were added; 'I' Stockton, 'K' Darlington, 'L' Middlesbrough and 'M' (Cyclist) Stockton in 1900. Transfer to the Territorial Force was as 5th Battalion Durham Light Infantry.

2nd Volunteer Battalion With headquarters at Bishop Auckland, the 2nd Durham Rifle Volunteer Corps had six companies: 'A' (Bishop Auckland), 'B' (Coundon), 'C' (Darlington), 'D' (Middleton-in-Teesdale), 'E' (Stanhope) and 'F' (Barnard Castle). In 1883 'C' Company was moved to Woodland. 'G' and 'H' Companies were added at Spennymore in 1886, then under General Order 181 of December 1887, the 2nd Corps became 2nd Volunteer Battalion Durham Light Infantry. 'D' Company was disbanded in 1899 and a new 'D' formed at Crook the same year. 'I' (Cyclist) Company at Bishop Auckland, 'K' and 'L' at Consett were added in 1900, 'C' moving yet again, this time to Shildon, in 1903. The 6th Battalion Durham Light Infantry was formed in 1908.

3rd (Sunderland) Volunteer Battalion The 3rd Durham Rifle Volunteer Corps was formed at Sunderland on 6 March 1860 and included six companies by 1862 with Major Lord Adolphus Vane Tempest in command. The sub-title The Sunderland was authorised in 1867. The corps became 3rd (Sunderland) Volunteer Battalion Durham Light Infantry in 1887, the change being notified in General Order 181 of December. A new company was added in 1900. The 7th Battalion Durham Light Infantry was formed in 1908.

4th Volunteer Battalion With headquarters at Chester-le-Street, the 4th Durham Rifle Volunteer Corps had ten companies: 'A' to 'C' (Durham), 'D' (Beamish), 'E' (Chester-le-Street), 'F' (Birtley), 'G' (Washington) and 'H', 'I' and 'K' (Felling). Under General Order 181 of December 1887 4th Durham RVC was re-designated as 4th Volunteer Battalion Durham Light Infantry. Headquarters moved to Durham in 1890, 'K' Company being disbanded in 1892 with a new 'K' added at Stanley. 'H' and 'I' Companies were amalgamated as 'H' in 1896, the 'I' position being taken up by a new company raised at Sacriston. 'H' Company transferred to the 5th Volunteer Battalion DLI as its 'L' Company in 1897 and at the same time a new 'H' was formed at Houghton-le-Spring. 'L' (Cyclist) Company was added at Stanley in 1900. Transfer to the Territorial Force in 1908 was as 8th Battalion Durham Light Infantry. 'C' Company, however, joined the OTC as part of the Durham University contingent.

5th Volunteer Battalion With headquarters at Gateshead, the 5th Durham Rifle Volunteer Corps had eight companies: 'A' to 'C' (Gateshead), 'D' to 'F' (South Shields), 'G' (Blaydon Burn) and 'H' (Winlaton). The corps was designated as 5th Volunteer Battalion Durham Light Infantry by General Order 181 of December 1887. Two new companies had been added by 1887 and the battalion was subsequently reorganised as follows: 'A' to 'D' Companies at Gateshead, 'E' to 'G' Companies South Shields, 'H' Company Blaydon, 'I' and 'K' Companies Winlaton. In 1897 'H' Company of the 4th Volunteer Battalion DLI at Felling was transferred to the 5th Volunteer Battalion as its 'L' Company. 'M' (Cyclist) Company was formed at Blaydon in 1900. The 9th Battalion was formed in 1908.

Illustration credits: Anne SK Brown Military Collection, Brown University Library (555) and (556), Bruce Bassett-Powell and Bob Bennet (552)

HIGHLAND LIGHT INFANTRY

71st (Highland Light Infantry) Regiment

Raised 1777 by John, Lord Macleod as the 73rd Regiment and re-numbered as 71st (Highland) in 1786. From 1808 the title was 71st (Glasgow Highland) and after 1810, 71st (Highland Light Infantry). The regiment provided the 1st Battalion Highland Light Infantry in 1881. The regiment had buff facings and the badge of a French bugle-horn.

74th (Highland) Regiment

The regiment was raised in 1787 for service in India by Sir Archibald Campbell, his commission being dated 12 October. The title at first included the word Highland, but this was removed in 1816, but later restored in 1845. The 74th provided the 2nd Battalion Highland Light Infantry in 1881. White facings were worn, WY Carman pointing out that in the beginning full Highland dress was expected to be in use, 'but no doubt the eighteen years in India brought modifications.' When the regiment returned to Scotland, full Highland uniforms were ordered, but the reductions of 1809 saw normal infantry dress supplied. The year 1845, which saw Highland return to the regimental title, also saw Highland dress restored, but not the kilt. For its services in India, and in particular at the Battle of Assay, the 74th was authorized to adopt an elephant as a badge. For the same reasons, an Imperial Crown, as seen on the Collar of the Order of the Star of India, was also adopted.

Regular Battalions

1st and 2nd Battalions The 1st Battalion was formed by the 71st (Highland Light Infantry) Regiment, the 2nd by the 74th (Highland) Regiment. The regiment proved to be a popular subject for many of Britain's leading military artists. In **(559)** we see the work of Richard Simkin, the image being painted by him as part of his 'Military Types' series for the *Army and Navy Gazette,* and in **(560)** one of the many watercolours by Harry Payne that were used for postcards produced by the Aldershot firm of Gale & Polden. The same company published a wide range of six-postcard sets, each featuring one particular regiment. For the Highland Light Infantry, the work of Edgar A Holloway was chosen, his subjects: officers in review order **(561)**, a church parade **(562)**, musketry inspection **(563)**, a piper and bandsmen **(564)**, a platoon inspection **(565)** and **(566)**, which is set during the early weeks of the First World War.

Militia Battalions

3rd and 4th Battalions In 1883 the 3rd

Battalion, which had been formed by the 1st Royal Lanarkshire Militia in 1881, was divided as 3rd and 4th Battalions. Headquarters of both were in Hamilton.

Territorial Battalions

One of the paintings by Richard Caton Woodville chosen to illustrate the City of Glasgow Territorial Force Association in Walter Richards's *His Majesty's Territorial Army* featured a private of the Highland Light Infantry **(567)**. The photograph shown at **(568)** is certainly of a Territorial battalion, the T over number over bugle over HLI shoulder tiles unfortunately not clear enough in the image to identify battalion.

5th (City of Glasgow) Battalion Formed from the former 1st Volunteer Battalion with headquarters and all eight companies at 24 Hill Street, Garnethill, Glasgow.

6th (City of Glasgow) Battalion Formed by the former 2nd Volunteer Battalion with headquarters and all eight companies at 172 Yorkhill Street, Glasgow.

7th (Blythswood) Battalion Formed by the former 3rd (The Blythswood) Volunteer Battalion with headquarters and all eight companies at 69 Main Street, Bridgeton, Glasgow.

8th (Lanark) Battalion Formed by the former 9th Lanarkshire Rifle Volunteer Corps with headquarters at Lanark and companies at: 'A' (Lesmahagow, Stonehouse, Coalburn and Blackwood), 'B' (Lanark, Biggar, Ponfeigh and Douglas), 'C' (Shotts, Cleland, Salsburgh and Harthill), 'D' (Carluke), 'E' (Forth and Tarbrax), 'F' (Law and Overtown), 'G' (Newmains) and 'H', Wishaw.

9th (Glasgow Highland) Battalion Formed by the former 5th (Glashow Highland) Volunteer Battalion with headquarters and all eight companies at 81 Greendyke Street, Glasgow. Affiliated to the battalion was the Glasgow Telegraph Messengers Cadet Corps which was re-designated as 1st (Glasgow Highland) Cadet Company in 1912. Headquarters were at the Head Post Office, Glasgow.

Volunteer Battalions

1st Volunteer Battalion The 5th Lanarkshire Rifle Volunteer Corps was re-designated as 1st Volunteer Battalion Highland Light Infantry by General Order 181 of 1887. The first headquarters of the corps were at 179 West George Street, Glasgow, its drill hall being in Parliamentary Road. In July 1874, however, new headquarters premises were taken over at 13 Renfrew Street, then again, in July 1879, at Ark Lane, Dennistoun. The next move was on 25 December 1879 when, as a result of a great storm during which the Ark Lane premises were blown down, the corps moved to Crown Halls, 98 Sauchiehall Street. These premises were rented until 1885 when a new headquarters and drill hall were purchased at 24 Hill Street, Garnethill. Transfer to the Territorial Force in 1908 was as 5th Battalion Highland Light Infantry, the

Glasgow Academy Cadet Corps, which had been formed and affiliated to the battalion in 1902, at the same time joining the OTC.

2nd Volunteer Battalion The 6th Lanarkshire Rifle Volunteer Corps was re-designated as 2nd Volunteer Battalion Highland Light Infantry by General Order 181 of December 1887. With headquarters at Yorkhill Street, Overnewtown, Glasgow, the battalion transfer to the Territorial Force in 1908 as 6th Battalion Highland Light Infantry. The Govan High School Cadet Corps, which had been formed and affiliated to the battalion in 1901, was eventually accepted by the OTC in 1911. Illustration **(569)** is by Lieutenant-General Sir James Moncrieff Grierson.

3rd (The Blythswood) Volunteer Battalion The 8th Lanarkshire Rifle Volunteer Corps was re-designated as 3rd (The Blythswood) Volunteer Battalion Highland Light Infantry by General Order 181 of December 1887. In 1902 a new headquarters and drill hall were built at 69 Main Street, Bridgeton at a cost of £12,000. Musketry was carried out at Gilbertfield near Cambuslang and transfer to the Territorial Force was as 7th Battalion, Highland Light Infantry. Illustration **(570)** shows a colour sergeant of the battalion wearing a blue collar which suggests that the photograph was taken prior to 1886 when yellow facings were introduced.

9th Lanarkshire Rifle Volunteer Corps With headquarters at Lanark and six companies: 'A' (Lesmahagow), 'B' (Lanark), 'C' (Biggar), 'D' (Carluke), 'E' (Douglas) and 'F' (Leadhills), the 9th Lanarkshire RVC became a volunteer battalion of the Highland Light Infantry (without change in title) in 1881. 'E' Company moved to Forth in 1894, 'F' to Law in 1901 and transfer to the Territorial Force in 1908 was as 8th Battalion Highland Light Infantry.

5th (Glasgow Highland) Volunteer Battalion The origins of the

10th Lanarkshire Rifle Volunteer Corps begin with a meeting held by the numerous Highlanders then resident in Glasgow on 24 April 1868. Some 800 men showed an interest in forming a corps and subsequently the services of the 105th (Glasgow Highland) RVC of twelve companies were accepted on 21 July 1868. Francis Robertson-Reid, late of the Royal Renfrew Militia, took command, and headquarters were established at 97 Union Street, Glasgow. Although recruited in general from all over Glasgow, 'C' Company was made up by residents of the Patrick area, 'E' from Crosshill, 'F' by natives of Islay and 'G' by exiles from Argyllshire. The 105th made its first appearance at the laying of the new Glasgow University building foundation stone by HRH the Prince of Wales on 8 October 1868. In June 1880 the 105th was renumbered as 10th and designated 5th (Glasgow Highland) Volunteer Battalion Highland Light Infantry by General Order 181 of December 1887. A Cyclist Company was added in 1900. Blairlodge School Cadet Corps, which had been affiliated to the battalion on 1891, was disbanded in 1904. General Grierson in *Records of the Scottish Volunteer Force* notes that in the latter years of the battalion's history, 'A' Company was recruited from Highland residents of Springburn, 'B' from Whiteinch, 'C' from Partick, 'E' from Queen's Park, 'M' from Hillhead and 'F', as always, from natives of Islay. The last headquarters and drill hall were at 81 Greendyke Street, Glasgow, the rifle range being at Patterton. Transfer to the Territorial Force was as 9th Battalion Highland Light Infantry. Illustration **(571)** is by Lieutenant-General Sir James Moncrieff Grierson and shows a private and lieutenant.

SEAFORTH HIGHLANDERS (ROSS-SHIRE BUFFS, THE DUKE OF ALBANY'S)

72nd (Duke of Albany's Own Highlanders) Regiment

The regiment was numbered as 78th when raised towards the end of 1777 by Kenneth Mackenzie, Earl of Seaforth. The facings were yellow from the beginning. Re-numbering as 72nd came in 1786, the additional Duke of Albany's Own Highlanders being added to the title in 1823. The 72nd provided the 1st Battalion of the Seaforth Highlanders in 1881. Interesting are two of the regiment's nicknames: The King's Men, which derives from the motto *Cuidich 'n Righ* (Help the King), and The Wild Macraes coming from the fact that when the 72nd was raised in 1777, many of the recruits came from the Clan Macrae. The motto, together with a stag's head, come from the founder's family and featured on the regiment's badges and Colours.

78th (Highlanders) (Ross-shire Buffs) Regiment

Raised by Francis Humbertson Mackenzie, Lord Seaforth, in 1793, the 78th wore buff facings until providing the 2nd Battalion Seaforth Highlanders in 1881. The badge of an elephant with the word Assaye was authorized in April 1807.

Regular Battalions

1st and 2nd Battalions The 1st Battalion was formed by the 72nd (Duke of Albany's Own Highlanders) Regiment, the 2nd by the 78th (Highlanders) (Ross-shire Buffs) Regiment. Illustration **(572)** from Bruce Bassett-Powell shows items of officers' insignia. The regiment was to find its way via the studios of several leading military artists, to the general public via prints and postcards. Richard Simkin's No 97 in his 'Military Types' series is shown at **(573)** and a postcard after Harry Payne in **(574).** The Aldershot firm of Gale & Polden produced a fine series of six-per-set regimental cards calling upon various artists to provide the artwork. Ernest Ibbetson was chosen for the Seaforth set, his caption for each card being: 'The Commanding Officer' **(575)**, 'The Colours and Escort' **(576)**, 'Drum-Major and Pipers **(577)**, 'Relieving Sentry' **(578)**, 'Parade Drill Order' **(579)** and 'A Gallant Charge' **(580)**. On the photographic side we have the officers of the 1st Battalion in India **(581)** and a member of a cyclist section **(582)**.

Militia Battalion

3rd Battalion Formed by the Highland Rifle Militia with headquarters at Dingwall.

Territorial Battalions

4th (Ross Highland) Battalion Formed by the former 1st (Ross Highland) Volunteer Battalion with headquarters at Dingwall and companies: 'A' (Tain, Nigg, Fearn, Edderton and Portmahomack), 'B' (Dingwall), 'C' (Munlochy, Avoch, Rosemarkie, Culbokie, Muir of Ord and Fortrose), 'D' (Gairloch, Opinan, Poolewe, Kinlochewe and Torridon), 'E' (Ullapool, Coigach and Braemore), 'F' (Invergordon and Kildary), 'G' (Alness and Evanton) and 'H' (Maryburgh, Strathpeffer, Garve, Strathconon and Fairburn).

5th (The Sutherland and Caithness Highland) Battalion Formed by the former 1st Sutherland (The Sutherland Highland) Volunteer Rifle Corps with headquarters at Golspie and companies: 'A' (Golspie, Melvich and Bettyhill), 'B' (Dornoch and Rogart), 'C' (Bonar Bridge, Lairg, Lochinver and Elphine), 'D' (Brora, Helmsdale, Kildonan and Kinbrace), 'E' (Thurso and Reay), 'F' (Wick and Lybster), 'G' (Halkirk, Watten and Westfield) and 'H' (Castletown, Dunnet, Mey and Bowermadden).

6th (Morayshire) Battalion Formed by the former 3rd (Morayshire) Volunteer Battalion with headquarters at Elgin and companies: 'A' (Forres and Altyre), 'B' (Elgin, Lossiemouth and Pluscarden), 'C' (Elgin and Lossiemouth), 'D' (Rothes and Archiestown), 'E' (Fochabers and Bogmuir), 'F' (Grantown-on-Spey, Nethy Bridge and Carrbridge), 'G' (Garmouth and Lhanbryde) and 'H' (Lossiemouth, Hopeman, Pluscarden and Burghead).

Volunteer Battalions

1st (Ross Highland) Volunteer Battalion The 1st (Ross Highland) Rifle Volunteer Corps had nine companies: 'A' (Tain), 'B' (Dingwall), 'C' (Fortrose), 'D' (Munlochy), 'E' (Ullapool), 'F' (Invergordon), 'G' (Evanton), 'H' (Moy) and 'I' (Gairloch). Headquarters were at Dingwall. The corps was re-designated as 1st (Ross Highland) Volunteer Battalion Seaforth Highlanders by General Order 181 of 1887. In the same year 'G' Company moved to Dingwall (with a detachment at Alness) and 'H' to Fairburn near Moy on the Brahan estate. Transfer to the Territorial Force was as 4th Battalion Seaforth Highlanders.

1st Sutherland (The Sutherland Highland) Volunteer Rifle Corps The 1st (Sutherland Highland) Rifle Volunteer Corps had ten companies: 'A' (Golspie), 'B' (Dornoch), 'C' (Brora), 'D' (Rogart), 'E' (Bonar Bridge), 'F' (Lerwick), 'G' (Thurso), 'H' (Wick), 'I' (Halkirk) and 'K' (Watten). Headquarters were at Golspie and the corps became a volunteer battalion (without change in title) of the Seaforth Highlanders in 1881. 'F' Company was disbanded in 1884, a replacement being formed at the same time at Lairg. 'L' Company was added at Wick in 1890 and 'M' at Reay in 1901. Transfer to the Territorial Force was as 5th Battalion Seaforth Highlanders.

3rd (Morayshire) Volunteer Battalion The 1st Elgin Rifle Volunteer Corps had ten-and-a-half companies located: 'A' (Forres), 'B' and 'C' (Elgin), 'D' (Rothes), 'E' (Fochabers), 'F' (Carrbridge), 'G' (Urquhart with a half-company at Pluscarden), 'H' (Forres), 'I' (Garmouth) and 'K' (Grantown). The 1st Corps was linked with the Seaforth Highlanders in 1881 and in December 1887 re-designated as its 3rd (Morayshire) Volunteer Battalion—Morayshire an alternative name for Elginshire. In the same year the

576 SEAFORTH HIGHLANDERS The Colours and Escort

577 SEAFORTH HIGHLANDERS Drum-Major and Pipers

578 SEAFORTH HIGHLANDERS Relieving Sentry

579 SEAFORTH HIGHLANDERS Parade—Drill Order

580 A Gallant Charge

headquarters of 'F' Company were moved from Carr Bridge to Abernethy. Ten years later the half-company at Pluscarden was increased to form 'L' Company, its headquarters, however, moved to Alves in 1904. 'G' Company transferred from Urquhart to Lhanbryde in the following year. By 1905 'D' Company had added a detachment at Archiestown and 'K' one at Cromdale. Battalion headquarters were located at Cowper Park, Elgin and transfer to the Territorial Force was as 6th Battalion Seaforth Highlanders.

Illustration credits: Alan Seymore (581), Bruce Bassett-Powell and Bob Bennet (572)

GORDON HIGHLANDERS

75th (Stirlingshire) Regiment

The 75th (Highland) Regiment was raised for service in India by Colonel Sir Robert Abercrombie in 1787, his commission being dated 12 October. Full Highland dress with yellow facings was worn but was lost from 1809 until 1862 when it was in part restored. Highland was also removed from the title in 1809, 1862 seeing the introduction of Stirlingshire as a suitable replacement. The 75th provided the 1st Battalion Gordon Highlanders in 1881. Authorized in July 1807 was the Royal Tiger badge as a commemoration for the regiment's services in India.

92nd (Gordon Highlanders) Regiment

Raised in 1794 as the 100th (Gordon Highlanders) by George Gordon Marquis of Huntly. The regiment was mainly recruited throughout Aberdeenshire and wore red coats with yellow facings. The tartan was Gordon with a yellow distinguishing stripe. Re-numbered as 92nd (Highland) in 1798, Gordon Highlanders being added to the numerical designation in 1861. The 92nd provided the 2nd Battalion Gordon Highlanders in 1881. Authorized as a badge in July 1802 was the Sphinx superscribed Egypt. A crowned thistle was also worn.

Regular Battalions

1st and 2nd Battalions The 1st Battalion was formed by the 75th (Stirlingshire) Regiment, the 2nd by the 92nd (Gordon Highlanders) Regiment. For No 98 in his 'Military Types' series of supplements to

the *Army and Navy Gazette,* Richard Simkin chose to feature a piper, officer and sergeant from the regiment **(583)**. For one of Gale & Polden's military postcards, Harry Payne was employed to provide the artwork shown in **(584)**, the subject this time being an officer, notebook in hand, addressing a private standing to attention having ordered arms. Gale & Polden also published a set of six cards featuring the regiment, this time the artist being Edgar A Holloway, three of which are illustrated here, **(585)**, **(586)** and **(587)**.

In illustration **(588)** we see a photograph of three members of the regiment, a printed label on the reverse of the image revealing that the men are from left to right: Private H Hefferon, Pipe Major C Dunbar and a Private McGeechan. The label also tells how the picture was used for a recruiting poster 1906-1923. The actual poster is shown in **(589)**, the artist having chosen to promote Private Hefferon to corporal and given Private McGeechan some additional good conduct stripes.

Militia Battalion

3rd Battalion Formed by the Royal Aberdeenshire Highlanders Militia with headquarters at Aberdeen.

Territorial Battalions

Members of the regiment's Territorial battalions appear in illustrations **(590)**, identified as such from the three tier shoulder title and the efficiency stars worn on the lower right arms, and **(591)**. In the latter, three tier titles are again in evidence, as is the unique to Territorials, Imperial Service brooch being worn by the soldier on the extreme left.

4th Battalion Formed from the former 1st Volunteer Battalion with headquarters and all eight companies at Aberdeen.

5th (Buchan and Formartin) Battalion Formed by the amalgamation of the former 2nd and 3rd Volunteer Battalions with headquarters at Peterhead. The eight companies were located: 'A' (Strichen, New Pitsligo, New Aberdour, New Deer and Maud), 'B' (Peterhead, Longside and St Fergus), 'C' (Peterhead, Boddam and Hatton), 'D' (Turriff, Fyvie and Cuminestown), 'E' (Ellon, Auchnagatt, Methlick, Skilmafilly and Newburgh), 'F' (Old Meldrum, Tarves, Newmachar and Pitmedden), 'G' (Fraserburgh and Rosehearty) and 'H' (Fraserburgh and Lonmay).

6th (Banff and Donside) Battalion Formed by the amalgamation of the former 4th and 6th Volunteer Battalions with headquarters at Keith. The eight companies were located: 'A' (Banff, Aberchirder, Cornhill and Portsoy), 'B' (Dufftown, Aberlour, Chapeltown, Glenrinnes and Minmore), 'C' (Keith and Grange), 'D' (Buckie. Findochty and Cullen), 'E' (Inverurie and Pitcaple), 'F' (Alford, Cushnie, Lumsden, Glenbuckat, Strathdon, Corgarff and Towie), 'G' (Bucksburn and Dyce) and 'H' (Huntly, Insch and Rhynie).

7th (Deeside Highland) Battalion Formed by the former 5th Volunteer Battalion with headquarters at Banchory. The companies were located: 'A' (Banchory, Durris and Torphins), 'B' (Portlethen), 'C' (Stonehaven), 'D' (Laurencekirk, Auchenblae, Bervie, Fettercairn, Fordoun and Marykirk), 'E' (Ballater, Crathie and Braemar), 'F' (Aboyne, Tarland, Finzean and Logie Coldstone), 'G' (Skene, Blackburn, Monymusk and Echt) and 'H' (Peterculter and Countesswells).

Shetland Companies Formed from the former 7th Volunteer Battalion with headquarters at Lerwick. There were just two companies: 'A' (Lerwick) and 'B' (Lerwick and Scalloway).

Volunteer Battalions

1st Volunteer Battalion With headquarters at Aberdeen, the 1st Aberdeenshire Rifle Volunteer Corps had nine companies lettered 'A' to 'I'. Re-designation as 1st Volunteer Battalion Gordon Highlanders was in 1884. 'L' Company was formed in October 1895, 'H' disbanded in 1898, while at the same time Aberdeen University raised a company lettered 'U'. In 1905 'D' and 'I' were amalgamated as 'D', and 'E' and 'L' as 'M'. The battalion maintained a rifle range at Seaton Links just over two miles from Aberdeen and transfer to the Territorial Force in 1908 was as 4th Battalion Gordon Highlanders.

2nd Volunteer Battalion With headquarters at Aberdeen, the 2nd Aberdeenshire Rifle Volunteer Corps had seven companies: 'A' (Methlick), 'B' (Ellon), 'C' (Newburgh), 'D' (Turriff), 'E' (Fyvie), 'F' (Old Meldrum) and 'G' (Tarves). Re-designation as 2nd Volunteer Battalion Gordon Highlanders was in 1884, headquarters moving to Old Meldrum in 1899. Three companies ('D', 'E' and 'F') of the 5th Battalion Gordon Highlanders were formed in 1908.

3rd (The Buchan) Volunteer Battalion Buchan is the name given to the area of north-east Aberdeenshire extending along the coast from the Ythan to Deveron rivers, a distance of some forty miles. With headquarters at Old Deer, the 3rd Aberdeenshire Rifle Volunteer Corps had nine companies: 'A' (New Deer), 'B' (Peterhead), 'C' (St Fergus), 'D' (Old Deer), 'E' (Strichen), 'F' (Longside), 'G' (Fraserburgh), 'H' (New Pitsligo) and 'I' (Cruden). Headquarters moved to Peterhead in 1883 and in the same year 'H' Company went from New Pitsligo to Fraserburgh and a new company was formed at Boddam. The corps was re-designated as 3rd (The Buchan) Volunteer Battalion Gordon Highlanders in 1884. Over the next seventeen years numerous changes were made within the battalion's company structure. In 1885 'C' moved to Crimond changing location yet again to Lonmay in 1888, 'K' went to Peterhead in the same year and in 1900 'I' was disbanded. 'C' Company was absorbed into 'E' and 'K' as 'C' in 1901. In 1908, headquarters and five companies ('A', 'B', 'C', 'G' and 'H') of 5th Battalion Gordon Highlanders were formed upon transfer to the Territorial Force.

4th (Donside Highland) Volunteer Battalion With headquarters at Aberdeen, the 4th Aberdeenshire Rifle Volunteer Corps had seven companies: 'A' (Huntly), 'B' (Kildrummy), 'C' (Insch), 'D' (Alford), 'E' (Inverurie), 'F' (Kemnay) and 'G' (Auchmull). Re-designation as 4th Volunteer Battalion Gordon Highlanders was in 1884, the additional title 'Donside Highland' being granted in 1893. Several new companies were later formed: 'H' at Auchmull in 1897, followed by one each at Kintore and

592   4TH VOL. BN. GORDON HIGHLANDERS

Kildrummy in 1899. Other changes were in 1899 when 'B' Company moved from Kildrummy to Strathdon, in 1903 when 'G' and 'H' went to Bucksburn and 1906 which saw 'B' and 'C' amalgamated as 'B' at Kildrummy. Transfer to the Territorial Force in 1908 was as four companies ('E', 'F', 'G' and 'H') of the 6th Battalion Gordon Highlanders. From Lieutenant-General Sir James Moncrieff Grierson's *Records of the Scottish Volunteer Force 1859-1908*, the several uniforms worn by the 4th Volunteer Battalion and its predecessors **(592)**.

5th (Deeside Highland) Volunteer Battalion With headquarters at Banchory, the 1st Kincardineshire and Aberdeenshire (Deeside Highland) Rifle Volunteer Corps had ten companies: 'A' (Banchory), 'B' (Laurencekirk), 'C' (Portlethen), 'D' (Durris), 'E' (Maryculter), 'F' (Echt), 'G' (Tarland), 'H' (Aboyne), 'I' (Ballater) and 'K' (Torphins). In 1883 a series of company mergers and changes in location began when on 28 November 'K' Company was amalgamated with 'A' and a new 'K' formed at Stonehaven. 'G' and 'H' were merged in May 1885, battalion headquarters moved to Aberdeen in May 1886 and in 1887 and 1891 respectively 'E' Company moved to Peterculter and 'F' to Skene. The corps was re-designated 5th (Deeside Highland) Volunteer Battalion Gordon Highlanders on 17 January 1884 and headquarters moved back to Banchory in July 1894. The 7th Battalion Gordon Highlanders was formed upon transfer to the Territorial Force in 1908.

6th Volunteer Battalion The 1st Banffshire Rifle Volunteer Corps had six-and-a-half companies: 'A' (Banff), 'B' (Aberlour), 'C' (Keith), 'D' (Buckie), 'E' (Glenlivet) and 'F' (Dufftown). Headquarters were in Keith and the half company at Glenrinnes. By General Order 12 of 1 February 1884, the 1st Banffshire RVC became the 6th Volunteer Battalion of the Gordon Highlanders, a new company ('G') being later formed at Aberchirder. Four companies ('A' to 'D') of

6th Battalion Gordon Highlanders were provided upon transfer to the Territorial Force. From Lieutenant-General Sir James Moncrieff Grierson's *Records of the Scottish Volunteer Force 1859-1908,* the several uniforms worn by the 6th Volunteer Battalion and its predecessors **(593)**.

7th Volunteer Battalion Since the disbandment of 'F' Company 1st Sutherland Rifle Volunteer Corps at Lerwick in 1884 there were no volunteers on the Shetlands until 1900 when three new companies—'A' and 'B' at Lerwick, 'C' at Scalloway—were raised as 7th VB Gordon Highlanders. Transfer to the Territorial Force was as The Shetland Companies Gordon Highlanders.

QUEEN'S OWN CAMERON HIGHLANDERS

79th (Queen's Own Cameron Highlanders) Regiment

Raised under a letter of service dated 17 August 1793 by Alan Cameron of Erracht and given the title of 79th (Cameronian Volunteers) Regiment of Foot. Records note that ten companies were authorized, each to be made up of fifty-seven rank and file. No man was to be enlisted who was over thirty-five or under five feet, five inches in height. The regiment was quickly raised and mustered for service at Stirling on 3 January 1794. The subtitle was changed to Cameron Highlanders in 1804, Queen's Own Cameron Highlanders in 1873. Little was changed in 1881 when, only the number was removed from the title. The original facings were dark green, changing to blue with the granting of the Queen's Own title in 1873. Badges featured the Sphinx superscribed Egypt, granted in 1802, and the Thistle ensigned with the Imperial Crown. The latter also in 1873.

Regular Battalions

1st and 2nd Battalions When the 79th Regiment became the Cameron Highlanders in 1881 it only contained one battalion. It would not be until 1897 that a 2nd was added. The regiment's badges are shown in Bruce Bassett-Powell's detailed image **(594)**, the uniforms beautifully painted in Richard Simkin's study of a private, officer and piper **(595)**. This colour plate was published on 7 March 1896 as a supplement to

the *Army and Navy Gazette*. Artist Harry Payne also included a piper in one of his Gale & Polden postcards, the musician on this occasion seen relaxing with a corporal as two drummers chat in the background **(596)**. The image is the original artwork supplied by the artist to the publisher.

Militia Battalion

2nd, later 3rd Battalion The Highland Light Infantry Militia at Inverness provided the regiment's 2nd Battalion in 1881, the re-numbering as 3rd being when the new regular battalion was formed in 1897.

Territorial Battalion

4th Battalion Formed from the former 1st (Inverness Highland) Volunteer Battalion with headquarters at Inverness. The eight companies were located: 'A' (Inverness), 'B' (Nairn, Cawdor, Ardersier, Auldearn, Croy and Petty), 'C' (Inverness and Moy), 'D' (Broadford, Torrin, Elgoll and Raasay), 'E' (Fort William, Corpach, Fort Augustus and Invergarry), 'F' (Kingussie, Dalwhinnie, Newtonmore, Kincraig, Insh, Aviemore and Ardverikie), 'G' (Beauly, Struy, Kiltarlity, Balnain, Inchmore and Drumnadrochit) and 'H' (Portree, Glenmore, Bernisdale, Edinbane, Sconser, Tarbert, Kilmuir, Dunvegan and Lochmaddy).

Volunteer Battalion

1st (Inverness Highland) Volunteer Battalion With headquarters at Inverness the 1st Inverneshire Rifle Volunteer Corps had ten companies: 'A' to 'D' (Inverness), 'E' (Fort William), 'F' (Kingussie), 'G' (Beauly), 'H' (Portree), 'I' (Ardersier) and 'K' (Roy Bridge). The corps became a volunteer battalion of the Seaforth Highlanders in 1881, transferring to the Cameron Highlanders in 1883 with the title 1st (Inverness Highland) Volunteer Battalion authorized under General Order 181 of December 1887. In September 1903 the headquarters of 'K' Company moved to Fort Augustus with a section at Drumnadrochit, transfer to the Territorial Force in 1908 being as 4th Battalion Cameron Highlanders. From Lieutenant-General Sir James Moncrieff Grierson's *Records of the Scottish Volunteer Force 1859-1908*, the several uniforms worn by the 1st Volunteer Battalion and its predecessors **(597)**.

Illustration credit: Anne SK Brown Military Collection, Brown University Library (596)

ROYAL IRISH RIFLES

83rd (County of Dublin) Regiment

Raised 1793 in Dublin by Colonel William Fitch who was later killed in the Second Maroon War of 1795-96. An early nickname of the 83rd regiment was Fitch's Grenadiers, due to the exceptional height of most of the men. County of Dublin was added to the title on 29 October 1859 and the 83rd provided the 1st Battalion Royal Irish Rifles in 1881. Yellow facings were worn, the Harp, Crown and motto *Quis Separabit* (Who shall separate us) were authorized as badges on 26 March 1832.

86th (Royal County Down) Regiment

The regiment was raised throughout Shropshire, Lancashire and the West Riding by Colonel Cornelius Cuyler under the title of Shropshire Volunteers in 1793 and was soon numbered as 86th. The Leinster was added to the title in 1809, followed in 1812 by Royal County Down. The 86th provided the 2nd Battalion Royal Irish Rifles in 1881. The granting of the Royal title in 1812 was as a reward for the services of the 86th during the reduction of the island of Bourbon. At the same time the facings were changed from yellow to blue and the badge of a crowned Irish Harp was introduced, but not authorized until 26 March 1832. Another badge, a Sphinx superscribed Egypt was sanctioned in July 1802.

Regular Battalions

1st and 2nd Battalions 1st Battalion formed by the 83rd (County of Dublin) Regiment, the 2nd by the 86th (Royal County Down) Regiment. The regiment's badges are shown in **(598)** and **(599)**, the latter illustration being a postcard published by Falkner & Sons from artwork provided by J McNeill. The regiment's rifle green uniforms are shown in Richard Simkin's illustration for No 100 in the 'Military Types' series which appeared as a supplement to the *Army and Navy Gazette* on 4 April 1896 **(600)**.

Militia Battalions

3rd, later 4th Battalion The former Royal North Down Militia became the 3rd Battalion in 1881, but was re-numbered as 4th in 1908. Headquarters were at Newtownards.

4th, later 3rd Battalion The original 4th Battalion was formed by the Antrim (Queen's Royal Rifles) Militia in 1881, being re-designated as 3rd in 1908. Headquarters were at Belfast.

5th Battalion Formed by the Royal South Down Militia at Downpatrick.

6th Battalion Formed by the Louth Militia with headquarters at Dundalk. Disbanded in 1908.

Illustration credit: Bruce Bassett-Powell and Bob Bennet (598)

PRINCESS VICTORIA'S (ROYAL IRISH FUSILIERS)

87th (Royal Irish Fusiliers) Regiment

The regiment was raised in Ireland under an order dated 18 September 1793 by Colonel Sir John Doyle who would remain colonel for thirty-eight years. The uniform worn at the time is illustrated in Cannon's history and appears as a scarlet coatee, of closer fit than usual, with deep green facings. Regimental badges were the Harp and Crown and the Prince of Wales's Coronet, Plumes and *Ich Dien* (I Serve) motto. When raised, the regiment's subtitle was 'The Prince of Wales's Irish, the word Own was added in 1811, Royal Irish Fusiliers replacing the whole in 1827. Blue facing substituted the green at this time. In 1881, the 87th provided the 1st Battalion Princess Victoria's (Royal Irish Fusiliers). The Eagle and Wreath of Laurel badge commemorates the capture by the 87th of the 8th French Regiment at the Battle of Barrosa in 1811.

89th (Princess Victoria's) Regiment

Raised 1793 by Colonel William Crosbie who at the time was serving as Member of Parliament for Newark. Princess Victoria's was added to the title in 1866, the 89th providing the 2nd Battalion Princess Victoria's (Royal Irish Fusiliers) in 1881. The Sphinx superscribed Egypt was authorized as a badge in July 1802, the Cypher and Coronet of Princess Victoria coming with the title in 1866. The uniforms had black facings.

Regular Battalions

1st and 2nd Battalions The 1st Battalion was formed by the 87th (Royal Irish Fusiliers) Regiment, the 2nd by the 89th (Princess Victoria's)

Regiment. The officer shown in Harry Payne's watercolour **(601)** wears the Queen's and King's Medals awarded for service during the Second Boer War. Both regular battalions fought in South Africa, the 1st sailing from Alexandria, Egypt on 24 September 1899, the 2nd arriving in the following October. In **(602)** we see a commanding officer, his bugler at his side, mounted in front of his battalion. By Richard Simkin, this print was No 101 in the artist's 'Military Types' series for the *Army and Navy Gazette*, published on 2 May 1896.

Militia Battalions

3rd and 4th Battalions The 3rd Battalion was formed by the Armagh Light Infantry Militia, the 4th by the Cavan Militia and the 5th by the Monaghan Militia. The latter was disbanded in 1908.

Illustration credit: Anne SK Brown Military Collection, Brown University Library (601)

CONNAUGHT RANGERS

88th (Connaught Rangers) Regiment

Raised under an order dated 25 September 1793 by Colonel the Hon John Thomas de Burgh (afterwards Earl of Clanricarde), chiefly in Connaught. The 88th provided the 1st Battalion Connaught Rangers in 1881. From its formation, the regiment took into use yellow facings and the badge of an Irish Harp. The latter, however, was not officially authorized until December 1830. Another badge, the Sphinx superscribed Egypt was confirmed in July 1802.

94th Regiment

Although officially disbanded in 1818, the 94th (Scotch Brigade) regiment (see above) is considered to be the predecessor of the 94th raised (re-raised) in 1823 and which became the 2nd Battalion Connaught Rangers in 1881. Recruiting mainly in the Glasgow area, the officers for the new 94th were chiefly from the half-pay list of the old regiment. The colonelcy was given to Sir Thomas Bradford who later became in 1825, C-in-C, Bombay. The regiment received its first Colours in Gibraltar soon after its formation. Later service was in Malta, India, Aden. In 1874 the 94th was authorized to adopt the diced band to the shako, as worn by Lowland regiments, and the Elephant Caparisoned badge and Peninsular honours of the old Scotch Brigade. Bluish green was the first facing colour noted, Lincoln Green being that noted in later Army Lists.

Regular Battalions

1st and 2nd Battalions The 1st Battalion was formed by the 88th

(Connaught Rangers) Regiment, the 2nd by the 94th Regiment. Illustration **(603)** is the original artwork provided by artist Harry Payne for one of Gale & Polden's uniform postcards, **(604)** being one of Richard Simkin's 'Military Types' series for the *Army and Navy Gazette*.

Militia Battalions

3rd Battalion Formed by the South Mayo Militia with headquarters at Westport. The battalion was amalgamated with the 6th in 1889, then disbanded in 1908.

4th, later 3rd Battalion The original 4th Battalion was formed in 1881 by the Galway Militia, being re-numbered as 3rd in 1908.

5th, later 4th Battalion Formed by the Roscommon Militia at Boyle and re-numbered as 4th in 1908.

6th Battalion Formed by the North Mayo Militia at Ballina and amalgamated with the 3rd Battalion in 1889.

Illustration credit: Anne SK Brown Military Collection, Brown University Library (603)

PRINCESS LOUISE'S (ARGYLL AND SUTHERLAND HIGHLANDERS)

91st (Princess Louise's Argyllshire Highlanders) Regiment

The 98th (Argyllshire Highlanders) was raised under the colonelcy of Duncan Campbell of Lochnell in 1794, a post which he would hold for some forty-one years. The uniform facings were yellow, and the regiment was re-numbered as 91st in 1798. Princess Louise's Argyllshire Highlanders was added to the title in 1872, the 91st providing the 1st Battalion Princess Louise's (Sutherland and Argyle Highlanders) in 1881. The Boar's Head of the Argyll family, and Myrtle of the Campbell Clan were authorized as badges on 14 March 1872.

93rd (Sutherland Highlanders) Regiment

The 93rd (Highlanders) was raised by Colonel William Wemyss of Wemyss in 1799. This officer had commanded the 3rd Sutherland Regiment of Fencibles, which was disbanded in 1798 after serving in Ireland, from which he drew the majority of his recruits. About 460 men coming in from Sutherland, others from Ross and adjacent counties, the regiment mustered up to 1,000 rank and file when it assembled in Guernsey. Sutherland Highlanders was added to the title in 1861, the 93rd providing the 2nd Battalion Princess Louise's (Argyll and Sutherland Highlanders) in 1881. This was the regiment that inspired Robert Gibb's famous 1881 picture 'The Thin Red Line'. The facing were yellow, badges featuring the Wild Cat and Butcher's Broom of the Sutherland Clan.

Regular Battalions

1st and 2nd Battalions The 1st Battalion was formed by the 91st (Princess Louise's Argyllshire

Highlanders) Regiment, the 2nd by the 93rd (Sutherland Highlanders) Regiment. The regiment could be easily identified by the badger head sporran top seen here in Richard Simkin's 'Military Types' series featuring the regiment **(605)**. Published on 4 July 1896, the image also features a private and piper. It can also be seen in one of the plates from the artist's book *Our Armies,* published by Day & Son **(606)**, and in William Barnes Wollen's 1901 study of an officer **(607)**. Artist EA Holloway also painted the regiment, producing six watercolours for one of Gale & Polden's regimental postcard sets. In **(608)** we see one of the cards set in a railway station and bearing the caption 'Going on Furlough.'

Militia Battalions

3rd and 4th Battalions The 3rd Battalion was formed by the Highland Borderers Light Infantry Militia at Stirling, the 4th by the Royal Renfrew Militia with headquarters at Paisley.

Territorial Battalions

5th (Renfrewshire) Battalion Formed from the former 1st Volunteer Battalion with headquarters at 34 Union Street, moving to Finnart Street, Greenock in 1911. The eight companies were located: 'A' to 'D' (Greenock), 'E' (Port Glasgow), 'F', 'G' (Greenock) and 'H' (Gourock and Inverkip). Many Territorial battalions received their first Colours from the hand of the King at Windsor in June 1909. Here in **(609)** we see the 5th Battalion just after the presentation.

    6th (Renfrewshire) Battalion Formed by the amalgamation of the former 2nd and 3rd Volunteer Battalions with headquarters at 66 High Street, Paisley. The companies were: 'A', 'B', 'C' (Paisley), 'D' (Renfrew), 'E' (Johnstone), 'F' (Thornliebank), 'G' (Barrhead) and 'H' (Pollokshaws).

    7th Battalion Formed by the amalgamation of the former 4th and 7th Volunteer Battalions with headquarters at Stirling. The companies were: 'A' (Stirling, Bannockburn and Bridge of Allan), 'B' (Stenhousemuir and Denny), 'C' (Falkirk and Bonnybridge), 'D' (Lennoxtown and Kilsyth), 'E' (Alloa), 'F'

(Alva, Dollar, Tillicoultry and Menstrie), 'G' (Kinross and Kelty) and 'H' (Alloa, Sauchie and Clackmannan).

8th (The Argyllshire) Battalion Formed from the former 5th Volunteer Battalion with headquarters at Dunoon. The companies were: 'A' (Inveraray, Lochgoilhead, Auchnagoul, Dalmally, Furnace, Cairndow, Strachur and Kilchrenan), 'B' (Campbeltown), 'C' (Southend, Campbeltown, Glenbarr, Tayinloan, Stewarton and Drumlemble), 'D' (Dunoon and Sandbank), 'E' (Lochgilphead, Kilmartin, Tighnabruaich, Glendaruel, Ardrishaig and Tayvallich), 'F' (Ballachulish, Kinlochleven, Ardgour and Duror), 'G' (Bowmore, Jura, Port Ellen, Bridgend and Ballygrant) and 'H' (Easdale, Clachan, Oban, Cullipool, Toberonochy, Benderloch and Ardchattan). The Dunoon Grammar School Cadet Corps was affiliated.

9th (The Dumbartonshire) Battalion Formed from the former 1st Dumbartonshire Volunteer Rifle Corps with headquarters at Helensburgh, moving to Hartfield, Dumbarton in 1913. The companies were: 'A' (Helensburgh and Cardross), 'B' (Kirkintilloch, Cumbernauld and Lenzie), 'C' (Dumbarton), 'D' (Milngavie), 'E' (Jamestown and Bonhill), 'F' (Alexandria and Renton) and 'G', 'H' (Clydebank).

Volunteer Battalions

1st (Renfrewshire) Volunteer Battalion With headquarters at Greenock, the 1st Renfrewshire Rifle Volunteer Corps had nine companies: 'A', 'B', 'C' and 'D' (Greenock), 'E' (Port Glasgow), 'F' and 'G' (Greenock), 'H' (Gourock) and 'I' (Rothesay). Under General Order 181 of December 1887 the 1st Corps was re-designated as 1st (Renfrewshire) Volunteer Battalion Argyll and Sutherland Highlanders. A cyclist company was added in 1900, 'I' Company was disbanded in 1906. Headquarters of the battalion were at 37 Newton Street in Greenock. And transfer to the Territorial Force as 5th Battalion Argyll and Sutherland Highlanders.

2nd (Renfrewshire) Volunteer Battalion With headquarters at Paisley the 2nd Renfrewshire Rifle Volunteer Corps had eight companies: 'A' and 'B' (Paisley), 'C' (Johnstone), 'D' (Paisley), 'E' (Kilbarchan), 'F' (Lochwinnoch), 'G' (Renfrew) and 'H' (Paisley). A new company ('I') was added at Paisley in 1884 and the corps was re-designated as 2nd (Renfrewshire) Volunteer Battalion Argyll and Sutherland Highlanders under General Order 181 of December 1887. 'K' (Cyclist) Company was formed at Paisley in 1900, 'E' was disbanded, and 'F' moved to Elderslie with detachments at Howwood, Kilbarchan and Lochwinnoch in 1903. Battalion headquarters were in High Street, Paisley, its rifle range at Foxbar on the Gleniffder Hills. Transfer to the Territorial Force was as five companies of the 6th Battalion Argyll and Sutherland Highlanders.

3rd (Renfrewshire) Volunteer Battalion With headquarters at Barrhead, the 3rd Renfrewshire Rifle Volunteer Corps had eight companies: 'A' (Pollockshaws), 'B' (Barrhead), 'C' (Neilston), 'D' (Thornliebank), 'E' (Hurlet), 'F' (Barrhead), 'G' (Cathcart) and 'H' (Thornliebank). In 1881 headquarters moved from Barrhead to Pollockshaws, 'E' Company going to Newton Mearns in the same year. Re-designation as 3rd (Renfrewshire) Volunteer Battalion Argyll and Sutherland Highlanders was notified in General Order 181 of 1887 and two new companies, 'I' and 'K' (Cyclist), were added at Barrhead in 1900. 'I', however, was disbanded in 1903. Transfer to the Territorial Force was as three companies of the 6th

Battalion Argyll and Sutherland Highlanders.

4th (Stirlingshire) Volunteer Battalion With headquarters at Stirling the 1st Stirlingshire Rifle Volunteer Corps had ten companies: 'A' and 'B' (Stirling), 'C' (Falkirk), 'D' (Lennox Mill), 'E' (Lennoxtown), 'F' (Stirling), 'G' (Denny), 'H' (Bannockburn), 'I' (Carron) and 'K' (Kilsyth). In 1881 the headquarters of 'D' Company moved from Lennox Mill to Falkirk and in 1887 1st Stirlingshire RVC was re-designated as 4th (Stirlingshire) Volunteer Battalion Argyll and Sutherland Highlanders. In 1904 the headquarters of 'H' and 'I' Companies moved to Stenhousemuir 1904, 'F' transferring to Falkirk in 1906. Transfer to the Territorial Force was as four companies of the 7th Battalion Argyll and Sutherland Highlanders.

5th Volunteer Battalion With headquarters at Dunoon the 1st Argyllshire Rifle Volunteer Corps had eight companies: 'A' (Inveraray), 'B' and 'C' (Campbeltown), 'D' (Dunoon), 'E' (Glendaruel), 'F' and 'G' (Ballachulish) and 'H' (Kilmartin). In December 1882 the headquarters of 'G' Company were transferred from Ballachulish to Southend at the southern portion of Kintyre, about ten miles south of Campbeltown. The 1st Argyllshire RVC had been linked to the Argyll and Sutherland Highlanders in the previous year as one of its volunteer battalions, but it would not be until 1887 that re-designation as 5th Volunteer Battalion took place—notification of the change being made in General Order 181 of 1 December. As a result of the war in South Africa, new companies were raised in 1900: 'I' at Carradale, thirteen miles north-east of Campbeltown, and 'K' (Cyclist) which was at Campbeltown itself and recruited from all over the battalion. In the following year the Dunoon Grammar School Cadet Corps was formed and affiliated to the battalion. Around this time 'A' Company is noted as also having detachments at Dalmally and Furness, 'E' at Strachur, Tighnabruaich and Lochgoilhead, 'G' at Kilkenzie and Glenbar, 'H' at Ardrishaig and 'I' at Tayinloan. Transfer to the Territorial Force in 1908 was as 8th Battalion Argyll and Sutherland Highlanders. Illustration **(610)** is a detail from a painting by Lieutenant-General Sir James Moncrieff Grierson shows two privates in different uniforms. The man on the left wears that dated by General Grierson as 1874-1883, the other the dress worn 1902-1908.

1st Dumbartonshire Volunteer Rifle Corps With headquarters at Helensburgh the 1st Dumbartonshire Rifle Volunteer Corps had twelve companies: 'A' (Helensburgh), 'B' (Cardross), 'C' (Dumbarton), 'D' (Bonhill), 'E' (Jamestown), 'F' (Alexandria), 'G' (Clydebank), 'H' (Maryhill), 'I' (Milngavie), 'K' (Kirkintilloch), 'L' (Cumbernauld) and 'M' (Luss). The corps became a volunteer battalion of the Argyll and Sutherland Highlanders (without change of title) in 1881. 'M' Company at Luss was disbanded in January 1882 but replaced the following month at Renton. The disbandment of the Luss Company had been as a result of the direct defiance by the corps to change its uniform to that then in use by the whole battalion. 'L' Company was absorbed into 'K' as a detachment in 1884 and at the same time a new 'L' was formed at Yorker. A Mounted Infantry Company lettered 'O' was added at Maryhill in 1900, then in the same year 'Q' (Cyclist) was raised at Dumbarton. Transfer to the Territorial Force was as 9th Battalion Argyll and Sutherland Highlanders.

7th (Clackmannan and Kinross) Volunteer Battalion With headquarters at Alloa the 1st Clackmannan and Kinross Rifle Volunteer Corps had seven companies: 'A' (Alloa), 'B' (Sauchie), 'C' (Alloa), 'D' (Dollar), 'E' (Tillicoultry), 'F' (Alva) and 'G' (Kinross). A new section was formed at Clackmannan in 1882 which, in the following year having increased in number, became 'H' Company. The year 1882 also saw the purchase of the old Alloa Prison which was enlarged to provide headquarters, a drill hall, offices and an armoury. The battalion also had its own rifle range at Hillend near Alloa, 'G' Company using a 600-yard site at Blairadam. Dollar Institution formed a cadet corps which was affiliated to the battalion in 1902. General Order 181 of December 1887 notified re-designation as 7th (Clackmannan and Kinross) Volunteer Battalion Argyll and Sutherland Highlanders and transfer to the Territorial Force in 1908 was as four companies (three in Clackmannanshire, one in Kinross) of the 7th Battalion Argyll and Sutherland Highlanders. The Dollar Institution Cadets at the same time became part of the Junior Division, OTC. Illustration **(611)** is a photograph taken by A Pithie of Mill Street, Alloa.

PRINCE OF WALES'S LEINSTER REGIMENT (ROYAL CANADIANS)

100th (Prince of Wales's Royal Canadian) Regiment

This regiment owes its origins to a number of loyal Canadians who, at the outbreak of the Indian Mutiny in 1857, offered to raise a regiment for duty in India. The same volunteers had made a similar offer regarding the Crimean War, but this was refused. This time, however, the services of the Canadians were accepted and duly raised was the 100th (Prince of Wales's Royal Canadian) Regiment. The first colonel, Henry Dundas, 3rd Viscount Melville, was commissioned on 22 June 1858. Many of the officers and men were serving members of the Canadian Militia, among them Alexander Roberts Dunn who as an officer in the 11th Hussars had won the Victoria Cross at the Charge of the Light Brigade, Balaclava, Crimean War. He was the first Canadian to be awarded the VC. The 100th arrived in England, by which time the Mutiny had been suppressed. It subsequently did duty in Gibraltar and Malta, embarking for India, where it remained until 1895, in 1877. The 100th provided the 1st Battalion Prince of Wales's Leinster Regiment (Royal Canadians) in 1881. Royal blue facings were worn, the badge of the Prince of Wales's Coronet, Plumes and *Ich Dien* (I Serve) motto being authorized, together with a Maple Leaf.

109th (Bombay Infantry) Regiment

Raised 1853 in Poona as the Honourable East India Company's 3rd

(Bombay European) Regiment, some of the recruits coming from the HEIC's depot at Warley in Essex, England. The regiment became the 109th in 1861 and provided the 2nd Battalion Prince of Wales's Leinster Regiment (Royal Canadians) in 1881. White facings were worn.

Regular Battalions

1st and 2nd Battalions The 1st Battalion was formed by the 100th (Prince of Wales's Royal Canadian) Regiment, the 2nd from the 109th (Bombay Infantry) Regiment. Illustration **(612)** shows several items worn by the officers of the regiment. The colour plate at **(613)** is by Richard Simkins, **(614)** by Harry Payne.

Militia Battalions

3rd, 4th and 5th Battalions The 3rd Battalion was formed by the King's County Royal Rifles Militia at Paronstown, the 4th by the Royal Queen's County Rifles Militia with headquarters at Maryborough and the 5th by the Royal Meath Militia at Navan.

Illustration credits: Anne SK Brown Military Collection, Brown University Library (614), Bruce Bassett-Powell (612)

ROYAL MUNSTER FUSILIERS

101st (Royal Bengal Fusiliers) Regiment

The 101st has its origins in the Honourable East India Company's Bengal (European) Regiment of 1756. It underwent several changes in title, known as Fusiliers from 1846, until joining the British Line as 101st (Royal Bengal Fusiliers) in 1861. The regiment provided the 1st Battalion Royal Munster Fusiliers in 1881. Uniform facings were blue.

104th (Bengal Fusiliers) Regiment

The Honourable East India Company's 2nd Bengal (European) Regiment was formed in 1839, Fusiliers being added to the title in 1850. It became the 104th (Bengal Fusiliers) in 1861 and provided the 2nd Battalion Royal Munster Fusiliers twenty years later. The uniforms had blue facings.

Regular Battalions

1st and 2nd Battalions The 1st Battalion was formed by the 101st (Royal Bengal Fusiliers) Regiment, the 2nd by the 104th (Bengal Fusiliers) Regiment. Illustration **(615)** is by Richard Simkin, **(616)** being the original artwork by Harry Payne for one of Gale & Polden's uniform postcards. **(617)**, a fine photographic portrait of an officer taken in India.

Militia Battalions

3rd, 4th and 5th Battalions The 3rd Battalion was formed by the Kerry Militia at Tralee, the 4th by the South Cork Light Infantry Militia with headquarters at Bandon, the 5th by the Royal Limerick County Militia at Limerick.

ROYAL DUBLIN FUSILIERS

102nd (Royal Madras Fusiliers) Regiment

The 102nd has its origins in the Honourable East India Company's European Regiment of 1746. Madras formed part of the title from 1830, Fusiliers from 1843. The 102nd, designated as such from 1861, provided the 1st Battalion Royal Dublin Fusiliers in 1881. The regiment, after 223 years' service in India, was brought to England in 1868. Blue facings were worn, the Tiger badge being awarded for the regiment's service in India.

618 THE ROYAL DUBLIN FUSILIERS
102ND & 103RD FOOT

103rd (Royal Bombay Fusiliers) Regiment

The origins of the 103rd lie in the formation in 1662 of the Bombay Regiment. It formed part of the Honourable East India Company's forces under several titles, Fusiliers being added in 1843. The regiment joined the British Line as 103rd (Royal Bombay Fusiliers) in 1861 and provided the 2nd Battalion Royal Dublin Fusiliers twenty years later. The uniform facings were blue. An Elephant and Tiger, both for Indian service, featured on the badges.

Regular Battalions

1st and 2nd Battalions The 1st Battalion was formed by the 102nd (Royal Madras Fusiliers) Regiment, the 2nd by the 103rd (Royal Bombay Fusiliers) Regiment.

Militia Battalions

3rd, 4th and 5th Battalions The 3rd Battalion was formed by the Kildare Rifles Militia with headquarters at Naas, the 4th from the Queen's Own Royal Dublin City Militia and the 5th by the Dublin County Light Infantry Militia at Dublin. Illustration **(618)** is by Richard Simkin and **(619)** a group photograph of the 1st Battalion band which includes many young musicians. By Edgar A Holloway, **(620)** is the artist's impression of the regiment being welcomed in France in 1914.

RIFLE BRIGADE
(THE PRINCE CONSORT'S OWN)

Regular Battalions

1st, 2nd, 3rd and 4th Battalions The regiment dates from 1800 when it was known as the Rifle Corps. It was numbered as 95th Regiment in 1803, then designated as the Rifle Brigade in 1816. The title Prince Consort's Own was added in in 1862. Several badges are shown in Bruce Bassett-Powell's detailed image **(621)**. Illustration **(622)** is from Richard Simkin, **(623)** the work of Harry Payne, and **(624)** that of Edgar Holloway.

Militia Battalions

5th Battalion Formed by the Queen's Own Royal Tower Hamlets Militia with headquarters at Victoria Park Square, London.

6th Battalion Formed by the Prince of Wales's Royal Regiment of Longford Rifles Militia. Amalgamated with the 9th Battalion in 1899 then disbanded in 1908.

7th, later 6th Battalion Formed as 7th Battalion in 1881 by the King's Own Royal Tower Hamlets Militia with headquarters at Dalston, London. Re-designated as 6th Battalion in 1908.

8th Battalion Formed by the Leitrim Rifles Militia with headquarters at Carrick-on-Shannon. Disbanded in 1889.

9th Battalion Formed by the Westmeath Rifle Militia with headquarters at Mullingar. Amalgamated with the 6th Battalion in 1899.

Volunteer Battalions

7th Middlesex Rifle Volunteer Corps (London Scottish) The services of a rifle corps composed of Scotsmen living in the London area were accepted by the War Office on 2 November 1859. The corps consisted of six companies and was designated as the 15th Middlesex (London Scottish) RVC, Lord Elcho (afterwards Earl of Wemyss) being appointed as lieutenant colonel in command. Headquarters were established at 8 Adelphi Terrace, Westminster and the six companies were located: No 1 (Highland) 10 Pall Mall, East, No 2 (City) The Oriental Bank, No 3 (Northern) Rosemary Hall Islington, No 4 (Central) Scottish Corporation House Crane Court, No 5 (Southern) 68 Jermyn Street, No 6 (Western) Chesterfield House West London.

Members of the corps paid an entrance fee of £1 (abolished in 1862) and were required to provide their own uniforms and equipment. General Grierson in *Records of the Scottish Volunteer Force* notes that of the 600 men originally enrolled, 340 were artisans who paid no entrance fee and only a five shillings per year subscription, and of these only fifty provided their own uniforms, the rest being equipped from a central fund.

In 1861 No 2 Company became No 7 and a new No 2, together with a No 8, were raised. No 3 Company was absorbed into the rest in 1865 and the following year company numbers were replaced by letters. This required the following reorganisation: 'A' Company (formed by No 1), 'B' Company (newly formed), 'C' Company (from No 4), 'D' Company (from No 5), 'E' Company (from No 2 and No 6), 'F' Company (from No 7), 'G' Company (left vacant), 'H' Company (from No 8).

The 15th was renumbered as 7th in September 1880 and in the following year a new 'G' Company was formed. At the same time the corps became a volunteer battalion (without change in title) of the Rifle Brigade. Additions in 1884 were 'I' and 'K' Companies. Transfer to the Territorial Force in 1908 was as the 14th Battalion London Regiment, headquarters having moved to Adam Street in 1873, then 1 Adam Street, Adelphi, then James Street, Buckingham Gate in 1886. From the Anne SK Brown Military Collection, a Harry Payne painting of the London Scottish as the rest up within sight of London and St Paul's Cathedral **(625)**.

14th Middlesex Rifle Volunteer Corps (Inns of Court) Formed as 23rd Corps at Lincoln's Inn, London from members of the legal profession on 15 February 1860 with six companies under the command of Lieutenant Colonel Commandant William B Brewster, late of the Rifle Brigade. Renumbered as 14th in 1880 and became a volunteer battalion (without change in title) of the Rifle Brigade in 1881. The St Peter's College Cadet Corps, Westminster was affiliated in 1902 and shown as Westminster School from May 1904. It was the intention to transfer the 14th to the Territorial Force in 1908 as the 27th Battalion of the London Regiment, but the members were not happy with this decision and chose to continue service as the Inns of Court OTC instead.

15th Middlesex Rifle Volunteer Corps (The Customs and Docks) Formed as the 26th Corps with headquarters at Custom House, London on 9 February 1860 and recruited from Customs Officers in the London Docks—four companies under the command of Major Commandant Ralph William Grey. Joined the 5th Admin Battalion and amalgamated with 9th Tower Hamlets RVC in 1864 under the title 26th (The Customs and Docks). Absorbed the 42nd Corps, also a dockland formation, in 1866, and the 8th Tower Hamlets in 1868. Now with thirteen companies, was renumbered 15th in 1880 and became a volunteer battalion (without change of title) of the Rifle Brigade in 1881. By 1891 the establishment had been reduced to eight companies. Formed part of 17th Battalion London Regiment.

16th Middlesex Rifle Volunteer Corps (London Irish) The 28th Middlesex Rifle Volunteer Corps of eight companies was raised as a result of a meeting arranged by Mr G T Dempsey, an Irishman resident in London, at his rooms in Essex Street, Strand in the latter weeks of 1859. Headquarters were placed at Burlington House and the first officers' commissions were dated 28 February 1860. It is of interest to note that out of the nineteen officers recorded in the Army List

for December 1860, no less than five held tiles: the Marquis of Donegal (lieutenant colonel), Lord Otho A Fitzgerald (captain), Lord Ashley (captain), Lord Francis N Conynhham (lieutenant) and the Earl of Belmore (ensign). Headquarters were transferred to York Buildings, Adelphi in 1866, Leicester Square in 1869, King William Street in 1873 and Duke Street, Charring Cross in 1897. The 28th was renumbered as 16th in 1880 and became a volunteer battalion (without change of title) of the Rifle Brigade in 1881. Formed the 18th Battalion London Regiment in 1908. Illustration **(626)** is a group photograph which includes officers, a bugler and pioneer.

18th Middlesex Rifle Volunteer Corps A little over five years after the first railway passengers had boarded their trains below the iron work of Matthew Digby Wyatt's roof at Paddington Station, a short distance to the north in the Vestry Hall, the committee set up to establish a corps of riflemen in Paddington had agreed to present the plans gathered so far to the War Office.

January 10 1860, and another meeting on record indicates that as of that date, no sanction had yet been received from the War Office; but nonetheless, recruiting had gone well and within a few days sufficient numbers had come forward to man a full company. By 29 February, the date of the first officer's commission, a second had been raised and in March a captain commandant had been appointed in the form of Major General David Downing (late of the Indian Army) who, on the 7th, attended a levee of Volunteer Officers given by Queen Victoria at St James's Palace. By this time the Paddington Volunteers, their motto 'Arm for peace', had been ranked as 36th in the County of Middlesex.

A third company well underway, the 36th Middlesex held its first parade and march around the borough on 8 May, 1860. A band made up of Metropolitan Railway workers and musicians from the Working Men's

College at Paddington Green led the way. Weeks later, at the first Volunteer Review held in Hyde Park, Nos. 1 and 2 Companies took the field and earned much praise for their smartness and soldierly appearance from those present.

Well on the way to four companies now, a cadet corps had also been formed, along with a drum and bugle band. Situated in the grounds of St Mary's Church next to Paddington Green, the Vestry Hall provided headquarters, while across the Harrow Road at the Hermitage Street Fire Station, drills were carried out and weapons stored. The corps also had the use of two riding schools—Pearce's in Westbourne Grove and Gapp's in Gloucester Terrace.

In 1865 the 36th Middlesex provided the Guard of Honour when HRH the Prince of Wales laid the foundation stone of the Paddington Infirmary (later Paddington General Hospital) adjacent to the Workhouse in the Harrow Road near Lock Bridge. Four years later, as the Vestry Hall began to grow into the Town Hall, temporary headquarters had to be found in rooms above the King and Queen public house in Harrow Road. This was a location within view of the next move which took the 36th across Paddington Green to Greville House, once the premises of the Working Men's College, and before that the home of Emma Hart, the future Lady Hamilton and friend of Lord Nelson.

A gradual increase in establishment seems to have taken place over the first ten years of the corps' existence. Mention of a No 7 Company at Kensal Green made up mainly from employees of the Metropolitan Railway is noted in 1870 and in 1872, 'H' Company (presumably letters have replace numbers by now) is on record as having held a dinner on 10 September. The 36th was renumbered as 18th in 1880 and in the following year became a volunteer battalion (without change in title) of the Rifle Brigade.

The premises at Paddington Green becoming more and more crowded as the battalion grew—transport and ambulance sections had been added to the still growing number of companies, and the band was restricted to practising in the hallways—so in 1895 property was acquired at 207-209 Harrow Road which occupied enough land to permit the building of a drill hall and rifle range. On the evening of 31 March 1896, the 18th were marched out of Paddington Green for the last time. Making their way past St Mary's Church, Sarah Siddons in her white Carrara not yet looking on, and into the Harrow Road where the parade took the battalion past the old Vestry Hall (now Town Hall), Paddington Green Police Station (later made famous in the film *The Blue Lamp*), Porteus Road, where the local artillery volunteers met and drilled, over the bridge that crossed the Grand Junction Canal and took the road down to where it skirted the Great Western, past the Red Lion public house to headquarters. The journey today is in the most part within the shadow of the great Westway Flyover. Formed the 10th Battalion London Regiment in 1908.

19th Middlesex Rifle Volunteer Corps (St Giles and St George's Bloomsbury) Four companies were formed as 37th Corps with headquarters at the Local Board of Works, Holborn on 31 March 1860 with Major John W Jeakes in command. Joined the 4th Admin Battalion in August 1860 but was made independent in May of the following year. Headquarters moved in 1861 to the Foundling Hospital in Guildford Street, WC1. Comprised eight companies by 1866. The additional title St Giles and St George's, Bloomsbury was added in 1869 and in 1880 the corps was renumbered as 19th. Became a volunteer battalion (without change in title) of the Rifle Brigade in 1881. Headquarters moved to Chenies Street, Bedford Square, WC1 in 1887. The 19th Middlesex was amalgamated with 1st Middlesex to form the 9th Battalion London Regiment in 1908.

20th Middlesex Rifle Volunteer Corps (Artists) Formed as three companies with headquarters at Burlington House, London on 25 May 1860 with the painter, Henry W Phillips as captain commandant. Numbered as 38th, the corps was recruited from painters, sculptors, musicians, architects, actors and other members of artistic occupations. A private in the corps was Queen's Medallist and Engraver to the Signet

JW Wyon who was responsible for designing the Artists Rifles badge. An apt device, it included the heads of Mars, the god of war, and Minerva, the goddess of the arts. Later increased to four, then six companies. Headquarters moved to the Arts Club, Hanover Square in 1869, the word Artists being included in the title from 1877. Renumbered 20th in 1880 and as eight companies with headquarters at in Fitzroy Square became a volunteer battalion (without change in title) of the Rifle Brigade in 1881. A move was later made to Duke's Road. The University College School Cadet Corps was affiliated in 1904. Transfer to the Territorial Force in 1908 was as the 28th Battalion London Regiment, the University College School at the same time becoming a contingent of the OTC.

21st Middlesex Rifle Volunteer Corps (The Finsbury Rifle Volunteer Corps) Formed as the 39th Middlesex Corps of eight companies at Clerkenwell on 6 March 1860, Thomas H Colvill, late of the 74th Regiment of Foot, and at the time Governor of Coldbathfields Prison, being appointed as lieutenant colonel in command. Included in the 3rd Admin Battalion until 1861 and 'The Finsbury RVC' was added to the title in 1862. Increased to ten companies in the 1870s, renumbered 21st in 1880. Became a volunteer battalion (without change in title) of the Rifle Brigade in 1881, transferring to the King's Royal Rifle Corps in 1883.

24th Middlesex Rifle Volunteer Corps The formation of a Rifle Corps at the General Post Office in London was sanctioned by the War Office on 13 February 1868. Designated as 49th Middlesex, it was to consist of seven companies each recruited from the minor staff of the several London postal districts and departments—the senior members had enrolled separately and had, since 1860, formed part of the 21st Corps at Somerset House. With headquarters at the General Post Office, London, the seven companies were recruited: 'A', from EC District, 'B', Inland Office, 'C', Newspaper and Money-Order Offices, 'D', WC District, 'E', E, SW and S Districts, 'F', N and NW Districts, 'G', E and SE Districts.

In June 1869 a new 'H' Company provided by SW District was formed, this being followed in July 1870 by 'I' Company from the Telegraph Branch. By the end of 1876 sufficient numbers had been enrolled by the E and SE Districts to increase the establishment by one company and subsequently, from January 1877, 'G' Company was recruited from E District only while the SE men provided the new 'K'. The 49th was renumbered as 24th in 1880 and in the following year became a volunteer battalion (without change of title) of the Rifle Brigade.

On 18th July 1882 the War Office approved a scheme for the formation by the 24th Middlesex RVC of an Army Post Office Corps (APOC), the idea being that this would undertake all postal duties connected with an army on active service overseas. The APOC would be placed on the Army Reserve and consist of two officers and 100 men, all recruited from the 24th. It followed that on 8 August 1882, London postal workers embarked to join the expeditionary force then in Egypt.

In 1883 the telegraph company 'I' was recruited up to 200 and subsequently divided as two divisions, 'A' and 'B', and shown in the Army List as 'Field Telegraph Companies' (FTC). The formation of the FTC had been authorised to run along the same lines as the APOC, the FTC to consist of fifty rank and file. In 1889 both the APOC and FTC were constituted as companies of the 24th, the former becoming 'M' Company, while the telegraph personnel formed 'L'. Additional companies were raised by the 24th during the Boer War, the battalion supplying regular drafts for the front line. At the General Post Office in Aldersgate Street, opposite Gresham Street, a bronze tablet was erected to commemorate those who lost their lives. Became the 8th Battalion London Regiment in 1908. Unique among the Volunteer and later Territorial Forces was the battle honour 'Egypt 1882' which had been gained by the work of the 24th Corps during that campaign. Although 'South Africa 1899-1902' was soon to appear below the name of the regiment in the Army List, it would not be until 1908 that the honour gained in Egypt was recognised. Two privates

and an officer are seen in illustration **(627)**.

26th Middlesex Rifle Volunteer Corps (Cyclist) Notification of the acceptance of a corps of Cyclist in Middlesex was received on 11 February 1888. The new formation to rank after the 25th (Bank of England) Corps and to be made up of three troops lettered: 'A', 'B' and 'C—this would be the first battalion in the history of the British Army to be completely dedicated to a cyclist role. The cyclists functioned as scouts, signallers, pulled Colt machine guns into action attached to specially designed carriages and even, according to one source writing in the *Volunteer Gazette*, practised laying their machines down in the road so as to hinder oncoming enemy cavalry. The battalion's first headquarters was at Ashley Place where, seven years after formation of the corps, the first red bricks of John Francis Bentley's Westminster Cathedral would be set in place. By the end of 1888, however, a move had been made to Hare Court, this time in the City and within a few yards of the Temple Church and Fleet Street. Further moves would be made: first to 2 Queen's Road, West Chelsea (1890); 69 Lillie Road, West Brompton (1899) and Horseferry Road, Westminster (1904). Upon formation, the 26th Corps was allotted to the King's Royal Rifle Corps as one of its volunteer battalions. It transferred to the Rifle Brigade in 1889. Became the 25th London Regiment in 1908.

1st Tower Hamlets (The Tower Hamlets Rifle Volunteer Brigade Volunteer Rifle Corps Formed as the 2nd Tower Hamlets Rifle Volunteer Corps and soon comprised seven companies located: No 1 Hackney, No 2 Dalston, No 3 Bow, No 4, 5 and 6 at Poplar and Limehouse, No 7 Clapton. James Scott Walker, who was appointed as lieutenant-colonel in command, held a commission dated 6 April 1860. The original headquarters were at Arnold House, Richmond Road, Dalston, but were transferred by the end of 1860 to Pembroke Hall, Lamb Lane in South Hackney. One of the original officers was Captain Joseph D'Aguilar Samuda, the Jewish Thames shipbuilder. The 2nd Corps was amalgamated with the 4th Corps in 1868 under the title of 1st Tower Hamlets, The Tower Hamlets Rifle Volunteer Brigade. Headquarters were placed at Robert Street, Hoxton and the establishment of the new brigade was set at fifteen companies—seven from the 2nd Corps, eight from the 4th. With effect from 1 January 1874 the 1st Corps was amalgamated with the 6th of twelve companies at Dalston. Now with a combined strength of twenty-seven companies, it was ordered by the War Office that a reduction should be made to sixteen. The reorganisation went as follows: 'A' Company from 'A', 'L', 'M' and 'N' Companies of the 1st Corps, 'B' Company from 'A' and 'L' of 6th Corps, 'C' Company from 'B' of 1st Corps, 'D' Company from 'B' of 6th Corps, 'E' Company from 'C' and 'D' of 1st Corps, 'F' Company from 'C' and 'H' 6th Corps, 'G' Company from 'E' of 1st Corps, 'H' Company from 'D' of 6th Corps, 'J' Company from 'F', 'I' and 'K' of 1st Corps, 'K' Company from 'E' of 6th Corps, 'L' Company from 'G' of 1st Corps, 'M' Company from 'F' and 'G' of 6th Corps, 'N' Company from 'H' and 'J' of 1st Corps, 'O' Company from 'J' of 6th Corps, 'P' Company from 'O' of 1st Corps, 'Q' Company from 'K' of 6th Corps.

Headquarters of the new and enlarged 1st Corps were transferred to those of the 6th Corps at Shaftesbury Street, Dalston. There would be further reorganisations when in 1874 the War Office directed this time that the brigade should reduce its companies from sixteen to twelve. Regimental Orders of 28 November 1874 showed how this was achieved: 'A' Company to be formed by 'A' and 'P', 'B' Company to be formed by 'B', 'C' Company to be formed by 'O' and 'Q', 'D' Company to be formed by 'E' and 'C', 'E'

Company to be formed by 'J', 'F' Company to be formed by 'F', 'G' Company to be formed by 'G', 'H' Company to be formed by 'H', 'J' Company to be formed by 'N', 'K' Company to be formed by 'K' and 'D', 'L' Company to be formed by 'L', 'M' Company to be formed by 'M'.

The corps appeared in the Army List as one of the volunteer battalions allotted to the Rifle Brigade from 1881. There would be no change in title until May 1904 when, having been transferred, 1st Tower Hamlets became 4th Volunteer Battalion Royal Fusiliers. A cadet corps was formed in 1885, but this disappeared from the Army List during 1891. The Tower Hamlets Brigade had formed a Machine Gun Battery in 1886 and it was this, under the command of Captain E V Welby, that formed the nucleus of the machine gun section of the City Imperial Volunteers in South Africa. Transfer to the Territorial Force in 1908 was as 4th Battalion London Regiment.

2nd Tower Hamlets Volunteer Rifle Corps With headquarters in Whitechapel Road, London, the 2nd Tower Hamlets VRC had eleven companies: 'A', 'B', 'C' and 'D' (Stepney), 'E', 'F', 'G' and 'H' (Mile End) and 'I', 'K' and 'L' (Finsbury). From 1881 the 2nd Tower Hamlets RVC is shown as being one of the volunteer battalions allotted to the Rifle Brigade, but there would be no change in title. Headquarters moved to Bow in 1894 and transfer to the Territorial Force in 1908 was as part of the 17th Battalion London Regiment.

Illustration credits: Anne SK Brown Military Collection, Brown University Library (625), Bruce Bassett-Powell and Bob Bennet (621)

BIBLIOGRAPHY

Published works concerning regimental records are essential to a book of this kind. With far too many to list, I can offer an estimation that more than 200 have been consulted for the purpose of my book. For a comprehensive account of possibly all published regimental histories, I must recommend Arthur S White's *A Bibliography of Regimental Histories of the British Army*. Arthur Sharpin White was a former librarian at the War Officer Library and his invaluable reference book is now, after many years out of print, available again with additional entries from The Naval & Military Press. The following books have also proved essential:

Army List: Several editions covering period 1880-1914.

Army Museums Ogilby Trust: *Index to British Military Costume Prints.* 1972.

Carman, WY: *Richard Simkin's Uniforms of the British Army, Infantry Regiments.* Webb & Bower, Exeter, 1985.

Chichester (Henry Manners) and George Burgess-Short: *The Records and Badges of Every Regiment and Corps in the British Army.* Gale & Polden, Aldershot, 1900.

Frederick, JBM: *Lineage Book of British Land Forces.* Microform Academic Publishing, East Ardsley, 1984

Grierson, Lieutenant-General Sir James Moncrieff: *Records of the Scottish Volunteer Force 1859-1908.* William Blackwood & Sons, 1909.

Parkyn, Major HG, OBE: *(Military) Shoulder-Belt Plates and Buttons.* Gale & Polden, Aldershot, 1956.

Westlake, Ray: *A Guide to the British Army's Numbered Infantry Regiments 1751-1881.* Naval & Military Press, Uckfield, 2018.

Westlake, Ray: *A Guide to the Volunteers of England 1859-1908.* Naval & Military Press, Uckfield, 2019.

www.ingramcontent.com/pod-product-compliance
Lightning Source LLC
Chambersburg PA
CBHW061546010526
44114CB00027B/2947